LAW AND THE INTERNET
Regulating Cyberspace

Law and the Internet
Regulating Cyberspace

Edited by

LILIAN EDWARDS and CHARLOTTE WAELDE

·H A R T·
PUBLISHING

OXFORD

1997

Hart Publishing
Oxford
UK

Distributed in the United States by
Northwestern University Press
625 Colfax
Evanston
Illinois 60208-4210 USA

Hart Publishing is a specialist legal publisher based in Oxford, England.
To order further copies of this book or to request a list of other
publications please write to:

Hart Publishing, 19 Whitehouse Road, Oxford, OX1 4PA
Telephone: +44 (0)1865 434459 or Fax: (0)1865 794482 or 434459
e-mail: hartpub@janep.demon.co.uk

British Library Cataloguing in Publication Data
Data Available
ISBN 1–901362–30–2

Typeset in 10pt Sabon
by SetAll, Abingdon
Printed in Great Britain on acid-free paper
by Biddles Ltd., Guildford and King's Lynn

Contents

List of Contributors

Yaman Akdeniz is a Ph D student at the Centre for Criminal Justice Studies at the University of Leeds, researching into the governance of the Internet. He is the founder of Cyber-Rights & Cyber-Liberties (UK), a non-profit civil liberties organisation whose purpose is to promote free speech and privacy on the Internet.

Alastair Bonnington is the in-house solicitor to the BBC in Scotland. He is co-author of the sixth edition of *Scots Law for Journalists*, a part time lecturer at Glasgow and Strathclyde Universities, and Secretary to the Scottish Media Lawyers Society.

Paul Cullen was admitted to the Faculty of Advocates in 1982 and appointed QC in 1996. He was an Advocate Depute from 1992 to 1995, and Solicitor General for Scotland from 1995 to 1997. He is now in private practice at the Scottish Bar specialising in commercial law.

Lars Davies is Research Fellow at the Information Technology Law Unit at Queen Mary and Westfield College, London, which he joined in May 1995. He works in the area of electronic commerce, with particular reference to the Internet. Prior to training as a lawyer, he worked in the computer industry. He assists in the teaching of the LLM in Information Technology Law at QMW. He hates biographies of himself, but likes ties.

Sandra Eden is a Senior Lecturer at Edinburgh University with a special interest in taxation and pensions. She has collaborated with Lilian Edwards in the building of a computerised expert system dealing with inheritance tax.

Lilian Edwards is a lecturer in private law at the University of Edinburgh. Having qualified in both law and computer science, her primary research interests lie in the fields of law and artificial intelligence, legal expert systems, freedom of expression in cyberspace, and regulation of the Internet. She is Reviews Editor of the *International Journal of Law and Information Technology* and AI and Law representative to BILETA, the UK academic body for information technology and the law.

Stuart Gale was admitted to the Faculty of Advocates in 1980 and appointed QC in 1993. He acts as a temporary sheriff, and has a special interest in intellectual property and company law.

Ian Lloyd is Professor of Information Technology Law and co-director of the Centre for Law, Computers and Technology at the University of Strathclyde. He has written extensively in the field of computer law including the leading text *Information Technology Law* (Butterworths). He is Managing Editor of the *International Journal of Law and Information Technology* and Joint Editor of the on-line Web-based *Journal of Law and Information Technology*. He teaches a range of IT law courses including an LLM course which is delivered over the Internet on a distance learning basis.

John MacKenzie is an associate with the Glasgow law firm Bird Semple, specialising in civil litigation and professional negligence. He developed the Web Pages for his previous law firm, Carltons, where he also developed software applications for use in the firm.

Hector MacQueen is Professor of Private Law at the University of Edinburgh and Executive Director of the David Hume Institute. He has written extensively in the field of intellectual property law and is author of volume 18 of the *Stair Memorial Encyclopaedia* on Intellectual Property (1993) and *Copyright, Competition and Industrial Design* (2nd edn, 1995). He is Editor of the *Edinburgh Law Review*.

Andrew Terrett is a Legal Information Systems Advisor at the international law firm Masons where he is responsible for intranet development. Before joining Masons he was co-ordinator of the national centre for information technology and legal education based at the University of Warwick. He has written on a wide variety of law/technology related topics.

Charlotte Waelde is lecturer in private law at the University of Edinburgh and was previously in commercial practice as a solicitor. She has a special interest in intellectual property and Internet law and has written extensively in these fields. She is editor of the forthcoming *Kluwer International Yearbook of Intellectual Property*.

Table of Cases

Table of Legislation

PART 1
Introduction

1

Introduction

LILIAN EDWARDS and CHARLOTTE WAELDE

Any volume entitled *Law and the Internet: Regulating Cyberspace* must start by considering some preliminary questions. What do we mean by the Internet? What do lawyers have to do with it? Is there a law of the Internet in the sense that there is a law of contract or property? What are its contents? Is cyberspace a place that has a legal system like that of England, Scotland or California? Can it be regulated, *should* it be regulated, and if so why, how and by whom? The contributions to this volume have been assembled in an attempt at least to begin to answer some of these difficult questions.

Clearly, the first hurdle to be surmounted is understanding what the Internet is, how it works, and what all the acronyms beloved of computer buffs actually mean. Only then is it possible to understand the legal problems arising from the Internet. The first paper in this collection, by Andrew Terrett, covers these issues in clear and lively terms and equips the reader with the necessary tools to explore and understand the issues raised in the ensuing pages.

The question of what lawyers can do with the Internet – how they can exploit it to benefit and expand their professional practice – is taken up both by Terrett, and more extensively, by John MacKenzie at p. 27. MacKenzie draws on his experiences of setting up a Web site for Carltons, a small to medium-sized legal firm in the city of Dundee, Scotland, to discuss how the Web can actually enhance the business of the average law firm. He looks beyond the Web's predominant use in current legal practice as a sophisticated marketing tool, towards a future when delivery of digitised information both within a law firm, and directly to clients has the potential to transform the legal market. His conclusion, that "it is clear that the electronic provision of advice is not simply a marketing gimmick but an information tool that will prove in the future to be central to the business of law"[1] is one needing to be heard in a profession lagging behind banking and accountancy in its willingness to embrace new technology. Mackenzie also highlights some of the legal questions to be faced when setting up a Web site, such as the use and effectiveness of disclaimers of legal liability.

---

[1] MacKenzie, p. 36.

We move from these introductory essays to consider the subject matter of the law of the Internet in four broad areas. These are intellectual property and the Internet, electronic commerce, liability for content on the Internet, and finally electronic evidence and procedure. The coverage of these topics is not intended to be comprehensive, aiming instead to give readers an insight into some of the characteristic legal disputes and most pressing controversies that can arise in these areas. Throughout these essays, a key recurring theme is what type of regulation is appropriate, and how rules once discovered or formulated, can be enforced.

The Internet is a venue with very special problems in the field of regulation. For a start, for much of its fairly short history, many users of the Internet have considered it a law-free zone, or at most, subject not to national laws but only to a sort of ill-defined global or international law of cyberspace.[2] An imperfect analogy might be drawn with the high seas, which are not subject to the territorial laws of any one country, but are subject to the international law of the sea as laid down in international treaties and custom. The problem with such an analogy, however, is that while international law is now a mature legal regime in which the sources of law are well defined[3] and recognised by almost all states, any "international law of cyberspace" has yet to emerge and in particular, there is no body or court which has the authority to create or interpret law for the Internet. Although the conception of the Internet as law-free is often informed by little more than wishful ignorance or anti-authoritarian feelings, it does however have some core pragmatic reality, given the difficulties of enforcement of national law in relation to cyberspace activities. This topic is explored in many of the essays in this volume, and it is worth analysing in some detail.

Most jurisdictions, England and Scotland amongst them, have had neither the time nor the resources to develop a body of new law devoted to the Internet. Almost invariably what happens instead is the application of existing law to deal with legal issues arising out of Internet transactions and publications. Unsurprisingly, laws tailored to regulate the world of hard copy and tangible goods often turn out to be inappropriate or inapplicable, and to produce undesirable, even ridiculous results, when operating in the realm of the digital goods and services of the Internet. As many software publishers have discovered to their cost, for example, it is an expensive and losing game to invoke the law of copyright to prevent unauthorised copying when, in the nature of digital text and information, multiple copies can be made virtually cost-free and undetectably similar to the original. The problem intensifies on the World Wide Web, a medium which cannot actually be accessed without

---

[2] See for example, Nicholas Negroponte, the best selling Internet guru and author of *Being Digital*: "National law has no place in cyberlaw. Where is cyberspace? If you don't like the banking laws in the United States, set up your machine on the Grand Cayman Islands. Don't like the copyright laws in the United States? Set up your machine in China. Cyberlaw is global law, which is not going to be easy to handle." (*Being Digital*, 1995, Hodder and Stoughton, p. 236).

[3] See Art 38 of the Statute of the International Court of Justice.

the would-be reader making an unauthorised copy of the target Web page on his or her local computer. This problem of the legality of "transient copies" of Web pages is taken up by Hector MacQueen at p. 89. Another topical example of existing law interacting poorly with the Web, can be found in the Scottish case of *Shetland Times v Wills*,[4] discussed in this volume by both MacQueen and MacKenzie.[5] The Shetland Times controversy concerns the legality of "hyperlinks". The user-friendliness of the Web is to a very great extent based on the ease with which the browser can move from one Web page to another by clicking on buttons known as hyperlinks. Such links are found on most if not all Web sites, and are usually regarded as desirable by both Web authors and browsers. In the *Shetland Times* case, however, it was argued from a foundation of conventional UK copyright law that the making of a hyper-link from Web site A to site B was tantamount to illegal copying of material on site B by the owner of site A. Although the case is unresolved at the time of writing, it has already been widely reported throughout the world because it has the potential to inhibit the future expansion of the Web for the entire global community of net users. The case illustrates well that a mismatch between "terrestrial" law and the infrastructure of cyberspace can be potentially disastrous for the Internet community.

A final example of the problems caused by extending existing law to the Internet can be found in the chapter contributed by Ian Lloyd on legal barriers to electronic contracts. It is uncertain whether such contracts, lacking both conventional execution and signature, can meet the formal requirements for valid contracts laid down in statute in both Scotland and England, as well as many other countries, which may present a significant impediment to the development of electronic commerce. Lloyd, like several other contributors, highlights the recurring problem that existing legislative frameworks are often not elastic enough to adapt to the novel demands of the Internet.

Another problem with applying national law to cyberspace is that the Internet, like a river, tends to run through nations rather than being contained within their political and jurisdictional boundaries. In its nature, it ignores borders and frontiers. Both Lilian Edwards and Yaman Akdeniz, dealing respectively with the civil law of defamation and the criminal law relating to child pornography, note that since material published or distributed via the Internet habitually crosses national boundaries without check, and in huge amounts, it cannot be regulated or sanctioned effectively by a single state's laws. A Web site owner involved in the illegal distribution of pornography, for example, can effectively absent himself from the criminal penalties of (say) England by trafficking from a server based in a foreign country, where either the criminal laws, or more plausibly, the law enforcement mechanisms, are more lax. Sandra Eden, in her essay on the taxation of electronic commerce,

---

[4] 24 October 1996; The Times 21 January 1997; 1997 GWD 1-5; 1997 SLT 669; 1997 SCLR 160 (Notes).
[5] At , respectively, MacQueen, p. 70 and MacKenzie, p. 39.

dissects the problem of how electronic services and goods bought and sold across national boundaries via the Internet, can be effectively and suitably taxed when there is no place of physical import where duty can be imposed, or customs post to be passed through. Stuart Gale, in his consideration of the impact of information technology upon civil practice and procedure, acknowledges that the global nature of Internet disputes may lead to a corresponding demand for extraterritorial remedies which the courts may not always be in a position to grant.[6]

To acknowledge that the enforcement of national law in cyberspace is difficult, perhaps even cripplingly difficult, is not however the same as saying, as one net commentator recently has, that "digital technology is . . . erasing the legal jurisdictions of the physical world and replacing them with the unbounded and perhaps permanently lawless seas of Cyberspace."[7]

There are still more difficulties with regulation of cyberspace by the laws of a single jurisdiction. It is not just that national law is difficult to apply and enforce given the inherently transnational nature of the Internet. It is also sometimes impossible to discern *what* country's laws would be most appropriately applied. The fact that two or more legal systems may have something to say about a particular dispute is a phenomenon not restricted to the on-line world, and in most legal systems there are rules which exist to resolve questions such as which country's courts should have jurisdiction to hear a dispute, which legal system's rules should be applied to resolve the dispute (the "choice of law" rules), and whether the judgement of a court of another country should be recognised and enforced. These are the rules of international private law (IPL). The Internet, however, sometimes seems to have been set up purely to test the rules of IPL to destruction.

Consider for example a contract made on the Internet which is formed by an offer sent by email from Paris to London, and an acceptance sent by email from London to Paris. As Lars Davies points out in his essay on contract formation, determining where and when the contract was made, a vital preliminary to determining choice of law, will depend as much on unpredictable Internet network topologies as on known rules of contract law. As Davies puts it: "It is of no use whatever to suggest that somewhere in the soup of electronic communications that make up a series of messages a contract was formed, but it is not known exactly where or when; just that a contract was somehow formed. In order for there to be a contract the exact instant when it came into existence must be identified and not merely a vague or nebulous occurrence."[8]

If regulation by the laws of a single state is ineffective, or perplexing, or both, what are the alternatives? Those usually canvassed include regulation by

---

[6] Gale, p 255.

[7] John Perry Barlow, "Selling wine without bottles" in P Ludlow ed. *High Noon on the Electronic Frontier: Conceptual Issues in Cyberspace* (1996, MIT Press) at p. 13.

[8] Davies, p. 105, n. 19.

many states, joining together to formulate multinational treaties or policies which each state will agree to enforce; regulation by non-governmental bodies[9] or "quangos" charged with regulatory oversight of a particular sphere of activity (copyright, say, or Internet domain names) by state organs or the Internet community itself; and self-regulation by Internet users. Different approaches to different types of legal domain may be appropriate. Each style has its problems. Multinational treaties require copious investment of time and money to draft, and political will to force through, as each state has significant interests in retaining complete control over its own law which it will be reluctant to surrender. They are particularly difficult to bring to successful fruition where there are substantial differences between the laws of the different states, as with laws on pre-trial prejudice,[10] or where the issue is one which is close to the domestic interests of a state and its people, as with criminal law, especially that relating to obscenity and pornography.[11]

What about regulation by non-governmental bodies? This is a solution which has been particularly influential in the area of intellectual property rights, where organisations such as the World Intellectual Property Organisation (WIPO), have taken a leading role in forming world policy and co-ordinating multilateral conventions relating to copyright and trademark. Other non-governmental bodies however have run into difficulties when faced with the anarchic climate and shifting players of the Internet. Waelde describes at p. 45 the halting progress made by the body charged with responsibility for allocating Internet domain names, InterNIC, in dealing with the many disputes that have broken out lately relating to domain names and trademarks. In these disputes, typically trademark holders allege that their marks have been infringed by parties holding Internet domain names similar or identical to the trademark. Invariably an accompanying claim is that InterNIC itself is responsible for having allocated the domain name to the infringer. InterNIC seems to have found itself unable to resolve the number of differing commercial, state, and corporate interests (both within and outside the US) which currently jostle for room in the free market of the Internet. If there is a moral to this story, it would seem to be that no one body in charge of the distribution of a scarce resource such as Internet domain names can ever please all interested parties.

The final option is self-regulation by Internet users themselves. As a solution, this fits well with the mores of what might be seen as the traditional constituency of Internet users. Until the 1990s, the Internet was overwhelmingly the domain of students, academics, free thinkers, computer industry workers and the like, who mainly accessed the Internet for free and used it for

---

[9] Non-governmental bodies is here intended to include bodies established under the auspices of international organisations: for example, the World Intellectual Property Organisation (WIPO), discussed below, is a United Nations body.

[10] See further Bonnington, p. 199.

[11] See further Cullen at p. 212 and Akdeniz at p. 223.

non-commercial purposes. It was also used almost exclusively by North Americans (and males). As a result, certain values or norms have noticeably embedded themselves in the Internet community, and persist even now when as many users of the Internet pay for it on an hourly or monthly basis as access it for free, and when commercial use of the Internet vies with personal and entertainment use. These norms, or "rules for the virtual society",[12] include a prioritisation of freedom of speech and expression even where this might cause distress or economic loss;[13] a failure to identify with nation-states as having the right to regulate Internet activities;[14] a dislike of externally imposed rules and regulations; and a requirement that instead rules or norms relating to Internet conduct should be created by democratic and participatory procedures involving Internet users.[15] All of these values lead "traditional" Internet users to resist external regulation and to prefer self-regulation.

Even "non-traditional", commercial users of the Internet are can be forced to admit that self-regulation and extra-legal remedies work better on the Internet than conventional remedies imposed by courts. For example, it has recently been reported that there is a growing trend among law firms seeking Internet-related work to insert the names of successful Internet legal practices on their Web pages as "meta tags" – textual references which are picked up by search engines, but invisible to the person browsing the site. Effectively sites incorporating these tags are hoping to improve their own "hit rate" by piggy-backing on the goodwill attached to well known Internet law firms. The conventional remedy (if any) for such practices might lie in the law of unfair competition or passing off. However in reality such a novel suit would be difficult to win and expensive to conduct. A far more effective sanction would be to bypass the courts and instead to lobby the major search engines to "strike off" sites using misleading meta tags.

Self-regulation has been most discussed in the field of obscene and pornographic speech on-line, where freedom of speech interests, prized by the Internet community, meet state interests in protecting its more vulnerable citizens (notably children) head on. Akdeniz describes at p. 231 how the American attempt in 1996 to proscribe indecent and obscene speech on the

---

[12] The concept is taken from M Gould "Rules for the Virtual Society" (1996) 10 International Review of Law, Computers and Technology 199.

[13] See further Edwards, p. 187.

[14] See further Gould, op cit supra, n. 11, p. 205.

[15] A good example of this can be found in the somewhat baroque procedures for creating new newsgroups on the Usenet (see further, Terrett, p. 22). Any Internet user has the technical capability to create a new news-group that will form part of the Usenet hierarchy by simply issuing a "newgroup" command; but if everyone did so whenever they wished, the result would be an unmanageable explosion in the number of groups. Instead, therefore, there are prescribed procedures, including a call for discussion (CFD) and voting open to every Internet user as to whether the group should be formed. When the group uk.current-affairs, princess-diana was formed or "new-grouped" in September 1997 to discuss the Princess of Wales' untimely demise, without these procedures having been gone through in the interests of speed, there was considerable criticism from some Internet posters, despite a clear public interest (many thousands of messages were posted) in the speedy creation of such a group.

Internet by enacting the Communications Decency Act 1996, was vigorously opposed by the on-line and civil liberties communities. This opposition culminated in the successful challenge to the Act in *ACLU v Reno*[16] where the Supreme Court overturned it as an unconstitutional infringement of freedom of speech. Akdeniz goes on to contrast the approach taken by the authorities in the UK, where *inter alia* an Internet Watch Foundation has been founded to combat the spread of child pornography on-line by co-operation between Internet access providers and the UK government, and wonders whether this exercise in so-called self-regulation may yet prove itself to be too heavy handed a strategy. Acknowledging that the Internet poses a fundamental challenge to effective government, Akdeniz suggests it may be better to think of "governance" of the Internet, embracing a mixture of state control, multinational co-operation and self-imposed regulation of conduct by Internet users such as parents, children and access providers.[17] Such a mixed paradigm may in the end be a better solution than any of the three strategies alone, for many areas of law other than control of pornography.[18]

One of the questions we asked at the beginning of this introductory piece was whether cyberspace was a place, and whether there could be a law of the Internet in the same sense that there is a law of England or Scotland. It is certainly false to regard the Internet as a "lawless place".[19] It is much truer to say that the Internet is regulated by a hotch-potch of national laws. But it is more true still to acknowledge that very often, states have little or no ability to enforce observation of their laws in relation to Internet activity. Such observations bring us back to the question of whether we should consider a legal regime of cyberspace, a conception dismissed earlier as naïve. Such a regime has no current jurisprudential basis that would impress a lawyer – as the contents of this volume show very clearly, lawyers have had no hesitation in attempting to apply their national laws to transactions and activities taking place on the Internet according to conventional rules of jurisdiction – but its psychological appeal to non-lawyers is not hard to see. For many Internet users, cyberspace *is* a place, a location as real, sensual and involving as the non-virtual world. Bruce Sterling, science fiction writer and social historian of the Internet, puts it this way:

> [I]n the past twenty years, this electrical "space", which was once thin and dark and one-dimensional – little more than a narrow speaking tube, stretching from phone to phone – has flung itself open like a gigantic jack-in-the-box . . . Since the 1960s, the world of the telephone has crossbred itself with computers and television, and although there is still no substance to cyberspace – nothing you can handle – it has a strange kind of physicality now. It makes good sense today to talk of cyberspace as a place all its own.

[16] (1997) 2 BNA EPLR 664. Decided June 26, 1997. Available at http://www.bna.com/e-law/cases/renovacludec.html.

[17] Akdeniz, p. 225.

[18] See for example Waelde's call for self-restraint on the part of trademark holders seeking Internet domain names (p. 64).

[19] Akdeniz, p. 224.

Because people live in it now. Not just a few people, not just a few technicians and eccentrics, but thousands of people, quite normal people . . . People are making entire careers in modern cyberspace. Scientists and technicians of course; they've been there for twenty years now. But increasingly, cyberspace is filling with journalists and doctors and lawyers and artists and clerks. And there are children living there now . . . People have met there and been married there. There are entire living communities in cyberspace today: chattering, gossiping, planning, conferring and scheming, leaving one another voice mail and electronic mail, giving one another big weightless chunks of valuable data, both legitimate and illegitimate."[20]

For Howard Rheingold too, cyberspace is now the place where "virtual communities" live:

"A virtual community as [it] exists today is a group of people who may or may not meet one another face to face, and who exchange words and ideas through the medium of computer bulletin boards and networks. In cyberspace, we chat and argue, engage in intellectual intercourse, perform acts of commerce, exchange knowledge, share emotional support, make plans, brainstorm, gossip, feud, fall in love, find friends and lose them, play game and metagames, flirt, create a little high art and a lot of idle talk. We do everything people do when they get together but we do it with words on computer screens, leaving our bodies behind. Millions of us have already built communities where our identities commingle and interact electronically, independent of local time or location. The way a few of us live now might be the way a larger population will live decades hence."[21]

If virtual communities are the way of the future, what legal regime should govern them? Can lawyers find a way to conceive of virtual legal systems, applied to cyber-nations which might or might not correspond to today's real-world nation-states?[22] How can law be made in a community such as the Internet which wholly lacks a sovereign of the type Austin proposed as essential for the creation of law,[23] or even the rule of recognition beloved of HLA Hart?[24] What would substitute for the legislatures and courts of such communities?[25] Might the legal subjects of such virtual legal systems include not only the natural and juristic persons with which lawyers are familiar, but also the virtual personae often adopted by hardened Internet users and electronic role-players, which may differ in name, sex and race from the corresponding "real world" persona of that individual?

---

[20] B Sterling *The Hacker Crackdown: Law and Disorder on the Electronic Frontier* (Penguin, 1992), pp xii–xiii.

[21] H Rheingold *The Virtual Community* (1994, Secker and Warburg).

[22] For example, William Gibson, in the science fiction novel *Neuromancer* (Ace Books, 1984) from which the term cyberspace originally came, conceives of the territorial nation-state being replaced by the *zaibatsu* or corporation-state.

[23] See J Austin, *The Province of Jurisprudence Determined* (1832).

[24] See H.L.A. Hart, *The Concept of Law* (1961).

[25] One model for "virtual courts" might lie in the alternative dispute resolution (ADR) mechanisms which are currently widely used to solve international commercial disputes. An experimental on-line dispute resolution system can be found at the University of Massachusetts Centre for Information Technology and Dispute Resolution: see http://www.umass.edu/dispute/.

These are speculative and exotic questions, especially for lawyers. Yet there is a need to start asking, if not yet answering, such questions. Internet law as a discrete topic is barely five years old and the first textbooks have only just emerged.[26] So far, as with early texts in most fields, they are principally fire-fighting exercises: attempts to describe and provide answers to immediate sources of legal disquiet and dispute. In the future however there will be a need for a more thoughtful analysis, for the consideration of whether a jurisprudence of the Internet is possible. In a small way, the editors hope that that this collection is a first step in that direction.

The origins of this book lie in a conference held in Edinburgh in March 1997 and organised jointly by the Faculty of Advocates in Edinburgh, and the Department of Private Law at the University of Edinburgh. The articles in this volume have grown well beyond their beginnings as conference papers, but are still, we feel, inspired by the sense of enthusiasm and collective uncovering of new ground which was so stimulating on that day. We would like to thank all our contributors, for their sterling efforts and heroic adherence to unreasonable deadlines; the Faculty of Advocates, and in particular, John Sturrock and Zena Richardson with whom we worked in the conception, organisation and administration of the conference; David Berry and Murray Earle for providing research assistance and technical support; and Richard Hart for his sympathetic editorial hand.

Lilian Edwards and Charlotte Waelde
Edinburgh, September 1997

---

[26] See in the UK, Smith ed. *Internet Law and Regulation* (FT law and Tax, 1996), Gringras and Nabarro Nathanson *The Laws of the Internet* (Butterworths, 1997); in the US, Perritt *Law and the Information Superhighway* (J. Wiley, 1996), Rosenoer *Cyberlaw: the Law of the Internet* (Springer-Verlag, 1997), Cavazos and Morin *Cyberspace and the Law* (MIT Press, 1994).

2

A Lawyer's Introduction to the Internet

ANDREW TERRETT*

THE INTERNET—WHAT IS IT?

"The Internet is a huge electronic resource"; "The Internet is a network of computers that allows people to communicate with other people from all over the world"; "It's is a hacker's paradise and a computer security nightmare"; "It's the future of commerce"; "It's a jargon-ridden techno-jungle".

These are some of the views that one might encounter if asking a random sample of the population about the Internet. All of the above answers are partially correct. Using the Internet for the first time can be like travelling to a foreign land – the culture, the language and the symbols are all different. It can be quite intimidating but eventually the language and customs become familiar and even enjoyable. This chapter is designed to introduce the new Internet user to some of the terms that they will encounter when using this technology. In this chapter the key technologies, the building blocks that make up the Internet are introduced and an outline of how they fit together is offered, by describing the basic networking and data communication concepts. This chapter also attempts to demystify some of the jargon and three-letter acronyms that new users will very quickly encounter.

The excitement that surrounds the Internet today is not due to the underlying technology, important though it may be. One of the reasons for the Internet's recent phenomenal growth has been the increasing ease of Internet communication; any computer user who is reasonably familiar with the concept of computer application windows and a mouse or pointing device can quickly get started given an Internet connection and the appropriate software. Another key reason is the wealth of information available over the Internet. Indeed, it would be hard to think a topic that is not represented on the Internet. Therefore, this chapter also looks at the types of information the legal user can find and how one goes about finding such information[1]

---

* *(andrew.terrett@masons.com)*
LL.M, Solicitor and Legal Information Systems Advisor, Masons Solicitors, London

[1] For more details on both the technology of, and the services of, the Internet, there are a number of extremely good reference texts available. In particular, Krol, E. (1992) *The Whole Internet: Catalogue & User's Guide*. O'Reilly & Associates, Inc., Sebastopol, CA or Kehoe, B.P. (1992) *Zen*

A DEFINITION OF THE INTERNET

Although there is no official definition of the Internet, most industry commentators would agree upon a description of the Internet as a "network of networks." It is unclear exactly how many networks are attached to the Internet. Current estimates suggest that at least 30 million people have access to the Internet and this number is growing all the time.[2] The Internet is based around three key technologies; packet-switching (a means by which data to be transmitted across the network is encapsulated in addressed "packets" or envelopes); Client-Server technology (a technology that allows a computer to access and utilise the services available on another computer); and a set of software protocols known as TCP/IP (Transmission Control Protocol/ Internet Protocol.) Protocols are sets of specifications that allow computers to exchange information regardless of their make, type or operating system. Any computer that can recognise the TCP/IP set of protocols is what is known as "Internet-enabled." The facilities available over the Internet include email, Telnet, file downloading and uploading (using so-called File Transfer Protocol or FTP), Gopher, Usenet discussion groups, Internet Relay Chat (IRC) and most importantly, the World Wide Web (WWW or W3 or simply "the Web").

The definition of the Internet as a "network of networks" has been further complicated by the recent development of the term "Intranets". At the time of writing, there was much discussion about, but little implementation of so-called "Extranets." Intranets are internal company networks which use the same software as one would use to access the Internet World Wide Web but are configured to prohibit public access. They can be used to connect corporate "islands" of information that often exist on older corporate computer systems. Such intranets may be connected to the Internet across what is known as a "firewall."[3] Extranets also use the same technologies as the Web but link networks together beyond the firewall so that corporations can securely share data with their business partners, re-sellers or in the case of law firms, with their clients.[4]

---

and the Art of the Internet: A Beginner's Guide to the Internet. 2nd Edition (July). Prentice Hall, Englewood Cliffs, NJ., are excellent value.

[2] See for instance a recent survey by the Georgia Institute of Technology (June 1997) http://www.gvu.gatech.edu/user_surveys/survey-1997-04/

[3] A firewall is a combination of computer hardware and software that examines the source and/or destination of data packets and (is supposed to) prohibit unauthorised attempts to gain entry to a corporate network using Internet services. All corporate Internet-related data traffic will be routed via the corporate firewall.

[4] Perhaps the most famous example of an Extranet is the Federal Express website that allows customers to track the progress of their shipment.

If we consider the network of a hypothetical corporation, each department may have its own network that allows users of the network to share files and to perhaps share the use of printers. Such departmental networks may be connected together to form a so-called "Wide Area Network" across departments or between geographically disparate offices. These Wide Area Networks may, in turn, be linked to a corporate "backbone" (yet another network) and such backbones may be linked together at meeting points called "gateways". This matrix-type arrangement of networks is a microcosm of the physical skeleton of the Internet, (the term "Internet" being an abbreviation of the word "internetworking.")

HOW DOES THE INTERNET WORK?

The history of the Internet can be traced to a US defence-related academic research initiative in the late 1960's leading to the development of the ARPAnet (or Advanced Research Projects Agency network.) ARPAnet began its existence as a network of a mere four computers. Since that time, a large number of other additional networks have been attached to the original ARPAnet. However, the Internet only took its first real steps towards adulthood in the early 1990's when its commercial potential was recognised following the development of the World Wide Web. There are still many technical standards to be decided before the Internet evolves into the much-trumpeted information superhighway. In short, the Internet is undergoing quite a shaky adolescence.

Packet-switching, one of the key technologies of the Internet, was designed to ensure that the network could withstand a sustained missile attack. The concept behind packet-switching was that data to be transmitted across the Internet, would be encapsulated in addressed "packets" or envelopes. These packets would be examined by special purpose computers known as "routers" for the packets' address. The routers would consider the current best route to the final destination based on available information. Routers constantly scan accessible networks looking for breakage and data traffic jams. Thus packets with the same destination need not necessarily take the same route. Moreover, information packets tend not to take the most direct route between two points. Once the data reaches its destination, the addressee computer "unpacks" the packets, removes the envelope and offers the data to the user.

Another important Internet concept is that of client/server computing. Many Internet services are based around this paradigm. A server is a computer that delivers or "serves" information to a client software program on another computer which may be physically part of the same network or it may be located thousands of miles away. The benefit of this computing paradigm is that servers and clients can be using different operating systems. For example, on the World Wide Web, one of the most important client/server Internet services, a Web Server may operate on the UNIX operating system, while the Web client software may be operating on Macintosh, Windows, UNIX or any of the myriad other operating systems—it doesn't matter. The Web Server needs to store only one version of the information to be "served" because the client program will interpret that information and create the display as appropriate. TCP/IP (Transmission Control Protocol over Internet Protocol) is the final element of the three key Internet technologies. It is a suite of protocols or rather a set of rules consisting of various layers that ensure communication across the Internet occurs smoothly. It is far more important for the non-technical reader to simply be aware of its existence rather than how it works and what each protocol does – that is a book in itself.[5]

THE DOMAIN NAME SYSTEM (DNS) AND IP ADDRESSES

Every computer that is Internet-enabled will have both a Domain Name and an IP (Internet Protocol) address, similar to a telephone number. IP addresses consist of four sets of numbers each between 1 and 255. An example of an IP address might be;

$$130.132.59.234$$

Such an address can be analysed in the same way as one can analyse a telephone number by looking up the area code. However, IP addresses are hard to remember and easy to type incorrectly. Thus the Domain Name System (DNS) was established because it was felt that computer users would prefer to deal with computer names rather than numbers. The IP address is still essential however as it is this numerical address that is attached to each data packet. The system that converts domain names into IP addresses is a distributed DNS database spread across the Internet on various computers world-wide. When the idea of DNS was mooted in the United States, little regard was given to the potential of an international naming convention. For instance the original hierarchy did not have a geographical domain for the United States as it was assumed that all domains would be located in the United States! For the first few years of ARPAnet, this was not a problem; the first international connection to ARPAnet did not occur for four years. Thus there remain six top-level domain (TLD) names (.com for company, .org for organisation, .gov for government .net for network organisations, .edu for

---

[5] For a non-technical introduction to TCP/IP, try Yale University's *Introduction to TCP/IP* website (http://pclt.cis.yale.edu/pclt/comm/tcpip.htm)

academic establishments and .mil for military networks.)[6] In addition there are now also geographical domains for nearly every country in the world[7] and each may have its own variation on accepted naming convention.[8] The legacy of the original naming convention remains in that most domains in the United States still do not use the .us ending. Experienced Internet users can analyse a domain name and learn something about the host computer or its owners; For example, the computer called "law.aberdeen.ac.uk" tells us that this computer is based in the United Kingdom, is in the academic domain, is based at Aberdeen University and is law-related. Alternatively, a (fictional) computer with the name of "spock.law.indiana.edu" tells us that this computer is based in the educational domain at Indiana University, is law-related and that the Computer Administrator is probably a Star-Trek fan!

Internet addresses may also offer the user some clue as to the type of software they should use or the type of Internet service they will encounter and possibly also the complete directory path of the file in question. These addresses are known as URL's (which stands for Uniform Resource Locators.) For example, the following URL;

$$http://www.w3c.org/WWW/style.htm$$

tells the user to use a World Wide Web browser (http:// is the protocol of the Web), that the site belongs to the "organisation" domain and that the file in question (style.htm) is located in the WWW subdirectory.

WHO OWNS THE INTERNET?

The most straightforward answer is that no one does. There is no single body that controls activities on the Internet. Networks within different countries are funded and managed according to local policies and laws. This is both one of the Internet's greatest strengths and one of its main weaknesses. Ownership is distributed between countries and their own governments, corporations, universities and telecoms utilities. Each individual computer attached to the Internet will be owned by someone, whether a corporation, firm or individual. Telecommunications utilities own the physical wires over which data is transferred. Internet Service Providers (so-called ISP's), telecoms utilities or Universities will own the data routing equipment. Thus a wide variety of organisations each play a part in owning the Internet.

[6] At the time of writing there is some discussion by the so-called International Ad-hoc Committee regarding the establishment of a further seven top-level domains (TLD's)in order to ease the crush. These proposed TLD's are .firm, .store, .web, .arts, .rec (for recreation/entertainment), .info and .nom for individual or personal nomenclature. See further Waelde, p. 45.

[7] Interested readers will find a complete listing of countries and their Domain Name codes at ftp://ftp.nw.com/zone/iso-country-codes

[8] For example, the United Kingdom and Japan use ".co" instead of ".com" for its commercial domain and .ac instead of .edu for their academic domains.

HOW IS THE INTERNET MANAGED?

Each network that is attached to the Internet, whether commercial, academic, military or government will have its own user policies and procedures. Thus the Internet does have some measure of localised regulation but such policies and procedures cannot be enforced upon other areas of the Internet beyond the control of an individual organisation. Instead, rules and protocols between networks have to be negotiated and are usually agreed upon after proposal, trial and (often endless) electronic and face-to-face discussion. Thus the technology of the Internet is constantly in flux. However, the Internet does benefit from the existence of two organisational bodies; the Internet Engineering Task Force (IETF) which, in its own words is "a large open international community of network designers, operators, vendors, and researchers concerned with the evolution of the Internet architecture and the smooth operation of the Internet."[9] and the World Wide Web Consortium (W3C) based in Geneva which is an international industry consortium founded to develop common protocols for the evolution of the World Wide Web. These two bodies are the closest the Internet has to an executive. That said, there still remain a huge number of differing interest groups competing to control the way in which the Internet is used. These include Internet software vendors, software users, free speech advocates, advocates of censorship, Governments, information scientists, information providers (both commercial and non-commercial) network administrators and corporations interested in the commercial potential but concerned about the legal liabilities.

WHAT THE INTERNET IS NOT

Information providers such as Compuserve, America On-Line (marketed as AOL in Europe) and until quite recently the Microsoft Network (MSN), offer users access to electronically "ring-fenced" information resources in return for a monthly fee. Many people mistakenly believe that such services *are* the Internet – they are not. Although these information provides now offer users *access* to various Internet services, they use proprietary software that uses different protocols. At the time of writing, with at least one of the above information providers attempting to buy another and others under intense financial pressure, it may only be a matter of time before these services are pulled under financially by the massive wave of consumer enthusiasm for full Internet access using ISP's. There are also a large number of commercial datasets accessible over the Internet such as Dow Jones, Westlaw and perhaps best known within the UK legal context, LEXIS-NEXIS. However,

---

[9] http://www.ietf.org/overview.html

the Internet only serves as an access point for such services and unlike much of the content one finds on the Internet, these services are fee-based.

INTERNET SERVICES

Although there are a large number of different services available and each are addressed in this section, by far the most important to most Internet users are the World Wide Web and email. Amongst the "also-rans", there are services such as FTP, Usenet, Telnet, MUD's, Talk and Internet Relay Chat (IRC).

THE WORLD WIDE WEB

Arguably the most important Internet service, the World Wide Web ("WWW" or "the Web") is defined as a "wide-area hypermedia information retrieval initiative aiming to give universal access to a large universe of documents."[10] More simply stated it is a system of linking millions of documents on thousands of computers together across the Internet using hypertext links.[11] Although the World Wide Web and the Internet are terms that are used almost interchangeably, the WWW is actually only a subset of the Internet. However like the Internet, no one body owns the WWW. Individuals, organisations and corporations are each responsible for the documents they author and publish on the Web.

ORIGINS OF THE WEB

Since the end of the Second World War, information scientists have imagined a seamless library where users could interact with the sum of human knowledge. An article entitled "As We May Think"[12] written by Vannevar Bush, offered a startlingly relevant vision of the World Wide Web, at that time still some 40 years away. Bush envisaged a machine called the "Memex", a "device in which an individual stores all his books, records, and communications, and which is mechanised so that it may be consulted with exceeding speed and flexibility", and in addition would allow the user to follow their own associative trail of thought. This is very much the model of the Web except that in addition, the user is also able to look at electronic documents provided by others. The first major move towards Bush's vision came in 1989 with the

---

[10] See the WWW FAQ at http://www.boutell.com/faq/
[11] The term hypertext was coined by Theodore (Ted) Nelson who invented the word for "non-sequential writing."
[12] *The Atlantic Monthly*, July 1945 – an electronic copy can be found at http://www.press.umich.edu/jep/works/vbush/vbush.shtml

development of a prototype World Wide Web by Tim Berners-Lee and colleagues who, at the time were working at CERN (the European Particle Physics Laboratory) in Geneva. Berners-Lee was interested in finding an easier method of sharing information between researchers. The elegant solution that Berners-Lee and colleagues developed was not to impose standards on hardware or software but rather on the data itself. This standard is HTML (or Hypertext MarkUp Language) and is the glue of the World Wide Web.

There are three features of the World Wide Web that have made it the *de facto* standard for Internet communication and information dissemination. First, it understands the difference between various types of files. There is no need for the user to appreciate that she/he is downloading, for example, a sound-file. The Web browser "knows" that the file should be transmitted via the computer's speaker. Secondly, hypertext linking allows the user to seamlessly follow links according to their own interests whether linking between machines on their own Local Area Network or across the Internet. Finally, WWW browsers offers the user a Graphical User Interface (i.e. no typing of commands) in order to navigate the Internet. In addition, developers have built into Web browsers the facility to access other Internet services such as FTP Gopher, Telnet and even email thereby making it the most widely used tool for Internet navigation.

FROM A PASSIVE MEDIUM TO AN ACTIVE ONE

The World Wide Web is now undergoing further development. From its beginnings as an essentially passive medium, whereby the user obtained an electronic copy of a static document, users can now input information through the use of on-line forms. It is now quite common for Web users to fill in forms in order to take part in surveys, register preferences or even purchase every-day items electronically. This inter-activity has allowed Web-based commerce to develop at a frightening pace. In addition computer programmers have introduced animation, sound and even video onto web-pages. Furthermore, the introduction of new Internet-compliant and platform-independent computer languages such as Java[13] have made it possible for software to be distributed over the Internet or Intranet at the time of need. This, in turn has called into question the current model of computing with expensive PC's storing software on the computer's hard drive until needed. The alternative is a cheap Internet-enabled machine which has much lowers costs of ownership and has been labelled by the computing press as the "Network Computer."

---

[13] Developed by James Gosling of Sun Microsystems. For more information on Java, see Sun's excellent web site http://java.sun.com

FINDING WEBSITES

How does a user find information on the World Wide Web given that there is no indexed guide to all available Internet websites. There are two main methods. Certain organisations have set about indexing websites through the use of computer programs (so-called "spiders") which are sent out onto the web and follow the links between websites and add every new website address to a central database. Internet users can then interrogate this database using the Web. Well known trade names in this area include Altavista,[14] Infoseek[15] and Lycos.[16] There are many others.

Secondly, it is possible to make an educated guess as to the address of many organisations. For example, every user of the Internet will have heard of the software company Microsoft and know that it is a corporation based in the U.S. All U.S. corporations register their websites with the .com suffix. Therefore, it would be a reasonable guess to assume that Microsoft's website is www.microsoft.com and that is indeed the case. Such methods can often be as quick as using a search engine.

EMAIL

Electronic Mail or "email" is the most commonly used Internet service based around client/server technology. It is an asynchronous one-to-one communication link – you do not have to respond to email at the time that it is received and therefore is an incredibly convenient method of communicating both with friends and work colleagues whether in the next office or thousands of miles away. Email can also be used for one-to-many communication with groups of like-minded people. This is achieved through electronic discussion lists known as listserv's. By joining a listserv-type discussion group, you can deliver a message to the electronic mailboxes of all the individuals who also subscribe to the discussion list. For example, the UK Higher Education community enjoys the benefit of a service called Mailbase[17] which offers academics and students access to many hundreds, if not thousands of discussion lists on a wide variety of discipline-specific issues. In the UK there are approximately ten academic law-related discussion lists and in the US there are many hundreds.[18]

---

[14] http://www.altavista.digital.com
[15] http://www.infoseek.com
[16] http://www.lycos.com
[17] http://www.mailbase.ac.uk
[18] A full list of U.S. law-related discussion lists can be found at http://www.lib.uchicago.edu/~llou/lawlists/lawlists.txt

Invented at the University of Minnesota, (it also happens to be their mascot) Gopher services were in many ways a predecessor to the Web. A Gopher service allows the user to access documentary information resources on the Internet using a simple text-oriented menu-driven hierarchy. Gopher services are now more rare on the Internet as usage of the graphically-enhanced WWW increasingly dominates. Most Web browsers can now access both Gopher and Web services. However, Internet users will still occasionally encounter Gopher sites.

USENET

Usenet is a close relative of the email listserv. To quote directly from the Usenet FAQ,[19] "Usenet is a world-wide distributed discussion system. It consists of a set of "newsgroups" with names that are classified hierarchically by subject. "Articles" or "messages" are "posted" to these newsgroups by people on computers with the appropriate software – these articles are then broadcast to other interconnected computer systems via a wide variety of networks." This an asynchronous one-to-many form of communication similar to listserv-type email discussion lists. However, in order to access Usenet newsgroups, a user needs to have a special "newsreader" program. There are many thousands of Usenet groups and new groups are established virtually every day. However, individual Usenet groups are usually controlled by a single person, the "owner." That person, often in conjunction with members of the group will decide the parameters of the discussion. Some newsgroups are "moderated", that is, they will have strict guidelines governing acceptable content and tone of the discussion taking place. However, the majority of Usenet groups are unmoderated and therefore are tantamount to an electronic discussion "free-for-all." Not surprisingly, it is Usenets that give rise to the largest number of "flame wars" (the exchange of highly personalised abusive messages) and potential libel claims. Usenet also contain large numbers of discussion groups that morally conservative organisations would wish to see restricted or even banned and may well be illegal in certain jurisdictions. In addition, given the high percentage of unmoderated groups, the so-called "signal-to-noise ratio" (that is, the amount of discussion that is actually useful as opposed to that which is merely opinionated) can be quite low.

---

[19] List of Frequently Asked Questions, found on the WWW at http://www.mug.com/help/what_is_usenet.html

FTP AND TELNET

File Transfer Protocol or FTP is the method by which a user can send a copy of a file from one computer to another across the Internet. There are two forms of FTP. In the first, you sign onto the remote host computer using a login or ID code which is supplied to you by the administrator of the host. The second form of FTP, known as "anonymous FTP", allows any user to sign on as a guest provided they offer some basic details about themselves such as an email address. Anonymous FTP is a very useful Internet function in that it allows Internet users to obtain digital information, either documents or computer software for no charge. Computer software houses often make software updates and so-called "bug-fixes" available to the world using anonymous FTP as it is far cheaper than using the traditional mail service.

Telnet is a simple Internet service that allows a remote user to access the facilities of their home network as if they were directly connected to it. For example, a user could retrieve their email from their own mailbox using Telnet. Similarly a number of reference libraries world-wide have make their library catalogues available over the Internet using Telnet.

TALK AND INTERNET RELAY CHAT (IRC)

A one-to-many communication, IRC is the CB (Citizen's Band) radio of the Internet. Unlike other Internet services, IRC allows the user to engage in synchronous conversation by typing into a keyboard and watching his/her own comments and the responses of others appear directly on screen, key by key. There are many thousands of IRC Channels offering discussion on a wide variety of topics. However given that conversations can occur between users from widely differing cultures and backgrounds, the results can often be quite anarchic. IRC has its own culture and "netiquette."[20] Talk is a more controlled and comprehensible one-to-one version of IRC. All that is required for this service is a Terminal Emulation program (usually available in the UNIX operating system), an email address and of course, someone at the other end willing to respond and chat.

These then are the major services that a user can obtain from the Internet. There are others such as MUD's which can stand for any of; Multi User Dimension, Multi User Dungeon, or Multi User Dialog. This is software in which many user interact and is primarily used for gaming purposes. Another area that has not been addressed in this chapter is the emergence of three dimensional worlds on the Internet built using a language called VRML (Virtual Reality Markup Language). In due course, we will see many current

---

[20] More information about IRC can be found on the WWW at http://www.undernet.org including a FAQ.

two dimensional websites evolve into three dimensional sites built using VRML. At the time of writing we are still some way from the delivery of such sites.

As with all new technological breakthroughs, all users whether corporate or individual need to consider their legal responsibilities and liabilities in their use of the Internet. From a practising lawyer's point of view, and as this book reveals, the Internet is a source of new legal problems and therefore a potentially lucrative source of new legal work. However, the Internet has at least four other uses;

• First, a technology as simple as Internet email can have dramatic benefits. Instead of using expensive and environmentally wasteful resources, organisations can save themselves thousands of pounds each year by distributing internal memo's, newsletters, and news releases via email. Some UK law firms already use email for this task and in addition use Internet email extensively for communication with remote offices and with clients as it is far cheaper than facsimile or the traditional postal service. However, given the inherent insecurity of the internet such firms appear to be a minority.

• Secondly, the Web can be a excellent source of useful legal and law-related information whether case reports, statutes, legal "grey" literature, or as a method of obtaining up-to-date information about the marketplace in which lawyers operate, information about a law firm's clients or potential clients (much of which would be difficult and/or expensive to obtain from other sources). There is a wealth of legal information already available. In the US, all Supreme Court decisions, the US Code, Treaties and vast amounts of both Federal and State law are freely available over the Internet. The position is similar in Australia. The UK has been a little slower to embrace this technology but since November 1996, all House of Lords judgments, new Statutes and Statutory Instruments[21] have been made available free of charge.

• Thirdly, the Web is a means by which a law firm can advertise its presence and market its skills to a world-wide audience, via its corporate website.[22] Many UK law firms have already established their virtual presence. Notably however, few law firms have yet to provide substantive legal services across the Internet, but there are exceptions.[23]

---

[21] See the Parliamentary website; http://www.parliament.uk

[22] See further, MacKenzie, p. 29.

[23] See for instance, the Blue Flag website (http://www.blueflag.com), a joint venture involving the City of London firm, Linklater and Paines and other european law firms offering substantive legal information about doing business in Europe and other legal matters relating to European law. See also the website of Kaye Tesler and Co, (http://www.kt.uklaw.net/) which offers a Web-based will drafting service. A similar service for Scots law is available at <http://www.golds.co.uk>

• Finally, the WWW can be a cheap, simple and secure method by which lawyers and support staff can disseminate internal information using intranet technologies. Intranets require a four elements – a network, computers with WWW browsers installed, a Web Server (the computer which stores the information) and the relevant information in an appropriate HTML format.

THE LAW FIRM INTRANET

Given that the World Wide Web was developed in order to encourage the academic sharing of knowledge, it would seem to be a tailor-made technology for sharing information between lawyers. Information that might be contained on an law firm intranet might include internal memoranda, press releases, IT support information, starting points for legal research and employee information from departments such as Human Resources, Accounts, and Marketing. However, an Intranet may become truly cost effective in the dissemination of law firm knowhow. Law firms are, in essence, know-how companies – other organisations become clients in order to solve their own legal problems and in doing so purchase a firm's applied knowledge. Hence the firm's knowhow is an extremely valuable strategic asset. Unfortunately, lawyers have in the past tended to horde their knowledge rather than share it. Breaking this cultural barrier may be as much a hurdle as the technical problems of developing an Intranet. Nevertheless, there remains an enormous opportunity open to law firms to exploit this new technology.

WHERE IS THE INTERNET GOING?

Almost by the day, new Internet-related technological developments are announced. The Internet and particularly the World Wide Web have become most important new computing initiatives. Within the last two years we have seen the emergence of Java as a new computing language designed to work on the Web. We have seen Microsoft, the world largest software company perform a multi-billion dollar re-analysis of its current strategy and subsequent redesign of all it's existing corporate software products so that they could interact with the World Wide Web. We have also seen the emergence of a new commercial force in the computing industry in the form of Netscape Communications Corporation which has grown from a two-man start-up to a billion dollar company. The World Wide Web browser has now become ubiquitous and is set to become the new electronic window on information of all descriptions whether originating on the Internet, a corporate database or CD-ROM. These are turbulent technological times.

INTERNET PROBLEMS AND POTENTIAL

There are still numerous business, technical and legal problems facing the Internet. Besides the legal problems such as trademark and copyright infringement, pornography, privacy and encryption, etc., many which are addressed in the following chapters, another major problem is information overload. In the words of Mitch Kapor, the founder of Lotus Corporation, "trying to get information off of the Internet is like trying to get a drink from a firehose." Reading one's email, belonging to a few discussion lists and exploring websites of interest can be a full-time job in itself. There is also a desperate need for *quality* rather than quantity of information. Information scientists worldwide are currently working on standards for metadata (data about data) which would allow more effective information search and retrieval but these are still some way from ratification and adoption.

To conclude, we are still some way from the much-hyped information superhighway, where every house, school, library, shop and office will have high-speed connections to the vast resources of the Internet as well access to video-on-demand, on-line shopping for everything from the holiday of a lifetime to a loaf of bread and interactive virtual-reality games. Indeed, the hype surrounding the Internet has made this term one of the most woeful clichés in technology. Yet, given the rate of change on the Internet in the last five years, the de-regulation of telecommunications world-wide, the establishment of global satellite networks[24] to carry Internet data traffic, and the enormously attractive commercial potential, such a scenario is likely to be with us much sooner than we expect.

---

[24] In 1998, the Iridium global phone network will be complete. See http://www.iridium.com for more information. In 2002, the Teledisic global Internet network will be operational. See http://www.teledesic.com for more information.

3

Setting up a Legal Web Site: Pitfalls and Promises

JOHN S MacKENZIE[1]

INTRODUCTION

Nicholas Negroponte, the guru of the information revolution, recently made forecasts about how computers will transform the way we live and work:

"Computing is not about computers anymore. It is about living. The giant central computer, the so-called main frame, has been almost universally replaced by personal computers. We have seen computers move out of giant air-conditioned rooms into closets, then onto desktops, and now into our laps and pockets, but this is not the end.

"Early in the next millennium your right and left cufflinks or earrings may communicate with each other by low orbiting satellites and have more computer power than your present PC. Your telephone won't ring indiscriminately; it will receive, sort and perhaps respond to your incoming calls like a well-trained English butler. Mass media will be redefined by systems for transmitting and receiving personalised information and entertainment. Schools will change to become more like museums and playgrounds for children to assemble ideas and socialise with other children all over the world. The digital planet will look and feel like the head of a pin."[2]

"The information industry will become more of a boutique business. Its market place is the global information highway. The customers will be people and their computer agents. Is the digital market place real? Yes, but only if the interface between people and their computers improves to the point where talking to your computer is as easy as talking to another human being."[3]

With such extravagant promises raising high expectations about computers and what they can provide for the ordinary user, it is unsurprising that the legal profession has become suffused with enthusiasm about the latest development on the Internet, the World Wide Web (WWW).[4] But is this enthusiasm justified or merely hype? Is the WWW really something that can benefit

---

[1] Solicitor, Bird Semple, Glasgow.
[2] Nicholas Negroponte, *Being Digital* (Coronet, 1995), p 6.
[3] Ibid., p 85
[4] For a description of the World Wide Web, see Terrett p. 19.

the ordinary solicitor in practice? To answer these questions, it is necessary to step back from the hype and analyse what the WWW can and cannot do.

The WWW can display text, pictures, video and sound. It can store and transmit that data at low cost. It is easy to search for and retrieve the information which has been stored. That information can also be updated both quickly and cheaply. These functions can be of enormous benefit to the practice of law. Historically the business of law has involved lawyers who have sole access to legal materials, largely as a result of the practical difficulties in locating the source material which is often stored in specialised libraries. These libraries can be rather intimidating to the layman. For an individual to locate and interpret the law on his particular problem would involve wading through numerous volumes of statutes, case reports and textbooks to find the relevant law. He would then have to interpret his findings—a task that is often difficult for the trained solicitor.

There is no reason however why these vast quantities of legal information should not be stored on a computer and accessed in the same way as any other information on the WWW. Indeed, much already is available, such as House of Lords judgements.[5] However, this information tends to be stored on an ad hoc and unsystematic basis. With further development of the search and retrieval facilities ("search engines") that are commonplace on the WWW, in the not too distant future an individual will be able to simply specify a particular legal topic such as trade marks, and the search engine will pick out both source materials and items of interest and relevance to trade marks. The information that is stored in this way will then form part of an enormous electronic library accessible to lay as well as legally trained persons.

But if an individual can find the law on a particular topic so easily, what will the role of the lawyer be? Some tasks will clearly remain in the province of the trained lawyer and indeed new jobs may be created. Specialised legal knowledge will be required, for example, to help prepare and index legal information for storage in an electronic format. Looking at existing tasks, there will always be a need for legal agents to fight an individual's case in court and to do the work preparatory to litigation. However, the routine work which is the bread and butter of the legal profession—conveyancing, personal injuries work, taxation, executry or probate—may well come under threat.

Compare legal work to the game of golf. Golf is a complex activity which is difficult to do properly. People who have problems with their golf swing may seek the advice of the golf professional. In the vast majority of cases, the golfing amateur will be provided with some basic instruction and told to go away and practice. On the Internet at present there resides the virtual golf professional. The surfer completes a series of questionnaires about his or her golf swing and upon submitting these details to the virtual golf professional, is provided with a list of topics detailing how their golf might be improved.

---

[5] http://www.parliament.the-stationery-office.co.uk/pa/ld199697/ldjudgmt/ldjudgmt.htm.

These topics have been automatically selected to suit their own golf swing. Standard questions can be prepared and, based on those standard questions, "personalised" responses can be given. The golfing student can take it from there. "Automation" and "empowerment" are the key concepts here.[6]

If we turn now to look at routine legal activities, such as the sale and purchase of houses and land (conveyancing), the process can be similarly turned into a standard set of questions and answers, and the individual empowered to carry out the process themselves. On-line help can provide step by step assistance. There is already software on sale in wide use in the UK and the United States which can assist the individual on the completion of tax returns and the preparation of wills, and reputedly, some firms have already automated their conveyancing practice to the extent that much of the work can be carried out by paralegals rather than associates or partners. Advocates and barristers may feel that their work will be less compromised by the introduction of new technology. But although for the foreseeable future, representation of clients in court may require the human touch (and voice), a substantial portion of the work of those at the Bar involves not oral advocacy but the giving of advice on legal points in the form of opinions. If information is readily accessible and helpfully indexed and signposted on the Web, then the scope for opinion work, a significant proportion of which involves simply identifying the applicable law, may become much reduced.

So the future of the legal profession is intrinsically bound up with the use of computers. But what of the present? Why should solicitors want an Internet presence, and if they do, how should they go about it? At Carltons, a small to medium sized firm of solicitors in Dundee, Scotland, the decision was taken that an Internet presence should be established with the intention that the experience gained would enable Carltons to exploit emerging Internet opportunities as they arise. This article explains some of the experience gained in setting up a Web site for Carltons and the information strategy that was implemented. The site can be examined at http://www.carltons-dundee.co. uk/. It should be noted that very different strategies might be needed for medium and large-scale firms.

SETTING UP A WEB SITE

Getting on line

Assuming that a firm wishes to embark on the route to electronic provision of advice, where should it start? For a small to medium sized firm, the best idea is usually to invest in a straight forward dial-up account with a mainstream Internet service provider (ISP). It will provide an e-mail account,

---

[6] These concepts are developed in R Susskind, *The Future of Law* (Clarendon Press, 1996), p. 195.

usually with multiple IDs or mailboxes, and space on their server where a basic Web site can be established. Some ISPs, such as CompuServe[7] and America On-line[8] provide their own content, in the form of discussion groups and other information services, in addition to the basic Internet services. Others, such as Scotland On-line[9] and Demon,[10] concentrate on providing high speed Internet connections, but tend not to provide their own information services. It is obviously desirable to select an ISP with a local dial-up node so that on-line time is charged at local telephone rates.

Once an account with a service provider has been put in place, what then? How can this account best be used to profit your firm and your clients?

E-mail

Possibly the most well known, and certainly the most used area of the Internet is that of electronic mail or e-mail.[11] This is simply a program for sending electronic messages between computers. E-mail can be of enormous use in the business office. First, solicitors can use it to communicate quickly and easily both with each other, and with their electronically minded clients. How frustrating it often is to phone a colleague or a client only to find that the telephone at the other end is continually engaged, or the person you are trying to contact is unavailable; how much quicker and easier simply to type in a message and press the 'send' button. In addition, word-processed documents in various formats can be attached to an e-mail message. Thus, for example, if you are acting for a lessor, a copy of a lease agreement can be attached to a covering e-mail, and easily sent to the agent acting for the lessee.

The Web site

As mentioned, many ISPs make space on their server available to subscribers as part of the basic monthly subscription cost. So once you have established an account, the next question is what to put on your Web site? A conventional beginning is to take the firm's brochure, expand the contents so that it provides information about the firm, for example, pictures of partners and staff, details of work handled and maps of the area. Then set up a features and articles section, using the firm's in-house newspaper in electronic form. If personnel are available to administer a question and answer section, where prospective clients have the chance to put queries by e-mail, so much the

---

[7] http://www.world.compuserve.com/.
[8] http://www.aol.com/.
[9] http://www.scotland.net/.
[10] http://www.demon.net.
[11] For a full description of e-mail, see Terrett p. 21.

better.[12] If the firm runs an estate agency business, consider placing properties for sale on the Web site.[13]

These first steps in establishing the ISP connection, the e-mail account and the Web site can be regarded as part of the overall process of incorporating technology into the firm's overall marketing strategy. Creating and publicising the Web site will enhance the firm profile and improve its image at relatively little cost. But after these first steps have been taken taken by the firm so that it can deal with electronic transactions and clients on-line, then the system is ready to be extended further. Let us now consider what can be done with a Web site of a more sophisticated character than the basic model described above.

Law firms and the Web

Around the middle of 1996, law firms in the UK increasingly began to establish Web sites. There was some degree of concern that a law firm should have a presence on the Internet or be left behind in the technological revolution. Web pages were often published without a great deal of thought going into why this was being done, or how the Web pages were to be developed. Establishing a Web site may appear easy, but there are a number of important steps and decisions which require to be taken before a firm goes "on-line".

One of the most important initial steps for a firm is to ensure that an appropriate domain name is secured.[14] This is a simple and relatively cheap way of making a fairly dramatic marketing impact. The name makes no real difference from a technical point of view, but it is crucial to making the Web site instantly recognisable and easily remembered. The domain name is the identity of the site. Why have a domain name "service-provider.co.uk/firmname" when you can have "firmname.co.uk"? Potential clients surfing the Web will not need to remember that the address will start off "http://www." and will usually remember that it ends ".co.uk". If all they have to remember is the firm name, the site is far more likely to be visited than if they have to remember the name of the service provider as well.

Any firm that does not yet have a Web presence should take steps to register their domain name now. ISPs can register names, and most company formation agents will also offer this service.[15] Businesses in the UK can secure the .co.uk suffix from Nominet, the responsible body in the UK, but if the business is of an international nature then they should consider applying for

---

[12] See eg http://www.carltons-dundee.co.uk/the-firm/quest.htm; http://www.aldavidson. demon.co.uk/feedback.html.

[13] See eg http://www.carltons-dundee.co.uk/property/index.htm;http://www.georgesons. co.uk; http://www2.southforrest.co.uk/southforrest/Property/sfpfs.html. See further de Wert "The Internet and its Future Role in Selling Property" (1997) 42 JLSS 242.

[14] For discussion of potential problems with domain names, see Waelde p. 47.

[15] On-line domain name registration services also exist: see eg Netnames at http://www.net-names.co.uk/.

the global .com suffix with InterNic in the US. Within three to five years (the realistic timescale of any formal business plan) a great deal of correspondence and legal advice is going to be carried out by way of either the Web or e-mail. For a fairly minimal cost a firm can ensure that it is not left behind. Lawyers may also gain credibility by being aware of the opportunities for their clients to register their businesses as US domains as well as UK domains, and it may be good practice to offer to register clients' domain names for them.

A Web site should be given as much if not more care and attention in preparation than a corporate brochure. Take some time to think about the layout and about the firm's corporate identity. If the firm has a corporate logo, it should be prominent on the Web site. Use it on each page so that a site identity is built up. However if the site is being developed to present large quantities of text based information, as is often the case with legal sites, think carefully about using a lot of fancy graphics. Downloading graphics takes a lot of time for a surfer, and many clients may be using home or work based PC's and may not have fast Internet connections. If graphics are desired, one useful approach may be to present two alternative versions of the site, one graphic-heavy and one mainly text-based; or at least to advise that those with slow Internet access use their browser controls to turn off the downloading of images.

Statistics: Keeping track of usage

How effective is a Web site as a marketing tool? How many clients or prospective clients are likely to access it? An important part of having an Internet presence being able to monitor how often the information that you provide is being accessed by surfers. One way to assess this is by the "hit rate". This is a count of how many times the Web site is accessed in a given period of time. People promoting their own sites often bandy about very large "hit rates". This is especially true if their aim is to sell advertising space on the site. To gather accurate statistics for a site it is important to instruct the Internet service provider to provide reports. The Web server will produce "log reports" which can be delivered daily. The following is an example of one line from the Carltons Web site log report.

"topcat.uk.gdscorp.com—[04/Feb/1997:13:01:46 +0000] "GET /features/employ. htm HTTP/1.0" 200 10805 194.247.68.35"

This information shows the domain name of the person looking at the Web pages [topcat.uk.gdscorp.com]; the date and time that person requested a particular file [04/Feb/1997:13:01:46 +0000]; the file that was requested [/features/employ.htm]; and whether that request was successful.

Obviously for a busy Web site, with thousands of visitors, it will be a struggle to analyse information like this line by line. To help with analysis there are a number of software applications available. One such application is Analog,[16] which is a freeware application. This programme reads all of the log report files and provides a report which gives the total number of hits, reports on location of browsers and the time at which they visited the Web site.

Care must also be taken in interpreting the data available. Statements that a site has had so many million hits are frequently misleading. A "hit" is a simple request for a computer file. This will include the .htm file, and any graphics files that are on that particular page. Thus a request for one .htm file may produce 10 (1 .htm plus 9 graphics) hits. Software like Analog provides a straightforward report showing the number of times that a .htm file was requested. This is more helpful than the number of "hits" as it gives a better indication of the number of times that the text has been read.

The remote host is the identity of the computer that requested the file from the service provider. It cannot identify the user of the computer, but can at least say whether or not the user is in the UK or elsewhere. For a firm whose main business targets are local rather than international, for example, it may be useful to know if the bulk of those examining the Web pages are local potential clients, or mere voyeurs poking around the Web from the US and Australia. It is also possible to distinguish corporate from academic hosts, and still more information will be available if and when the proposed new top level domain names (such as ltd.co.uk and plc.co.uk) come into use.

The most interesting figures emerging from the Carltons Web pages showed the time of day at which the Web site was being used. While there was activity throughout the day, this reached a low during the early hours of the morning, gradually increased through late morning, and peaked mid afternoon and early evening. This tended to suggest that people using the Carltons Web pages were at work, had access to PCs and were in the UK. This conclusion was supported by a dip in activity at the weekend.

At present around 150 to 170 remote hosts, (let's call them people) access Carltons' Web pages each week, which is a more than satisfactory figure for a small legal firm outwith the central belt in Scotland. Compare this activity to our property shop. We would be delighted if there were 150 people coming into our property shop each week!

Does it matter what level of activity there is on a site? The answer is, helpfully, yes and no. It is useful to assess where the activity is so that you know which areas of the Web site are popular and which need improvement. At the present time, the main current purpose of a Web site is to promote the firm. If the site generates exposure in the conventional media then it is paying for itself. As long as clients are happy, the actual number of people visiting the Web site is less than crucial.

---

[16] http://www.statslab.cam.ac.uk/~sret1/analog/.

The benefits of being involved

Being involved in the Web also means that the firm keeps up-to-date with the latest advances in technology. Office technology of the future is likely to be based around Internet technology. Java programming is a system which allows mini-applications ("applets") to be stored on a central computer and sent to a user's PC only when needed. At a basic level this has allowed the development of animations on the WWW.[17] At a higher level it is hoped that word processing and database applets can be developed allowing users to download applications with only the features they need. If the firm has an Internet presence it will be kept aware of the latest trends and advances in automation and the information world..

Intranets

The technology of the Web need not simply be confined to transmitting information across, or retrieving information from, the outside world via the Internet. It can also be used to distribute information within the office on what is termed an "intranet".[18] Information can be exchanged between members of the firm which can range from the most mundane matters, such as reminders to fee earners to fill in time sheets, to more important matters such as synopsis of recent cases; counsel's opinions, whose value can extend to cases other than the ones for which they were initially ordered; details of ongoing transactions; requests for assistance; and so on. A limited amount of the information that is available on the intranet can be made available to clients of the firm, with the result that the practice of giving legal information can be changed almost beyond recognition. An "Advice Shop" can be set up with perhaps four or five PC's and a connection to the firm's own intranet. Clients can "come into" the Advice Shop, log on to one of the PC's and "ask" the usual preliminary questions discussed at an initial meeting. For example with a divorce case, the same questions come up time and time again, and often the solicitor will spend 40–45 minutes reciting the law on a particular topic. Those questions can be answered in digital format either by way of a video presentation, or in text form. If the general public have access to that advice on a PC, at little or no charge, then they are better informed when they first contact the solicitor for advice rather than information.

This distinction between information and advice is crucial to an understanding of how computer technology and the Web can be made to work for a law firm. When a client first approaches a solicitor, he or she is generally

---

[17] For a basic example, see http://www.carltons-dundee.co.uk/. An international example can be found at http://jumbo.com.hk/.

[18] For more information on intranets, see Terrett, p. 25.

simply looking for information that is of a fairly generic character. Once armed with that information, the client will look for somebody to guide or to advise on the best course of action in relation to his or her particular problem. A distinction can thus be drawn between the business of providing generic information, and the business of specifically advising a client. Recognising this distinction helps us to understand what shape the computerised law firm of the future should take.

Future developments in Web sites for law firms

The law firm Web site of the near future will have three levels of information which represent three levels of value. Information at the most basic layer will be accessible world wide via the Internet. The second layer will be accessible by the general public but only through the medium of the "advice shops" mentioned above. The third level will be accessible to fee earners within the firm. These three levels of information can be compared with the "information continuum" which Richard Susskind talks of in his treatise *The Future of Law*.[19]

At the first level of value, the information will be free. The information provided to the casual enquirer will be of the kind now found on most legal Web sites, namely features on legal developments and recent cases, articles on topics of interest to the public, and perhaps a question and answer section. This is similar to the kind of information often currently delivered via a firm's "hard copy" newsletter or mailshot.

The second level of information will be provided to what might be termed the "client in need". This level will contain detailed legal information, including some practical guidance and will, where appropriate, refer to cases and statutes. In essence, it will contain the information that would be provided to a client at an initial meeting. Thus for divorce, a client will be able to select information about the grounds for divorce, the position relating to children, residence and contact orders etc, and a detailed run through of the law relating to financial provision on divorce. If further information is required after this detailed level of information is exhausted, the client is directed towards a particular solicitor. This information is valuable and a charge should be made for access. The concept of "micro-charging" is important here. Micro charging is a system whereby a user inputs his or her credit card details at a single registration point. The credit card is debited for each page that is accessed by the user. Thus the user pays only for as much information as he or she wishes to read. There are certain attractions to this concept. The user does not feel that they are being charged large amounts of money but on the other hand, the information provider recovers enough to recoup the cost of providing that information. If Carltons were to charge £1 for each time that

---

[19] Op cit supra n. 6, p. 86.

a request had been made from our quality pages on our Web site, we would have generated £10,000, at a very early stage.

The third level of the information hierarchy is the detailed source material from which the lawyer will work for a fully paid up client. In essence, this level will be a 'digital library'.[20] The digital library will include statutes, statutory instruments, textbooks, internal memorandums, style documents, case reports, office manuals, instruction manuals and so on. The fee earner will also have access to the generalised legal advice that was being made available to "clients in need". Access to this level of information will be restricted to those employed by the firm.

When viewed in this light it is clear that the electronic provision of advice is not simply a marketing gimmick but an information tool that will prove in the future to be central to the business of law.

MANAGEMENT OF THE WEB SITE

It is vitally important that any information that is provided electronically is kept up to date, as much of the value of the system lies in keeping the contents current. As the Web site, including all three levels of information, becomes more detailed and assumes a greater importance in the running of the firm, it will become clear that management of this asset cannot be left to a junior member of the firm, or even to the partner I charge of information technology, as may be the case in many firms at present. It is likely that in the future, most firms will appoint in addition to the usual office manager and network manager or systems administrator (the person who manages the hardware of the network), an information manager who will assume overall responsibility for both actual and editorial content of the Web site as the firm's prime information asset. The initial construction of the Web site will be daunting enough, but maintaining its value by keeping it current will be crucial. It is an investment that should not be left to harried and overworked partners or assistants who need to focus on billing hours.

POINTS OF DANGER

Security implications

One of the problems with digital communication and the storage of data in a digital format is security. No system will ever be wholly secure but efforts should be made to ensure that the very latest techniques are employed to defeat any attempt to gain unauthorised access to the information held on the

---

[20] This is the theme developed by Nicholas Negroponte in *Being Digital*, op cit supra n. 2.

firms PC's. If a dial-up account is being used, and the Web site is stored on the server belonging to the ISP, then the information is stored remotely, and information on the office computers should be secure.[21] If however the firm has a direct connection to the Internet and the Web pages are delivered from its own server, software known as a "firewall" is available to prevent unauthorised access to the information on the firms PC's.

The position of employees and their use of the firms PC's should be clearly spelt out. Systems should be put in place to ensure that employees do not introduce unauthorised software onto the network. Even installation of software can cause systems crashes, which are frustrating, time consuming, and costly. A firm policy may also be required to deal with employees' use of the Internet. Decisions need to be made about whether personal use should be monitored or even prohibited during firm time. Modern operating systems have sophisticated tracking facilities, and these, combined with effective disciplinary procedures should ensure that use of the Internet is restricted to firm business and that employeees are not diverted by its alternative role as leisure facility.

Legal risks arising from Web sites

Liability for advice given

One of the difficulties of giving information by way of a Web site is that it is possible that a solicitor will never see the person who chooses to rely on the advice, and that the information given may be inappropriate to the particular circumstances of that person and cause loss. Such persons may not generally be what are regarded as "clients" but certainly, when the practice of micro charging is adopted, funds will be received from individuals who never come in physical contact with an office. Potentially worrying questions may then arise as to the liability of the firm.

Disclaimers

At present some solicitors appear to be fairly comfortable with a general disclaimer along the lines of: "Any advice given is worth what you paid for it!"

This general disclaimer is designed to fit in with the current Internet culture. This is a culture that rebels against restrictions and lengthy disclaimers. There is often a feeling (mistaken of course) that if information is provided on the Internet then you can do with it what you wish. Lengthy disclaimers tend to be counterproductive in the present climate, as surfers may not stay long enough to read the disclaimer. On the other hand, when considering the

---

[21] The question of safeguarding against viruses is however outwith the scope of this article.

paying client rather than the casual surfer, who is seeking specific information and is willing to pay for it, the liability of the firm for the information provided becomes an important issue. A firm must assess the risks of negligent misrepresentation and how these risks can be minimised. Some firms have therefore gone for fairly prominent disclaimers.[22]

If a case of negligent misrepresentation is plead against a firm as the result of advice given on a Web site, the question of how far liability may extend will require to be assessed by the courts after hearing evidence of how the Web operates, the information given on the site and a detailed examination of the relationship between the firm as host of information and the surfer as the one who reads that information. In *Hedley Byrne & Co v Heller & Partners Ltd*[23] the court held that a negligent, though honest, misrepresentation, spoken or written, may give rise to an action for damages for financial loss caused. Such liability may arise even though there is no contractual or fiduciary relationship between the advisor and the person who suffered loss. The law will impose a duty of care when a person seeks information from an adviser with special skill and trusts that adviser to exercise due care, and the adviser knew, or ought to have known, that reliance was being placed on his skill and judgement. It is however possible to avoid liability even if a court finds a duty of care existed and that duty was breached, by means of an express and valid disclaimer of responsibility. In *Hedley Byrne* itself, such a disclaimer was effective.

In *Anns v. Merton London Borough Council*[24] Lord Wilberforce said:

> "Through the trilogy of cases in this House, *Donoghue v. Stevenson*, *Hedley Byrne & Co Ltd v Heller & Partners Ltd* and *Home Office v. Dorset Yacht Co Ltd.*, the position has now been reached that in order to establish that a duty of care arises in a particular situation, it is not necessary to bring the facts of that situation within those of previous situations in which a duty of care has been held to exist. Rather the question has to be approached in two stages. First one has to ask whether, as between the alleged wrongdoer and the person who has suffered damage there is a sufficient relationship of proximity or neighbourhood such that, in the reasonable contemplation of the former, carelessness on his part may be likely to cause damage to the latter, in which case a prima facie duty of care arises. Secondly, if the first question is answered affirmatively, it is necessary to consider whether there are any considerations which ought to negative, or to reduce or limit the scope of the duty or the class of person to whom it is owed or the damages to which a breach of it may give rise (see the Dorset Yacht case, per Lord Reid)."[25]

This theme was introduced, along with the concept of reliance in *Hedley Byrne* when Lord Morris stated:

> "My Lords, I consider that it follows and that it should now be regarded as settled that if someone possessed of a special skill undertakes, quite irrespective of contract,

---

[22] See for example http://www.mcgrigors.com/disclaim.htm, http://www.shepwedd.co.uk/disclaimer.htm.
[23] [1964] A.C 465.
[24] [1978] A.C. 728.
[25] Ibid at 751.

to apply that skill for the assistance of another person who relies on such skill, a duty of care will arise. The fact that the service is to be given by means of or by the instrumentality of words can make no difference. Furthermore, if in a sphere in which a person is so placed that others could reasonably rely upon his judgement or his skill or upon his ability to make careful inquiry a person takes it upon himself to give information or advice to, or allows his information or advice to be passed on to, another person who, as he knows or should know, will place reliance upon it, then a duty of care will arise."[26]

It appears plausible then that those who provide information on the Internet to others might fall within the ambit of a relationship and a duty of care, but the question of reliance will be a crucial factor in determining whether that relationship exists. The whole purpose of Web pages is to provide information. However there is a clear intention (clear, at least, on the part of the solicitor) that the information is general in its terms and cannot be taken as being applied to specific situations. It is simply generic information that is being provided, not advice to an individual client. The position can be compared with the provision of information in a a book. It is for the reader to decide how the information provided in the book applies to his or her specific situation. The position can be contrasted with reliance upon a specific survey report relating to a specific property, where it is easy to see that the number of people who are likely to have access to the information will be restricted. Even when semi-specific information is provided, as in the case of simple reports, it has been held that the use of a disclaimer in clear and understandable terms will be sufficient to exclude liability under the common law.[27] It is likely therefore that where information rather than advice is given in general terms on Web pages, an appropriately worded disclaimer will successfully exclude liability.

Hypertext links

Continuing the theme of liability, the question of whether to include hypertext links ("hyperlinks") to other Web Sites is currently problematic. The dangers of linking to other sites have been illustrated by the Scottish case of *Shetland Times v. Wills*[28] and by the US case of *Washington Post & Others v Total News & Others*.[29]

In the *Shetland Times* case, the pursuers, who owned and published a newspaper called "The Shetland Times" took action against the defenders, who ran a news reporting service under the name "The Shetland News". Both busi-

[26] [1964] A.C 465 at 502.
[27] See *Robbie v Graham & Sibbald* 1989 SLT 870 (cf. *Melrose v Davidson & Robertson* 1992 SLT 395).
[28] 1997 SCLR 160. See the commentary by MacQueen at p. 70.
[29] The full text of the complaint can be found at http://www.carltons-dundee.co.uk/features/wpvtotal.htm.

nesses published news items on Web sites on the Internet. The pursuer's home page contained advertising material and headlines of news stories. By clicking on a headline, the browser was taken to that news story. The defenders published the pursuers' headlines verbatim on their own Web site, with hypertext links connecting these headlines to the full stories on the pursuer's web site. Effectively therefore, surfers looking at the Shetland News Web site could go straight to the news story on the Shetland Times site without first going through the Shetland Times home page (i.e. the first page of that Web site). The pursuers objected to this, principally because they were attempting to sell advertising space on their home (front) page. They sought interdict and interim interdict against the defenders.

In the course of his opinion on the question of interim interdict, Lord Hamilton noted:

> "It was fundamental to the setting up by the pursuers of their Web site that access to their material should be gained only be accessing their Web site directly. While there has been no loss to date, there is a clear prospect of loss of potential advertising revenue in the foreseeable future."[30]

We all know that the home page is the most popular area of a Web site. It is the gateway to the rest of the site. However the ability to bypass the home page and link directly to a particular Web page is surely fundamental to the continued success of the Internet. Indeed entire businesses have been created by indexing individual pages. Lord Hamilton seems to suggest that a loss will be incurred, and thus a right of action created, simply through a potential loss in advertising revenue. His Lordship's opinion was given after only a brief interim hearing, and in the view of this writer, the court entrusted with the final decision is likely to rule that it is for the Web site owner to ensure, using whatever techniques are available, that the site is only accessed in the way he or she wants. It is possible to protect Web pages by password or to make use of programming techniques which devise the text for a document from a database, thus preventing straightforward linking.

Liability of one Web site for the content of another Web site to which a hyperlink is made is also a source of some concern for some commentators. It is this writer's view that linking to another site will not cause any legal difficulty so long as the link clears the screen totally of the first Web site and substitutes the new Web site in its place. A danger arises, as illustrated by *Washington Post*, where a site is constructed around frames technology. In this case, the defendants, a five-person organisation, had built a Web site using the "frames" technique. The defendants had their logo and Uniform Resource Locator (URL) at the top of the screen and a list of links to major suppliers of information down the side of the screen. The main part of the screen contained the Web pages put together by the plaintiffs, who included The Washington Post Company, Digital Ink Co. Time, Inc., Entertainment Weekly

---

[30] 1996 SCLR 160 at 163.

Inc., Cable Network News, Inc., Times Mirror Company, Dow Jones & Company, Inc. and Reuters New Media Inc. As the surfer moved from one link (on the left-hand side of the screen) to another, the content of the main part of the screen changed, but the frames on the top and left, including the advertising banner, remained in place. The effect of this was to access information provided by other Web site providers, but 'encased' within the frames at the top and the bottom of the screen. It therefore would appear to a surfer that all the information appearing on the main part of the screen was endorsed or provided by those companies whose logos and names appeared in the frames at the top and the sides. The danger is then that it appears as if the information is being 'passed off' as that of the companies whose names appear within the frames. This is often done for profit in the form of advertising revenue; the plaintiffs suffer a loss in that the impact of the information they have provided on their Web site is diminished. It is therefore important that when a browser leaves the Web site, the screen is entirely cleared and the linked site substituted.

CONCLUSION

Information technology, its uses and abuses, is an area that is developing very fast, perhaps too fast for the law to keep up. National laws may not be sufficiently flexible to cope with the Internet and we are offered the tantalising prospect of cyber-law. National boundaries may fall or, perhaps more realistically, businesses on the Internet will contract out of national law and into a trans-national cyber-law. Lawyers will be needed to draft and interpret that law. Virtual courts may be established with representatives from around the world, fighting their client's case from their desktop. One thing is certain: there are exciting times ahead for lawyers.

PART 2
Intellectual Property Aspects

4

Domain names and Trade marks: What's in a name?

CHARLOTTE WAELDE[1]

The clash between ownership and use of domain names in cyberspace and trade marks in the terrestrial world is one of the areas of dispute currently at the forefront of legal debate in relation to the Internet. The issues that arise illustrate the struggle being played out between commercial users of the Internet as they strive to mould disputes arising out of the unstructured web of cyberspace into a form that more closely resembles the rules of legal engagement with which they are familiar. Traditional terrestrial rules of trade mark law are being employed to resolve clashes over domain names with some extraordinary results. In response, those currently charged with a supervisory role in relation to the allocation of domain names have formulated their own policies to deal with the clashes. These policies have in their turn led to yet more disputes, and resulted in international efforts to resolve the clashes, which in their turn have led to further criticism. The result is something akin to chaos. Despite this, the Internet continues to function, and indeed to grow at a phenomenal rate.

The purpose of this paper is firstly to examine and to comment on the basic issues of trade mark law and domain names in this area; secondly to look at the trends in the case law in the UK and the US and to highlight a number of the issues that flow, and in particular, to comment on whether the analyses of the disputes to date have been sufficient; and thirdly to explain the policies of the regulatory bodies and suggest how these policies could be improved.

WHAT IS A DOMAIN NAME?

Every resource on the Internet, such as a web page or a file of information has its own address—or Uniform Resource Locator (URL). A domain name

[1] Lecturer in Law, University of Edinburgh. Email: Charlotte.Waelde@ed.ac.uk I would like to express my sincere thanks to Sam Wilson, Postmaster at Edinburgh University for his very helpful comments on various drafts of this paper.

is part of this address which is assigned to each computer or service on the Internet.[2]

An example of a domain name is "ibm.greenock.com". Reading this from left to right, "ibm" is the name of the hostcomputer; "greenock" is the **second** level domain name, and is registered by the organisation or entity who wants to use the particular address. The last item "com" is the **top** level domain name and often describes the purpose of the organisation or entity who owns the second level domain name.

The InterNic Registry in the United States[3] handles applications for registration under a number of well known top level domain names. These are **".com"** used by commercial entities"; **".gov"** for US governmental organisations; **".edu"** for certain educational establishments; **".org"** for other non-profit organisations who do not fall easily into the other categories; **".net"** for the network providers and **".int"** for organisations established by international treaties

There are also registries in other countries around the world administered by other network information centres such as RIPE-NIC in Amsterdam and AP-NIC in Tokyo. These registries co-ordinate IP addresses with the domain names registered on the basis of geographical location. For example ".uk" for the United Kingdom and ".fr" for France. A company in the UK can register in the ".com" top level domain or it can register in the ".uk" top level domain. Because the top level domains administered by InterNic do not include a geographical location, they are viewed as having international connotations, thus making them attractive to those businesses who like to view their activities as having international appeal.

The domain name system maps names to a series of numbers or IP address—such as "198.41.0.5". These numbers are then linked with an easily read and remembered address—the domain name. The domain name need not change if the computer or service changes, whereas the series of numbers will. The domain name is intended to be more meaningful to human beings than the series of numbers. The numbers referred to above are linked with the domain name "rs.internic.net". People who are using the domain name can therefore choose an easily remembered, and importantly, easily recognisable names in cyberspace.

There are a number of factors that have brought the domain name system into opposition with the law of trade marks. It is argued that a domain name functions as a trade mark, and therefore any use of a domain name by a person not entitled to the trade mark, amounts to infringement. Interestingly, and importantly, most of the disputes to date have been in relation to the ".com" top level domain name. There are a number of reason for this: firstly, it is one of the oldest—in terms of original top level domains; secondly, it is a naming system which might utilise only two names, such as "Harrods.com", thus

[2] See Terrett p. 16.
[3] For further information on InterNic see below p. 59.

making the address easily and instantly recognisable. By contrast, under one of the country domains, the name would be "Harrods.co.uk". Thirdly, its association with commercial organisations is also important in that it is attractive to a commercial entity seeking to set up a web site; and finally, as mentioned above, the name has international connotations.

Another factor that has contributed to the controversies surrounding domain names is the development of browsers and search engines which make finding specific locations on the Internet relatively simple. Most browsers now allow a surfer to find the web site of a company by simply typing in the company name. If a browser such as Netscape is used, the surfer need only type in the word "apple", and the browser will add the rest of the URL; i.e., in this case "http://www.apple.com", in order to take the surfer directly to the home page of Apple computers. Prior to the development of these browsers, the surfer would have had to work much harder to find a particular address and the web page located at that address. Search engines, such as Infoseek, AltaVista and Yahoo! have also simplified the task of the surfer, allowing information to be found using only one key word, often a word that is used as part of a trade mark by a business.

THE PROBLEMS THAT ARISE WITH THIS SYSTEM OF DOMAIN NAMES

No two domain names can be identical. There can only be one "harrods.com". The word "Harrods" could however be registered under one of the country domains. Thus along with "harrods.com", "harrods.co.uk" can also be used as a domain name. In addition, variations on the name "harrods.com" can be registered, for example "harr0ds.com" or harrods1.com. The permutations are limited only by the imagination.

There may be a number of people or entities who consider themselves to be "entitled" in the loose sense of the term to a particular domain name. Let us take the example of the name "Fellowes". In the UK, "Fellowes" may be the registered trade mark for office stationery, it may be the name of a regular street market in London, and of an art gallery in Aberdeen; there may be a solicitors firm named "Fellowes", it may be the unregistered mark for "Fellowes" kitchen utensils, and be registered for garden seed and other equipment. And indeed you may have different entities equally entitled to the same mark in other countries around the world, whether they operate within the same sphere of business or not. Trade mark law is, after all, territorial. Only one of these organisations will be able to register the name "Fellowes.com". The controversy is over who gets that domain name and why.

THE WAYS IN WHICH DISPUTES HAVE ARISEN

One way in which disputes have arisen is where a third party intentionally registers a domain name in the knowledge that someone else will want it, such as "windows95.com". This domain name was registered by a student in Utah. The intention may be to hold the company or business who wants to use the domain name to ransom, and demand financial reward for giving up the domain name. Another example is where "Mcdonalds.com" was registered by a journalist, Mr Quittner in 1994. To secure return of the name, McDonalds were forced to make a donation for computer equipment for a primary school. These have become known as "cyber-squatter" disputes.

A second way in which disputes arise is where a domain name is registered by someone who knows it is the same as a trade mark belonging to someone else, or very similar to such a trade mark, but intends to use it for their own purposes. Visitors to the site may be surprised to find that the goods or services which are advertised are not those they would normally have associated with the mark that they know and understand. Teubner & Associates, a high technology software company found themselves in just such a position. A competitor of Teubner's registered the name "tuebner.com", which is a common misspelling of Teubner. "Tuebner.com", after negotiation, has been reassigned to Teubner & Associates.

Thirdly, disputes can arise over "innocent" registrations. This is where registration is made of what would be a logical choice of a domain name. Our example of "Fellowes" above provides one such scenario. The winner of the race to the register for the domain name "Fellowes.com" could be the stationery company. Imagine the surprise of the computer literate clients of the firm of solicitors, or devotees of Fellowes grass seed when they access the home page and find out it is totally unrelated to the products or services that they associate with the name.

The permutations are endless, as are the potential grounds for dispute. Interlaw Ltd, an international legal organisation, registered the domain name "interlaw.org". Interlaw Ltd complained about the registration of the domain name "inter-law.com" by the "Lectric Law library, a popular legal site. Someone else has registered the domain name "interlaw.com"; and yet someone else "Electric-Library.com".

Most of the litigation to date has involved instances where there has been intentional pirating of domain names, as in the cases of "Tuebner.com" and "McDonalds.com".

REPORTED DISPUTES AND DECIDED CASES

Rumours and stories of domain name and trade mark controversies are rife. A number of cases have reached the court, particularly in the US.[4] To date (31 July 1997), three cases have been heard in court in the UK, although unfortunately, due to their specific facts, have not contributed significantly to the development of a UK jurisprudence in relation to the domain name/trade mark controversy.

The basis on which actions for infringement of trade marks by the use of domain names have been brought in the US to date rest on two main grounds, that of confusion, and that of dilution. This article will look first at the question of confusion. During this discussion, one of the themes that will be highlighted is that there is a distinction to be drawn between the domain name and the underlying goods and services that are offered at the address, and that this distinction needs to be taken into account in trade mark and domain name disputes.

Confusion in the US

A trademark in the US is defined in the Lanham Act 1984 as "any word name, symbol, or device or any combination used or intended to be used to indicate the source of the goods". The touchstone of liability under this Act is that of confusion.[5] Liability for infringement of a trade mark is strict. In other words, there is no need for intent or negligence. Liability arises when the infringer uses a mark which may be confused with the trade mark of the infringed party, when used in conjunction with similar goods or services.

Trade mark confusion and similar domain names was considered in the case of *Maritz Inc. v Cybergold Inc.*[6] Maritz alleged trade mark infringement against CyberGold. Maritz used the unregistered "GoldMail" name in conjunction with its GoldMail service. This service, provided on the Internet, was designed to provide financial incentives and rewards for reading electronic mail. Their URL was ".goldmail.com". CyberGold were developing a similar Internet service, using the domain name "cybermail.com". The court was prepared to consider the matter of confusion between the marks, "GoldMail" and "CyberMail", stressing that the use of the allegedly infringing mark must "create a likelihood of confusion, deception or mistake among an appreciable number of ordinary buyers as to the source of or association between the two names".[7] In addition there must be the "likelihood that an appreciable

---

[4] For details of some of the cases that have arisen in the US see http://www.bna.com. This is the home page of the Bureau of National Affairs, Inc. in Washington DC.

[5] *Polaroid Corp. v Polaroid Electronics Corp.* 287 F 2d 492.

[6] 1996 US Dist Lexis 14977 29 August 1996.

[7] *Duluth News-Tribune v Mesabi Publishing Co.* 84 F 3d 1093 8th Cir 1996.

number of ordinarily prudent purchasers are likely to be misled, or simply confused as to the source of the goods in question".[8] Factors pertinent to a finding of confusion included: the strength of the trade mark; the similarity between the marks; the competitive proximity of the products; the intent to confuse the public; evidence of actual confusion and the degree of care reasonably expected of customers. [9]

The court found that it was not shown that the use of the "CyberMail" mark created a likelihood of confusion, deception or mistake among an appreciable number of ordinary buyers as to the source or association of the Internet services offered by the two companies.

This case dealt with different names, "GoldMail" and "CyberMail". Subsequent cases in the US have dealt with names that were the same and have based themselves on dilution rather than on confusion, an argument that is only possible if the marks that have allegedly been infringed are famous within the meaning of the US Trade Mark Dilution Act 1995 which came into force on 16 January 1996.

Confusion in the UK

There have been three cases on domain names that have reached court so far in the UK, the first of which dealt with domain names, trade marks and passing off, the second of which looked at domain names and passing off only as neither party had a registered trade mark, and the third of which relied on the concept of unfounded threats of litigation under the Trade Marks Act 1994.

The first case was *Harrods Ltd v UK Network Services Ltd and Others*[10] where the domain name "harrods.com" was registered by Michael Lawrie. Harrods, the famous department store in London wanted this domain name to advertise themselves and their wares on the Internet. Michael Lawrie was ordered by the court to hand the domain name over to Harrods, on the grounds that his potential use of the domain name constituted "trade mark infringement and passing off". Sadly, as Michael Lawrie did not turn up in court, the arguments to support this contention were not outlined and discussed in full.

The second dispute was that of *Pitman Training Limited and PTC Oxford Ltd v Nominet UK Ltd and Pearson Professional Ltd*.[11] which was based on the common law tort of passing off as neither party had a registered trade mark. The dispute was over the domain name 'pitman.co.uk' which was claimed by

---

[8] *Centaur Communications* 830 F2d.

[9] *Anheuser-Busch Inc. v Balducci Publications* 28 F 3d 769 8th Cir 1994.

[10] High Court, Ch D December 9, 1996. For comment on this case see "Protecting Your Name on the Internet". Gardner (1997) 8 Computers and Law 23.

[11] Unreported. High Court Ch D 22 May 1997. For further information see http://www.open.gov.uk/1cd/scott.htm

Pearsons plc who operate a publishing business, and Pitman Training Limited who operate a training and correspondence course business. Both were equally entitled to use the trading name 'Pitman' in the UK within their respective spheres of business. Nominet, the body in the UK responsible for allocating domain names under the top level domain 'co.uk' originally allocated the name to Pearsons plc. For some unknown reason, when Pitman Training Limited asked Nominet to register the same domain name several months later, it was duly allocated to them, thus depriving Pearsons plc of their registration. Pitman Training Limited proceeded to set up a web site and email service using the domain name, and it was only a period of months later, when Pearsons were ready to go "live" with their web site that they discovered that they no longer had the registration. After much correspondence between the various parties, Nominet re-allocated the domain name to Pearsons plc. On application for interlocutory injunction, the court ordered that it should revert to Pitman Training Limited, pending the full hearing. At the full hearing, Pitman Training Limited argued that because they had used the domain name for a period of months, the general public would associate that name with their business, and should it revert to Pearsons plc, that would constitute passing off. The court disagreed that a case of passing off had been established on the rather thin evidence presented (two e-mail messages had been sent to Pitman Training Limited during the months that the site had been in operation) and ordered that the domain name should be allocated to Pearsons plc on the basis that they had registered it first with Nominet.

While the case does not contribute to our knowledge of the trade mark and domain name controversy, it is interesting for a number of factors. First because, in distinction to many other cases, it dealt with the ".co.uk" domain rather than the ".com" domain. Secondly, it could have been argued that Nominet were negligent in their procedures in re-allocating the domain name to Pitman Training Limited when it had already been allocated to Pearsons plc. Nominet operate a first come first served policy on the registration of domain names. However, suing Nominet for damages would not have been a sufficient remedy for either party as what they wanted was the domain name rather than monetary compensation. Thirdly, it is notable that the court upheld Nominet's policy on first come first served registrations.

The third case which was heard before the High Court on 31 July 1997 was *Prince plc v Prince Sportswear Group Inc. (Prince)*.[12] Prince plc is an IT company registered in the UK. For the past two years it has operated a web site under the domain name "prince.com". Prince Sportswear Group Inc., a company registered in the US, notified InterNic that it was the owner of the Federal trade mark "Prince" and that the use of the domain name "prince.com" by Prince plc was a dilution of its famous mark. As with Nominet, InterNic operates a domain name allocation policy on a first come,

---

[12] For further information see http://www.prince.com/prince. 31 July 1997 High Ct. Ch. D

first served basis.[13] However, if a second person is able to come forward and show that they are the owner of a registered trade mark pertaining to that name, then the first person who has registered the domain name loses that registration. Such a loss of registration can be put on hold if the first party can either prove that they have a trade mark registration, or have commenced proceedings in a US court to protect that domain name. When InterNic wrote to Prince plc intimating that that they were about to re-allocate the domain name, Prince plc could neither show they owned a trade mark, nor confirm that they had commenced proceedings in a US Court, and so were in danger of losing the domain name in favour of Prince Sportswear Group Inc. However, at the last minute, Prince plc filed suit in the High Court in London, alleging that the statements made by Prince Sportswear Group Inc. that Prince plc were "infringing and diluting their trade mark rights" constituted groundless threats in terms of section 21 of the UK Trade Marks Act 1994. Although InterNic domain name policy refers to an action being raised in a US court, they have applied this flexibly, and have said, at least for the time being, that an action before any court will suffice. How long this policy will be operated in this way remains to be seen. On 31 July the High Court found that Prince Sportswear Group Inc. had indeed made groundless threats in terms of Section 21. At the time of writing the full text of the judgement was still awaited. What is particularly interesting in this case is the international flavour it is bringing to this area. US cases have dealt mainly with litigants in the US. The two UK cases have involved litigants in the UK. This one has litigants on either side of the Atlantic each equally entitled to use the same mark, albeit, in this instance, in different spheres of business. Indeed, Prince Sportswear Group Inc. have now filed an action in the US (*Prince Sports Group Inc. v Prince plc* DC NJ, Civil Action No 97-03581 submitted 17/9/97) alleging unfair competition and trade mark delution. In response, Prince plc argue that the court in New Jersey does not have jurisdiction to hear the case because it does not do business and has no contacts there. These arguments are in keeping with a number of other cases that have been brought in the US on questions of jurisdiction and the internet, each of which is contributing to a fascinating jurisprudence in this area that has yet to achieve a consistent approach.

Despite the fact that UK trade mark law has not yet been analysed in detail in connection with these disputes, there are interesting developments dealing with terrestrial trade mark rights which may well prove useful in the battle in cyberspace. Under the UK Trade Marks Act 1994, s 10(2), the question of confusion and similarity of goods was considered in *British Sugar v James Robertson*.[14] Six factors were taken as important in establishing similarity of the goods and services: the users of the goods and services; the uses of the

---

[13] For the latest revision and details of this policy see http://www.rs.internic.net/policy/internic/internic-domain4.txt.

[14] [1996] RPC 281.

goods and services; the physical nature of the goods or acts of service; the trade channels through which the goods or services reach the market; whether in self service stores the goods are found together or apart; the extent to which the goods or services are competitive. Similar considerations are likely to arise in assessing the similarity of the services or goods offered on the Internet. Clearly the most pertinent factor is the respective channels through which the goods or services reach the market.

If the goods and/or services are similar, then the second test to find infringement is that there must be a likelihood of public confusion between the trade marks which are appended to the goods and services used, which includes a likelihood of association.

This was considered in *Wagamama Limited v City Centre Restaurants plc and others*.[15] Wagamama owned the WAGAMAMA trade mark which was registered for restaurants. City Centre Restaurants decided to open a restaurant under the name Rajamama. Wagamama sued for infringement of trade mark and passing off. It was held that there had been infringement and that a case of passing off had been made out. In the judgement much discussion revolved around the phrase 'likelihood of association'. It was argued that the inclusion of the words in the section meant that there could be infringement of the trade mark even if there was no confusion in the minds of the public. The effect of this argument was to say that the grounds on which a case of infringement could be established under this section had been extended, such that, if there was an association between the marks in the mind of the public, this was sufficient for infringement, and that there was no need to show confusion. In other words, the function of a trade mark was not just to indicate origin, but included non-origin association, a much wider test, the effect of which would be to give the trade mark proprietor a much wider monopoly in the trade mark. This argument as to likelihood of association was dismissed. The court found that the wording of the section clearly states that there must exist a likelihood of confusion in the minds of the public, and included in, but not separate to that test, was a likelihood of association. Nevertheless, in this case the court concluded that there did exist confusion in the minds of the public as to the origin of the trade mark in that it was shown that the public thought that the Rajamama restaurant might be connected with WAGAMAMA.

The finding in this case re-inforces the view that the prime function of a trade mark is the "origin function", in other words, the function of a trade mark is to signify origin of goods and services; the touchstone of liability is that of confusion.

So, for goods and services provided on the Internet, is a surfer likely to be confused if the name "Fellowes.com" is chosen as the domain name for the company supplying office stationery if in fact she is a client of the law firm of

---

[15] [1995] FSR 713

the same name? This will depend on whether the domain name is viewed as associated with the web site only, or the underlying goods and services. And this is where a fundamental problem lies in associating domain names with trade marks. A domain name is an address used to call up a specific location on the Internet such as a Web page. Until you access the Web page, the domain name has no associations relating to the underlying goods or services. There is nothing in traditional trade mark law to prevent a business from using the same mark as that belonging to someone else, but using it for *dissimilar* goods and services so long as it is not likely to cause confusion. Does the domain name refer to the Web page, or to the underlying goods and services? If it is regarded as a trade mark (or an infringement of a trade mark), where is the point of confusion? At the point of access to the Web page? Or at the point of finding out what goods and services are being offered at that site? If the latter, then arguably confusion is unlikely to occur.

Perhaps an analogy could be drawn with those non-Internet related cases on trade marks and passing off which deal with the question as to the point at which confusion arises. These cases generally view post sale confusion as irrelevant; in other words, confusion must be present at the time at which the customer is making up his or her mind as to what to purchase before there is infringement of a trade mark. In *Bostik v Sellotape*[16] the court found it irrelevant that a customer might find the colours of the "blu-tack" offered by competing brands confusing after they had torn open the packets, because that confusion would only arise after the sale was made. The problem with domain names is almost the inverse of this; there may be confusion at the point of accessing the address, but once the relevant page is accessed, there need not be any confusion thereafter.

In *Reckitt & Colman Products Ltd v Bordman Inc. & Ors*,[17] the "*Jif*" *lemon* case which concerned the similarity of packaging of two products comprising lemon juice packaged in a plastic lemon, the court held that the crucial point of reference for a shopper who wishes to purchase a lemon is the shape of the lemon itself: "Virtually no, if any attention is paid to the label which that lemon bears"; when the shopper gets home, the label is taken off as it "performs no useful function and is easily detachable, so that it is not thereafter any part of the purchased product". Can an analogy be drawn here with the function of a domain name? Once the Web site is accessed the domain name is discarded; what matters is the mark at the point of sale. Where is the equivalent of the point of sale on the Internet? Not at the point at which you log on, but rather the point at which you actually reach the Web site and make your decisions as a purchaser.

Taking this approach to the question of confusion, it would be perfectly legitimate to register any number of domain names using the key phrase "Fellowes", under different top level domains, such as ".com"; ".plc.uk";

[16] [1994] RPC 556
[17] [1990] RPC 341

".ltd.uk"; and so on. The underlying goods and services are different, and there is no question of confusion once accessed.

However, this argument will fail if registration of a domain name as a trade mark is made in class 38 of the UK Register of Trade Marks. There have apparently been a number of applications filed for registration of domain names in the UK in this class, although it is not clear as to whether they have actually been registered as yet. Class 38 covers Telecommunications, specifically services allowing communication including the transmission of messages to one another. If the application is made in this class, then there can only be one mark, and the registration of a very close mark is going to be disallowed on the basis of similarity of services. However, if the registration is allowed, but relates rather to the underlying goods or services, then registration of similar domain names in different classes should pose no problem.

Trade mark dilution in the US

The second main ground on which trade mark and domain name infringement actions have been pursued, is on the grounds of trade mark dilution. The anti-dilution doctrine seeks to enable the trade mark proprietor to protect his mark against the sorts of use where public confusion is absent. The doctrine does not seek to protect ideas of origin, but rather the quality which the trade mark embodies. For example, if the mark "Rolls-Royce" which is associated with quality cars were to be used in association with low grade safety pins, the quality associated with the mark would be diluted.

Prior to January 1996, only 25 US States had dilution laws, defining dilution as "the blurring of a marks product identification or the tarnishment of the affirmative associations a mark has come to convey".[18] Dilution protection was extended to federal marks on January 16 1996 by virtue of the Federal Trademark Dilution Act of 1995. This Act created a federal cause of action for the owners of well known or famous marks, and did away with the requirement that a likelihood of confusion be established. There are a number of different scenarios in which dilution of trade marks by domain names has been considered by the courts.

Firstly, there is the use of a domain name which impacts on the underlying goods. In *Hasbro Inc. v Internet Entertainment Group Inc.*[19] the court granted a preliminary injunction preventing Internet Entertainment Group from using the domain "candyland.com" for its Web site which featured sexually explicit materials. Hasbro produces a game Candy Land for young children, and the court was persuaded that 94% of mothers were aware of this game. The court found that the name "Candy Land" was being diluted by use by the

---

[18] *Mead Data Central Inc. v Toyota Motor Sales* USA 875 F 2d 1026 A 1031.
[19] Case C96 130 WD.

Internet Entertainment Group. The court may well have been influenced in this case by the sexually explicit nature of the materials.

Other cases on dilution have dealt with names of companies which serve as trade marks indicating the origin of the goods or services offered under the mark.

In *Panavision International LP v Toeppen*,[20] Dennis Toeppen registered the domain name "panavision.com". Panavision sued for dilution of its trade mark. The court found that Panavision's mark was a famous mark and that Toeppen had made commercial use of the mark by attempting to sell the domain name to Panavision. The court did much to limit the effect of its judgement by stating that it did not give trademark owners pre-emptive rights in domain names but held that registering a famous mark as a domain name merely for the purpose of trading on the value of the mark by selling the name to the trademark owner violated dilution statues, a point which also emphasis the need for some trading activity for a finding of dilution. This case was decided on November 21 1996.

The judgement in a previous case concerning the same defendant, that of *Intermatic Inc. v Dennis Toeppen*,[21] decided on 3 October 1996, was very much wider. Toeppen had registered the domain name "intermatic.com". The court found that Intermatic were entitled to summary judgement on the issue of dilution because "Toeppen's action lessens the capacity of a famous mark "Intermatic" to identify and distinguish goods or services as a matter of law". It was found that the Intermatic mark was famous within the meaning of the Federal Trade Mark Dilution Act 1995; Toeppens' use of that mark was commercial, evidenced by his intention to resell or license the domain name; and that the use of the name in connection with the Internet constituted "commerce" under the Act (thus fulfilling the requirement that there be some trading activity). By attempting to licence or sell the mark Toeppen caused dilution of the distinctive quality of the mark by lessening Intermatic's capacity to identify its goods to potential customers and destroying the mark's advertising value. This reasoning would suggest that the courts in the US would find that there was dilution of a trade mark in all cases where there was an intention by the person who registered a domain name resembling a famous trade mark to sell that domain name for financial reward.

Trade mark dilution in the UK

It may be difficult to argue that a trade mark has been infringed by dilution where there is no element of confusion under s 10(2) of the UK Trade Marks Act 1994 given the stance taken by Laddie J in *Wagamama* discussed above.

---

[20] 19/09/1996 http://www.jmls.edu/cyber/cases/panavis.html.
[21] No 96 C 1982 ND 1II.

However, if the notion of dilution is raised in an action concerning the hijacking of a company name by a third party seeking to make a profit from selling it on, then those carrying out such activities may find that a court has very little sympathy for them. In *Direct Line Group Ltd v Direct Line Estate Agency*,[22] a trade mark infringement action was brought against the directors of a number of companies with names such as YSL Limited; Virgin Jeans Limited; and the Nike Clothing Company Limited. Direct Line Group Limited objected to the registration of the names Direct Line Estate Agency Limited and Direct Line Estates Limited. Laddie J took a robust approach to the defendants' line of business remarking: "[the directors] have a track record of taking or being associated with the taking of famous trade marks belonging to third parties, either for the purpose of carrying on business which siphons off the goodwill belonging to other traders, or for the purpose of offering those marks back to their rightful proprietors, no doubt as a profit". He went on to say "I think it only right to say that this court will view with extreme displeasure any attempt by traders to embark upon a scam designed to make illegitimate use of other companies" trade marks".

Such a robust approach would dispose of a number of complaints of the type that have reached courts in the US, such as those lodged against Dennis Toeppen. This would then leave open the door for a proper examination of the more difficult issues in relation to trade mark/domain name disputes, such as where a number of businesses are entitled to use the same mark, whether within one country or world wide. How should those problems should be resolved?

Famous marks and domain names

The US cases on dilution discussed above concern "famous names" within the meaning of the Federal Trade Mark Dilution Act 1996. There is also provision in the UK Trade Marks Act 1994 concerning the protection of "famous names" which may be of significant value to trade mark owners in their domain name fight, in particular given the international nature of the Internet.

Section 56 of the Trade Marks Act 1994 incorporates Article 6bis of the Paris International Convention into UK law. In terms of this section, if a person can show that his mark is "well known" (in the Paris Convention sense) then irrespective of whether he carries on business or has goodwill in the UK, he may stop a third party using a similar mark in relation to identical or similar goods, where that use is likely to cause confusion. The section is subject to the limitation that the mark must be well known in this country, and that needs proof of a substantial degree of recognition. What standard of proof this will require is not known, although Cornish suggests that the German

[22] Ch D 12 September 1996.

methodical approach requiring 80 percent recognition may set the standard.[23] Cornish uses an interesting example concerning the store "Macy's" situated in New York. The name Macy's will be "well-known" (subject to sufficient evidence) in UK for the goods that the store sells. Therefore, a British applicant could not register "Macy's" as a trade mark for department store goods. The question for the Internet then is whether "Macy's" could be used as a domain name by a UK business selling different goods or services?

Under the Trade Marks Act 1994, Macy's could object to the use of the name "Macy's" in connection with dissimilar goods or services, such as services provided on the Internet, if they could show the name Macy's had a reputation in the UK, and that the use of the name by a third party took unfair advantage of, or caused detriment to their own mark.[24] There is no requirement for confusion under this section, but rather it embodies the doctrine of dilution. What is in contemplation is the use of a mark which has been registered and/or used in another country, where the reputation of that mark has spread to the UK as a result of, for example, advertising in newspapers, or publicity on television, radio or in films. In these circumstances, the mere fact that the famous name is adopted as a domain name could amount to taking unfair advantage of, or causing detriment to, Macy's, even if the business using it was selling dissimilar goods.

Thus, it would appear that there may be a similar remedy on the grounds of dilution of a famous mark in the UK as is found in the US. However, this theory is as yet untested and will have to overcome judicial reluctance to embrace the notion of dilution in UK trade mark law if confusion is not present.[25]

Conclusion on UK law and domain names and trade marks

If the matters that have so far troubled this question of domain names and trade marks are teased out, the question of using recognised trade marks and

---

[23] W R Cornish, *Intellectual Property: Patents, Copyright, Trade Marks and Allied Rights*, 3rd edn (1996) Sweet & Maxwell p. 542.

[24] Trade Marks Act 1994, s 5(3).

[25] The reluctance of the judiciary to embrace the doctrine of dilution is exemplified by *Baywatch Production Co. Ltd. v The Home Video Channel* [1997] FSR 22 where the High Court considered the ambit of s 10(3) of the Trade Marks Act 1994, which outlaws infringement of registered marks with "a reputation in the UK". The court considered that section 10(3) only applied where:

1. a sign is similar to the trade mark, so that there is a likelihood of confusion on the part of the public, is used in relation to goods and services which are not similar to the mark; and
2. the mark has a reputation in the UK; and
3. the use of the sign, being without due cause, takes advantage of, or is detrimental to the distinctive character or the repute of the trade mark.

However, doubt has been expressed as to whether this interpretation of s10(3) is correct as there is no reference to confusion in the wording of the section.

company names as domain names becomes easier to deal with. Beyond that, if a domain name is seen as synonymous with a trade mark, then there appears no reason why actions for trade mark infringement should not succeed based on either confusion or dilution. The courts can then be left to analyse the far more tricky questions in this area, such as the distinction between the domain name and the underlying goods and services which are being promoted; how to reconcile conflicts where two or more parties are equally entitled to use the same trade mark in the terrestrial world, albeit for different goods and services; and the equally intractable problem of international conflicts where two or more parties are equally entitled to use the same trade mark for the same goods and services but are situated in different jurisdictions.

ALLOCATION AND REGULATION OF DOMAIN NAMES

The ferocity of the storm in the US over the ownership of domain names has been caused by two main factors. The first factor, as discussed above, was the Trade Mark Dilution statute of 1996, which introduced Federal protection against dilution of famous marks. The second factor has been InterNic's registration policy. To investigate this further, we must briefly examine the institutional structures currently in place for regulation of Internet domain names.

THE REGULATION OF DOMAIN NAMES: *INTERNIC*

The Internet Assigned Numbers Authority (IANA) acts under authority from the US Government and the Internet Society (ISOC) which is funded by the National Science Foundation (NSF). IANA allocates blocks of numeric IP addresses to Network Solutions Inc. (NSI), who have overall authority for IP addresses, domain names and other Internet parameters. As mentioned above, the function of allocating domain names is then further delegated by NSI to InterNic.[26] Several domain name allocation policies have been created by InterNic.[27] The latest includes the following provisions:

1. Domain names are registered on a first come first served basis. No investigation is carried out to determine whether the applicant is entitled in any way to the name which he seeks to register.

---

[26] See Terrett p. 16 and http://www.internic.net.

[27] For perceptive discussion on the policy and various revisions see:

C Oppendahl *"Avoid the Traps in the New Rules for Registering a Domain Name"*. New York Law Journal. 8 August 1995. http://www.patents.com/nylj3.sht.

C Oppendahl. *"NSI Domain Name Dispute Policy puts Owners at significant Risk"*. New York Law Journal 21 May 1996 http://www.patents.com/nylj6.sht..

C Oppendahl. *"Fourth Domain Name Policy Leaves Owners with Few Options"*. New York Law Journal 3 September 1996 http://www.patents.com/nylj7.sht.

2. If a second party comes along claiming to have superior right to the name by way of a trade mark, then they must first contact the domain name holder. The trade mark holder must furnish InterNic with a copy of the trade mark certificate which registers the name which is disputed as a trade mark.

3. Where the domain name was registered prior to the registration of the trade mark, the domain name holder may continue to use the domain name pending resolution of the dispute; if the registration of the domain name was made after the registration of the trade mark, then the domain name holder may have to forfeit the domain name to the registered trade mark holder. The domain name holder must indemnify InterNic against damages it may suffer in relation to the dispute.

A registered trade mark from any authority is sufficient for InterNic as proof ownership of a registered trade mark. This has meant that where a dispute arises, the holder of the domain name, who has no registered trade mark, generally does all he can, at great speed to obtain a registration. A good example is Road Runner Computer Systems who offers Internet services. In December 1995, Warner Bros. owner of the registered trade mark "Road Runner" complained to InterNic about the registration and use of the domain name "roadrunner.com" by the computer company. InterNic informed Road Runner that it would place its domain name on hold. Road Runner then applied for, and got a trademark registration in Tunisia. However, in this instance InterNic still refused to allow Road Runner to keep the domain name. Tunisia, unlike most other countries, will register a trade mark within a matter of days.

It was this policy of re-allocating the domain names, to the registered trade mark owner that fanned the flames of the fire. The policy completely ignored any claims that prior unregistered mark owners may have, and also assumed that a domain name and a trade mark were synonymous. The policy is also unfair to non-US based businesses, as it is far more difficult for them to raise an action in the courts of the US. However, as mentioned above, InterNic are currently operating a flexible policy, indicating that the raising of an action in any court, US or otherwise, is sufficient to stay the action. How long this flexibility will continue remains to be seen given that InterNic itself may lose the right to allocate domain names in 1998. It is also noteworthy that part of the reason the first come first served policy to the allocation of domain names was adopted by InterNic was because they did not have the resources to carry out trade mark searches. This may also help to explain why priority was given to registered as opposed to unregistered trade marks—it does not cost InterNic anything simply to see a copy of a trade mark registration certificate.

Development of regulatory efforts

Over the past months, many developments have taken place in the domain naming system in a bid to reach solutions to the problems arising in courts in the US and elsewhere. One of the suggestions that has been on the cards for a while is the proposal to create many more generic top level domain names. The purpose would be to relieve the pressure on the ".com" top level domain, and to make room for every business to have its own generic top level domain, suited more closely to its particular function. Such generic top level domains may include ".reg" for registered trade marks, or ".biz" for unincorporated businesses. In this way every "Fellowes" could have a registered "commercial" address pertinent to their particular area of commerce for example "Fellowes.store" and Fellowes.firm".

Until recently NSI who, because they were in place at the start of the great expansion of the commercial use of the Internet have enjoyed a near monopoly in the allocation of top level domains, have been unwilling to accede to this request. There is however no central authority that is responsible for the monitoring and provision of the Internet. Rather, governance of the Internet is largely based on consensus together with a need to adhere to the technical constraints that are required because of the need for the equipment used around the world to be able to communicate; the computers need to be able to "talk to each other". The "monopoly" enjoyed by InterNic in the provision of top level domains has largely been *de-facto*, partly because of these technical constraints, and partly because it has such a lead in the market. It also registers names in the ".com" domain, which is the one that is seen as so attractive to commercial business.

Prima facie there appears to be no reason why other providers should not assign top level domains with ease. A company called "AlterNic" has challenged NSI's *de facto* monopoly by setting up and creating its own top level domains. The argument put forward by AlterNic is that if more top level domains were created, this would lessen the pressure on the ".com" domain and end the flurry of disputes. AlterNic has a series of servers to deal with the creation and management of these top level domains. In order to access AlterNic's servers and top level domain names, a few changes need to be made to the configuration of the browser and server software used to access Internet sites. Once done, the browsers can then recognise AlterNic's top level domains. Moreover, AlterNic's root servers will point towards NSI's root servers. In other words, if the correct configurations are made to the software, then your browser can recognise both AlterNic's and NSI's top level domain names. However, currently NSI's root servers will not point to AlterNic's top level domains thus limiting the utility of AlterNic's alternative naming system.

This approach, of creating more top level domains, is now being expanded. The International Ad Hoc Committee (IAHC) set up by a number of interested parties[28] to try and find a solution to the domain name problem, announced an increase in the number of top level domain names in May 1997 in a Memorandum of Understanding on Generic Top Level Domain Space of the Internet Domain Name System (MOU).[29] This MOU sets up an Internet self-governance system pursuant to the plan for increasing and administering generic top level domains. Seven new generic Top Level Domains are to be created, and more firms around the world are to be allowed to act as registrars. The new top level domains will be ".firm" for businesses or firms; ".store" for businesses offering goods to purchase; ".web" for entities with web activities; ".arts" for entities in the cultural and entertainment activities; ".rec" for recreation and entertainment activities; ".info" for information services, and ".nom" for individual or personal nomenclature.[30] Twenty eight new registrars will be established to deal with the administration under these top level domains, and each will also be able to register second level domains.

A number of arguments suggest that the creation of these extra top level domains will not signal an end to the disputes, but do little more than create further "techno-anarchy" in cyberspace. First, a number of businesses argue that they may lose associated good will if they are not able to use the ".com" domain, such is the current fixation on the word ".com". Secondly, there are already over 230 top level domains throughout the world , including such country domains as ".uk" for the UK and ".de" for Germany. This has not alleviated the problem. Thirdly, there is no reason to suppose that some business will not simply register under all the top level domains. It is still difficult to imagine that the owners of certain names would be happy to see their marks used by others. Harrods of London may now have "harrods.com", but that would not stop them objecting to "harrods.firm", or "harrods.info" being registered by someone else. It is likely to be argued that confusion and dilution will still occur if the name is used by anyone other than Harrods of London.

Before the ink had dried on the page of the MOU, the proposals it contains had come under fire from no less a person than Madeleine Allbright, the US Secretary of State,[31] who argued that the strategy suggested is not in the best interests of US residents. In addition, a group calling itself the Open Internet Congress met in July 1997 to formulate a plan to try and stop implementation of the proposals by the IAHC arguing that it represents an "unauthorised

---

[28] IHAC is a coalition of participants from the Internet community. Membership includes the Internet Society (ISOC), Internet Assigned Numbers authority (IANA), Internet Architecture Board (IAB), Federal Networking Council (FNC), International Trademark Association (INTA), and the World Intellectual Property Organisation (WIPO).

[29] See (1997) BNA 2 EPLR 747 for details

[30] For a response to this issue see http://www.nic.uk/iahc-com.html.

[31] For which see http://secretary.state.gov/www/statement/, and for comment http://www.news.com/News/Item/0,4,10198,00.html.

attempt to take over the Internet".[32] Most recently, the World Intellectual Property Organisation (WIPO) has stepped in and announced plans for a domain-name dispute resolution mechanism to commence in early 1998 after consultations with interested parties.

THE FUNDAMENTAL ISSUES TO BE RESOLVED

There is no doubt that there is currently a great deal of confusion surrounding the issue of trade marks and domain names. In this confusion there are a number of fundamental issues that have to be resolved concerning the interaction between the two.

At a very basic level, it is not at all clear why trade marks and domain names are necessarily seen as synonymous. A domain name is an address. We all have addresses, and there has never been any argument that a postal address should be seen as synonymous with a trade mark, no matter how similar the name is to a registered mark. However, it is true that on the Internet, a company's "address" (i.e. its URL) may raise a level of expectation as to the quality and origin of the goods that may be offered, or the information that may be offered in connection with that address. For example the name "next.clothes.com" may lead us to think that what we would be buying would be clothes and other goods from the store Next, a commercial entity, and that any merchandise would be of the quality expected from Next. Because these domain names may suggest quality, origin and identity, they may function as trade marks. However, careful consideration must be given to the separation of the domain name from the trade mark and the underlying goods and services, which should not automatically be seen as synonymous.

A further problem is over the use of the trade mark. Trade mark law is such that it permits multiple registrations of the same trade mark in different geographical locations, and for different goods and services where there is unlikely to be confusion. However, only one person can hold a particular domain name, and that is for world wide use. This question of competing international trade marks and domain names, mentioned only briefly above, must be rationally analysed to create an internationally workable policy.

Another fundamental problem revolves around the policy that InterNic has chosen to follow in giving priority in allocation of domain names to the holders of registered trade marks. Why should those who own registered trade marks have a superior claim to a domain name over those who use unregistered trade marks? Domain names can be of significant value to those who cannot obtain a registered trade mark. InterNic policy certainly fails to take account of the interests of the holders of unregistered marks.

---

[32] (1997) BNA 2 EPLR 748.

Initial relief from the courts

The hi-jacking of domain names by those intending to make a quick profit from selling them back to the true owner has been discussed above. If the courts continue to take the robust approach found in the *Toeppen* cases, then many of the types of disputes that have reached court to date will be solved with little problem.

However, there are, and will continue to be other circumstances which will need to be dealt with, such as when two or more entities are entitled to the same trade mark, whether based within the UK or abroad.

Self regulation and self restraint

A first solution would be for InterNic to revert to the policy of registering domain names on a first come, first served basis, and to halt the practice of re-allocating on the basis of a registered trade mark. Users would then have to accept these were the grounds on which the system operates, and quite frankly stop getting so excited about "domain name hijacking". There are plenty of variations on a particular name that can be registered with a little imagination. It is unlikely, because of the registration fee that is charged by InterNic, that those entitled (in the loosest sense of the word) to register a domain name will register all the possible variations. If someone else has your preferred name first, then you have to settle for something else. In addition, a number of companies register second level domains under the top level domains which could easily be used by others. For example, Proctor & Gamble have registered "pampers.com" as one of their domain names, along with many other ".com" addresses featuring their products. How much preferable if they were to register "pampers.p-and-g.com", and similarly register all their products under the one second level domain of ".p-and-g" thus freeing up more names for others.

Is such self-restraint and self regulation likely? Unfortunately not! Further disputes are almost bound to get to court: the courts are then going to have to make decisions.

Creation of more top level domain names

As discussed above, the proposal to create seven more generic top level domains has come under heavy criticism, and it is not at all clear whether their creation will solve the problems that have arisen. Nonetheless, the solution remains on the cards.

Cease allocating domain names: allocate numbers instead

As explained above, domain names are based on a series of underlying numbers. If the disputes over names do not cease, then users could simply be given a series of numbers, and no dispute over the name could arise. Clearly this solution would not be popular. Users of the Internet see value in having an easily recognisable and memorable name. Further, the domain name remains constant—for example, if the user changes service providers, then the underlying numbers change but the domain name remains constant. Therefore any change in service provider would entail consequent changes in corporate stationary and so on. But this is not a new problem. If a business moves, then stationery has to change; telephone numbers change, and again business information also has to change. The solution, however unpopular, would certainly not be impossible. Perhaps a better solution than tearing the Internet apart by litigation.

Create a global directory

The explosive growth of the Web and the lack of a global directory have contributed significantly to the domain name problems. Indeed, the domain name service is becoming confused with a directory service, which it is not. The optimal solution would be to create a global database that would map the name of a company to its web page. All the user would have to do would be to type in the name of the business, and possibly the products they provide. The directory service would find the requested web site by looking up the IP address. The web search engines do, of course, already carry out this function, but in an unstructured way. To create a truly global database would require investment and co-operation, and appears it would be some time away. What is needed is a solution now.

CONCLUSION

To date it appears that the courts have been prepared to rush in to the domain name trade mark dispute with little examination of the fundamental issues.

This has been partly spurred on by the policy that InterNic has adopted while at the same time exhibiting an unwillingness to be dictatorial in their approach to the question of regulation of domain names. This is understandable. The Internet and its users have always prided themselves that the Internet is unregulated—or rather self-regulated. The last thing that IANA or any of the other bodies involved want to do is to impose obligations on users.

The disputes over domain names and trade marks are not going to go away. However, with the increase in the number of top level domains available, education of the commercial Internet users that the ".com" domain is not the only solution to an Internet address, and self restraint, the problems can be overcome.

5

Copyright and the Internet

HECTOR L MACQUEEN[1]

INTRODUCTION

A major issue for copyright lawyers at the present time is how to deal with the arrival and rapid development of the Internet and the prospect of the "information superhighway", world-wide telecommunications systems which permit the rapid, indeed virtually instantaneous transmission around the world, at times chosen as much by recipients as by transmitters, of information and entertainment in all media—print, pictures still and moving, sound, and combinations thereof. The issues are manifold. Is the ease of perfect reproduction and manipulation of material in the digital form used by our communications systems the death-knell of the whole basis of copyright? Are we going to have to reconsider such fundamentals of copyright law as what constitutes publication, reproduction and public performance, or the old distinctions between categories of work such as literary, artistic, sound recording and film? Are we going to see the emergence of a genuine market-place in which producer and user bargain about the price for individual transfers of material, rather than requiring intermediaries such as publishers? Given the ready flow of material across national frontiers, does the international harmonisation of copyright laws need intensification, and should the classic rules of private international law on jurisdiction and choice of law be adapted to enable a party confronted with infringements in another country to sue effectively in his own country and have judgments recognised abroad?

The question of how UK copyright law applies to the Internet and the material appearing thereupon has not yet received much systematic treatment in the standard texts on the subject, even those the latest editions of which have appeared within the last year or two.[2] Accordingly this paper approaches

[1] LLB (Hons), PhD, FRSE, Professor of Private Law, University of Edinburgh, and Director, The David Hume Institute, Edinburgh. Email address Hector.MacQueen@ed.ac.uk. I am grateful to the editors for stimulating thought and providing references, but am alone responsible for what appears here.

[2] There are number of thoughtful comments in W R Cornish, *Intellectual Property: Patents, Copyright, Trade Marks and Allied Rights*, 3rd edn (1996): see e.g. 463-471. See also J Phillips and A Firth, *Introduction to Intellectual Property* Law, 3rd edn (1995), 332-335. The topic attracts no special attention in e.g. *Copinger and Skone James on Copyright*, 13th edn (1991) and First Supplement (1994); H Laddie, P Prescott and M Vitoria, *The Modern Law of Copyright*, 2nd edn

its complex subject in a very simple manner, by looking at the main rules of UK copyright defining what material may be subject to copyright, drawing attention to those subject matters which appear to be especially relevant to the Internet and sites thereon; and then turning to how copyright in that material may be infringed, again highlighting application of the rules to web-sites, and defences available against infringement. This will demonstrate some of the difficulties with which the Internet confronts copyright, and the paper will finish with some of the international proposals to develop the law and to meet these difficulties.

A few preliminaries may be helpful, however. Copyright first developed in the early modern period as a response to the growth of the printing technology which facilitated the rapid multiplication and distribution of copies of written works. The development of copyright has continued to be driven by technological advance in the means by which works can be presented to the public at large, and protection has been extended and adapted to cover photography, cinematography, sound recording, broadcasting, cable transmissions and computer programs. So there is no reason to suppose that, if the Internet does in fact present new problems for copyright, the law cannot be adapted to deal with them. The practical benefit of working within the copyright mould is the continued applicability of the international regime under the Berne Convention and other treaties, which ensures potentially world-wide protection for right-holders (a vitally important point in relation to the global Internet).

A second preliminary point concerns the functions of copyright. Two major conceptualisations of this can be identified in the world's legal sytems. The Anglo-American or Common Law tradition emphasises the economic role of copyright. Protection of copyright subject-matter against unauthorised acts of exploitation enables right-holders either to go to market themselves with a product based on the material, or to grant others the right to do so for what-ever seems an appropriate price. In the absence of copyright, which would enable free-riding by would-be users, it is unlikely that producers of the material would be able to earn any return for their work, and without that incentive production would dry up. Copyright is thus essentially a response to market failure, a means by which socially beneficial activities can be made financially worthwhile. In contrast, the Continental or Civil Law tradition sees copyright as springing from the personality rights of the producers of the subject matter. This perception is reflected in the name "author-law" given to the topic by the various continental systems—*droit d'auteur, urheberrecht,* and so on. Protection is given out of respect for the creative act of produc-tion, and extends beyond the merely economic to the so-called "moral rights": the right to be identified as the creator of a work, the right to have the integ-

(1995); and J Holyoak and P Torremans, *Intellectual Property Law* (1995). A useful discussion in a perhaps unexpected place to which my attention was drawn by Dr Athol Murray, is P Wienand, "The Legal Implications of Electronic Data Exchange", (1997) 18 *Journal of the Society of Archivists* 83–92.

rity of a work preserved, and others. The distinction between the two conceptualisations is sometimes summarised by saying that the Anglo-American tradition is centred on the entrepreneur, the Continental one on the author. The distinction is reflected in various rules: for example, where the Anglo-American tradition gives copyright protection to media works such as sound recordings and broadcasts, the Continental tradition uses a separate group of "neighbouring rights" for these non-author works. Again, where the Anglo-American tradition vests first ownership of copyright in the employer of an author making a work in the course of employment, the Continental tradition always gives it to the author. But it is important not to over-emphasise such distinctions. Continental copyright laws are also a basis for market operations and the author plays a fundamental role in Anglo-American copyright laws, where moral rights are now also developing.[3] Membership of the Berne Convention, which has been the basis of international copyright since 1886 and sets minimum standards for national copyright legislation, has embraced countries from both traditions for most of its history and since 1989 has included the USA. The convergence promoted by the Convention's minimum standards has been further advanced by the 1994 Agreement on Trade-Related Aspects of Intellectual Property Rights (TRIPS). During the 1990s, even more fundamental steps towards convergence have been taken within the European Union, by a policy of harmonisation of copyright law in its Member States through a series of Directives. The global nature of the Internet means that purely national responses to the copyright problems arising are inadequate, and that a convergent approach is required; but nonetheless the deep-seated differences in basic concepts have an effect upon international discussions, the outcome of which may sometimes reflect a somewhat uneasy compromise between the competing schools of thought.

The third preliminary is to observe that the legal system which has so far thrown up most of the actual cases about Internet copyright is that of the USA. These cases are of course immensely valuable in showing the kinds of question which are likely to arise elsewhere. But it is necessary to be somewhat cautious in assuming that courts in other countries would necessarily reach the same conclusions. US copyright law is characterised by its express basis in the American Constitution, which empowers Congress "to promote the progress of science and useful arts, by securing for limited times to authors and inventors the exclusive right to their respective writings and discoveries". The actual law is found in the Copyright Act 1976 with various additions and amendments thereto. The constitutional basis and the general American legal tradition encourage the courts to take a much more overtly policy-oriented approach to copyright questions than would be possible for a British or (even more so) another European court. In any event, as Jacob J once observed

---

[3] In the UK see Copyright, Designs and Patents Act [CDPA] 1988, ss 77-89. The USA has not enacted moral rights as such but other rights granted in US law have been accepted as satisfying the requirements of the Berne Convention on this matter.

when several American cases were cited to him in a case about software copyright, the language of the American statute is not at all the same as that of the British one, and one must therefore be careful of reasoning which may be dependent ultimately on the legislative wording.[4]

Lastly, this paper is a much compressed treatment of a very large subject, and space prohibits anything other than fairly abbreviated discussion of the issues. In particular, it is only possible to make the most incidental of references to the Database Directive of 1996,[5] which has important implications in this area of law, and to the problems of international private law.

SOME EXAMPLES

By kind permission of the *Shetland Times*.

It is always helpful to have good examples with which to illustrate discussion of a complex matter. For Internet copyright, fortunately, a particularly useful one is readily to hand in Scotland in the recent and very interesting case of *Shetland Times v Wills*.[6] *The Shetland Times* published by the pursuers is a newspaper the owner of which (Mr Robert Wishart) has established an Internet website or home page (*http://www.shetland-times.co.uk*). The opening or front page of the site used headlines from the newspaper upon which users clicked to gain access to the stories as printed under these headlines in the newspaper. Dr Jonathan Wills, who was once well-known as a student Rector of Edinburgh University and was also at one time editor of *The Shetland Times*, began to publish *The Shetland News* after falling out with Mr Wishart. Dr Wills also operates a website for his newspaper, using news headlines as the means of access to its stories (*http://www.shetland-news.co.uk*). From about 14 October 1996 *The Shetland News* page included *Shetland Times* headlines as hypertext links, and by clicking on these access could be gained to the relative stories on *The Shetland Times* website, bypassing the front page of that site altogether. *The Shetland Times* alleged infringement of copyright and sought interim interdict. The practical reason underlying the

---

[4] *Ibcos Computers Ltd v Barclays Mercantile Highland Finance Ltd* [1994] FSR 275 at 292.
[5] Parliament and Council Directive 96/9/EC.
[6] 24 October 1996; *The Times* 21 January 1997; 1997 GWD 1-5; 1997 SLT 669; 1997 SCLR 160 (Notes).

action seems to be that *The Shetland Times* hopes or hoped to sell advertising space on its website front page, and of course this commercial benefit would be lost if readers could access the news stories directly and bypass the front page.[7] *The Shetland Times* obtained its interim interdict before Lord Hamilton, and the case continues. At the time of writing (August 1997), a full hearing on the petition for permanent interdict was expected to take place in the Court of Session on 11–14 November 1997.[8]

The case seems to be not untypical of the copyright issues arising on the Internet. A parallel litigation in the USA, now settled, involved an organisation called Total News, from whose website a reader could link on to the web pages of other news organisations such as *The Washington Post*. Again the real issue appears to have been advertising on the respective sites, inasmuch as even after a link had been made to another site from the Total News one, the display was still "framed" with Total News advertisements. The settlement allows linking but not framing.[9] Another yet-to-be-decided case of this type (albeit one concerned mainly with trade mark rather than copyright questions) is *Ticket Master v Microsoft*, where the defendants have provided a link to the plaintiffs' website avoiding its home page. In essence the issue raised can be put as being whether providing hypertext links from one website to another infringes the copyright in the second site.[10]

Another type of case involves the creator of a website who puts other persons' copyright material on to his pages. In recent French cases, for example, Raymond Quenard's poem "Cente Mille Milliards de Poemes" was placed on two different websites without the authorisation of the owners of the copyright in the work.[11] In August 1997 the BBC obtained the removal from 19 private websites of unauthorised copies of pictures and texts from *Teletubbies*, the popular children's TV programme.[11a] A well-known American case of this type is *Religious Technology Center v Netcom On-Line Communication Services*,[12] in which one Denis Ehrlich unauthorisedly posted on an electronic bulletin board both published and unpublished works by L Ron Hubbard, founder of the Church of Scientology. The case raised the additional issue of whether the bulletin board operator and the service provider with which the

---

[7] It is perhaps worthy of note here that *The Shetland News* site seems to have been much more successful in attracting advertisers than *The Shetland Times* counterpart.

[8] The progress of the case can be followed on the respective websites. [9] For details of the settlement dated 6 June 1997, see http://www.bna.com/e-law/cases/ totalset.html.

[10] For details of this case see http://www.bna.com/e-law/docs/ticket.html; and for discussion see C Waelde, "Intellectual property and the Internet", in H L MacQueen and B G M Main (eds), *Innovation, Incentive and Reward: Intellectual Property Law and Policy*, 5(3) Hume Papers on Public Policy (1997), 64-81 at 72-73.

[11] (1997) 11 *World Intellectual Property Reporter* 266.

[11a] *The Scotsman*, 15 August 1997.

[12] 907 F Supp 1361 (ND Cal, 1995). See also *Religious Technology Center v Lerma*, US District Court for the Eastern District of Virginia, 4 October 1996 (http://www.bna.com/e-law/cases/lerma.html) and E. Cameron, (1997) 11 *International Review of Law Computers and Technology* 155–165.

board was based could be liable for infringement of copyright along with the person who made the initial copy. Finally there are the cases about those who access and download material from the Internet. Assuming that the material has copyright—as a literary, artistic or musical work, or as a computer program, sound recording or film—is such accession or downloading an infringement of copyright? An issue of this kind arose in *Sega Enterprises Inc v Maphia*,[13] where however the ultimate question was again the liability of the bulletin board operator who provided the service through which not only downloading, but also initial unauthorised uploading of copyright material (computer games), took place.

COPYRIGHT SUBJECT MATTER

The governing copyright statute in the UK is the Copyright Designs and Patents Act 1988, now several times amended. Under its provisions, the following subject-matter is protected:[14]

- original literary, dramatic, musical and artistic works
- the typographical arrangement of published editions of literary, dramatic or musical works
- sound recordings
- films
- broadcasts
- cable programmes

For convenience, literary, dramatic, musical and artistic works will be collectively referred to as "author works" in the remainder of this paper, and the other categories will be grouped as "media works".

To what extent are website contents capable of being brought within these categories of protected work? As will be shown below, several if not all of the categories are clearly applicable. The difficulty which may arise is the multimedia nature of the website; which of the categories is most appropriate?[15] The digital medium in which all works on the Internet are basically expressed means that distinctions based on form are hard to apply. However it may not be necessary to characterise the whole of the website in this way. Although the different categories of work are protected for different lengths of time, the periods are uniformly long and unlikely to have much practical impact, when the shortest is around fifty years from the establishment of the website.[16] Again, there are various kinds of infringement, but they all apply in more or

---

[13] 857 F Supp 679 (ND Cal, 1994); US District Court for the Northern District of California, 16 December 1996 (http://www.bna.com/e-law/cases/sega2.html).
[14] CDPA 1988, ss 1–8.
[15] This issue also arises with CD-Roms. See further Cornish, *Intellectual Property*, 465-466.
[16] See further below, 75, 78.

less the same way to each of the categories of work. Characterisation of the site may not therefore be necessary, and it may in any event depend on precisely which elements have been taken and which is regarded as forming the most substantial part of that taking.[17]

Literary works

A literary work is any work which is written, spoken or sung, apart from a dramatic or musical work.[18] However, the work must be recorded, in writing or otherwise, before copyright will arise.[19] The category includes compilations of material and computer programs.[20] Since a good deal of the material on a website will be written, albeit in digital form, it is therefore potentially protectable as a literary work. But there are still at least a couple of further hoops to be gone through. A literary work must be "intended to afford either information and instruction or pleasure in the form of literary enjoyment".[21] This has been taken to mean that in general a single word, or the title of a work, do not have copyright; similarly with advertising slogans consisting of stock phrases or commonplace sentences.[22] A recent Australian case has held that there is no copyright in the names of computer program commands, since they were merely "triggers" for a set of instructions to be given effect by the computer.[23] The requirement of "originality" also needs to be kept in mind as a threshold which a literary work must pass before it achieves protection. In the UK, "originality" is still best understood as meaning an independent form of expression achieved through the author's judgement, skill and labour,[24] although in the USA the Supreme Court has departed from the American version of this requirement, the "sweat of the brow" test, and added a need for a spark of creativity.[25] The result was to deny copyright protection to a telephone directory as a compilation. There have been some hints in British cases that skill and labour is not enough for originality,[26] and the European harmonisation of copyright may eventually push the threshold a little higher, the favoured formulation at present being that a work should be its "author's own intellectual creation". In particular this formulation is found in the

---

[17] See further below, 79.
[18] CDPA 1988, s 3(1).
[19] CDPA 1988, s 3(2).
[20] CDPA 1988, s 3(1).
[21] *Exxon Corporation v Exxon Insurance Consultants International Ltd* [1982] Ch 119.
[22] *The Laws of Scotland: Stair Memorial Encyclopaedia*, vol 18 (1993), para 951, gives the authorities.
[23] *Powerflex Services Pty Ltd v Data Access Corporation*, Federal Court of Australia, 4 June 1997, [1997] 11 *World Intellectual Property Reporter* 223.
[24] *Stair Memorial Encyclopaedia*, vol 18, paras 941-948.
[25] *Feist Publications Inc v Rural Telephone Service Co*, 499 US 340 (1991).
[26] Notably in *Interlego AG v Tyco Industries Inc* [1989] AC 217.

Database Directive,[27] the implementation of which in the UK is expected to take many compilations, electronic or otherwise, out of the protection of copyright.

The implications of these requirements for websites are of some significance. Much of the information gathered on websites will fall into the category of compilation, either as anthologies of material, or as expressions of raw data. The extent to which copyright protection will continue to be available is therefore in some doubt. Important individual elements within websites may well not be protected by copyright, notably the phrases or key words used for hypertext links. This was an issue in *The Shetland Times* case, where the *Times* home page used the newspaper headlines as links to the material deeper within the site, and the headline texts were then taken up by *The Shetland News* to act as the links on to the *Times* stories. Lord Hamilton held that the headline texts had copyright, so that the actions of the *News* in copying them for reproduction on its own website was an infringement. Although this view has been criticised in the light of the general denial of copyright to titles and slogans, the creation of a headline does involve skill and labour, in that the reader's attention has to be attracted, information about the relevant item conveyed, and (at least in the case of the tabloid press, which much favours punning and jokey headlines) entertainment provided. So it seems perfectly possible that a headline can be an original literary work, albeit one the protection of which would be very "thin", given the necessarily limited scope of the genre.[28]

Musical and dramatic works

The protection provided here is for the written rather than the performed version of such works; but there is no reason why a score or a script should not appear on the Internet. Given the use of fanfares and the like on some websites, it should be noted that the four notes constituting the Channel 4 TV theme have been held to be a musical work for copyright purposes.[29]

Artistic works

Websites are full of artistic material and indeed the sites themselves are very often designed with considerable artistic care. For the purposes of copyright protection, the concept of an artistic work embraces graphic works (which includes any painting, drawing, diagram, map, chart or plan), and photo-

---

[27] Parliament and Council Directive 96/9/EC, article 3(1). See also the Software Directive, Council Directive 91/250/EEC, article 1(3).

[28] By "thin", I mean that not very much variation from the first work would be required to evade a charge of infringement.

[29] *Lawton v Lord David Dundas*, 13 June 1985, *The Times*.

graphs, and there is no requirement that any of these possess artistic quality. The only requirement is originality, as discussed above.[30]

First ownership of literary, musical, dramatic and artistic copyright

The creator of the literary, musical, dramatic or artistic work is the first owner of any copyright in it, subject to the rule that if the work is made in the course of the creator's employment, the employer is the first owner (unless otherwise agreed).[31] The creator of a website is thus its owner, unless the website is created in the course of her employment. Employment should of course be distinguished from the contract for services under which a consultant creates a website under commission from another entity. If the commissioner wants the copyright as well as the website, it will be necessary to obtain an assignation or an exclusive licence from the creator, and both transactions will need to be in writing.[32] The UK Act also recognises joint ownership arising from joint authorship, where the contributions of two or more authors to a single work are not distinguished from each other.[33] Such a concept may become of great importance in a digital world, which greatly increases the scope and opportunities for the creation of single works by many hands.[34] UK copyright lasts for the lifetime of the author (or the last to die of joint authors) plus a further seventy years from the end of the year of death.[35]

Published editions

Copyright subsists in the typographical arrangement of a published edition of a literary, dramatic or musical work, the owner being the publisher.[36] Is a webpage published? Publication is defined in the copyright legislation as the issue of copies to the public which includes making it available to the public by means of an electronic retrieval system.[37] This last is clearly applicable to the Internet. So the author of the arrangement of a website has a copyright (albeit one only lasting twenty-five years from first publication).[38]

---

[30] CDPA 1988, s 4. See above, 73.
[31] CDPA 1988, s 9.
[32] CDPA 1988, ss 90 and 92.
[33] CDPA 1988, s 10. See further *Stair Memorial Encyclopaedia*, vol 18, paras 985-992.
[34] See further J Ginsburg, "Putting Cars on the 'Information Superhighway': Authors, Exploiters and Copyright in Cyberspace", in P Bernt Hugenholtz (ed), *The Future of Copyright in a Digital Environment* (1996), 189-219 at 192-197.
[35] CDPA 1988 ss 9-12.
[36] CDPA 1988, ss 8 and 9(2)(d).
[37] CDPA 1988 s 175(1).
[38] CDPA 1988 s 15.

Sound recording

A sound recording is a recording of sounds from which sounds may be reproduced or a recording of the whole or any part of a literary, dramatic or musical work from which sounds reproducing the work or part may be produced. It does not matter on what medium the recording is made or by what method the sounds are reproduced.[39] Thus if sounds are reproducible as part of a webpage, it will embody a sound recording, and that recording will have a copyright in its own right, regardless of whether or not the sounds themselves are a reproduction of another copyright work. The owner of the copyright is the producer of the recording.[40]

Films

For films, the definition is "a recording on any medium from which a moving image may by any means be produced".[41] If sounds accompany the film, they are to be treated as part of the film for copyright purposes, but this does not affect any copyright subsisting in the sound track as a sound recording.[42] Again, therefore, moving images produced on a webpage will have copyright protection. The breadth of the definition with regard to the medium and means of recording and production means that not only videos but also computer games are to be treated as films for copyright purposes.[43] Film copyright is owned jointly by the producer and the director: the latter seems unlikely to figure in Internet discussions, and the producer of a website is presumably the site's operator.

Broadcasts

The definition of a broadcast in the copyright legislation is in terms of "transmission by wireless telegraphy".[44] Since the Internet is dependent on the wires of the telecommunications system, transmission on the Internet is not broadcasting, and copyright protection is unavailable through this medium, at least for the moment.[44a]

[39] CDPA 1988, s 5A.
[40] CDPA 1988, s 9(2)(a).
[41] CDPA 1988, s 5B(1).
[42] CDPA 1988, s 5B(2) and (5).
[43] See *Sega Enterprises Ltd v Galaxy Electronics Pty Ltd*, 28 August 1996, Federal Court of Australia [1997] 2 EIPR D-37; *Golden China TV Game Centre v Nintendo Co Ltd*, 25 September 1996, Appellate Division, South Africa, [1997] 1 EIPR D-20; Cornish. *Intellectual Property*, 343.
[44] CDPA 1988, s 6.
[44a] Note however that a *reception* of a broadcast includes relay by means of a telecommunications system (CDPA 1988, s 6(5)).

Cable programmes

By contrast, and to the surprise of some,[45] the concept of a cable programme, in which the copyright is owned by the service provider,[46] was held entirely relevant to the Internet by Lord Hamilton in *The Shetland Times* case. Indeed the principal basis for his decision to grant an interim interdict in that case was the view that a website or items thereon were cable programme services or cable programmes. The 1988 Act defines a cable programme as any item included in a cable programme service, which in turn is defined as a service consisting wholly or mainly in *sending* information by means of a telecommunication system, otherwise than by wireless telegraphy, for reception at two or more places (whether or not simultaneously), OR for presentation to members of the public. Excluded from this definition are two-way or interactive communication systems, of which a very simple example is a telephone system.[47]

In *The Shetland Times* case two main arguments were presented against the website being a cable programme service. One was that it did not involve *sending* information but rather allowed information to be accessed by members of the public. The other argument was that the service was two-way or interactive inasmuch as members of the public could communicate information to the site as well as receive it, and so fell outwith the definition of a cable programme service. Lord Hamilton rejected both these arguments, while noting that little technical information was available to him at this interim interdict stage. His rejection of a narrow approach to the word "sending" used in the 1988 Act seems reasonable, since such an approach would end up excluding many services from the protection of copyright. At the very least a website operator enables the material to be sent. The inter-activity point is more difficult. It is necessary to quote the statutory exclusion in full:

> The following are excepted from the definition of "cable programme service"—(a) a service or part of a service of which it is an essential feature that while visual images, sounds or other information are being conveyed by the person providing the service there will or may be sent from each place of reception, by means of the same system or (as the case may be) the same part of it, information (other than signals sent for the operation or control of the service) for reception by the person providing the service or other persons receiving it.

The possibility of inter-action between *The Shetland Times* website and its readers arose because the webpage included a note inviting comments or suggestions to be sent in by electronic mail. Indeed this note was itself a hypertext link moving the reader into an already addressed email template. It was

---

[45] But cf Wienand, "Legal Implications of Electronic Data Exchange", at 85.
[46] CDPA 1988, ss 7 and 9(2)(c).
[47] CDPA 1988, s 7.

argued that this facility meant that there was the possibility of communication going beyond "the operation and control of the service" by the users. Lord Hamilton thought, however, that this was not an essential part of the service provided, or that it was at any rate a severable part of the service, and hence the exception did not apply. But, although the sub-section does talk about a need to show that inter-activity is an essential feature of the service, it only requires that *part* of the service be inter-active, perhaps eliminating the notion of severability as a way of evading the exception. The sub-section is also quite clear that only *potential* for inter-activity is necessary—information *"will or may be* sent from the place of reception . . . for reception by the person providing the service or other persons receiving it". This analysis suggests that the really crucial word in the sub-section is "essential", and it is on the meaning to be given to this word that Lord Hamilton's opinion will probably stand or fall.

A point which was not raised before Lord Hamilton is whether anything on the website was a cable programme, even if the site was a cable programme service. The definition in the 1988 Act already quoted provides the rather inert comment that a programme is an item.[48] But it can be argued that in the context of broadcasting and cable transmission a "programme" is an item with a content the sequence and length of which are determined by the provider, and that therefore, at least "in the case of data bases or other interactive information services . . . as a result of the severed tie between a single component and its predefined position in a sequential order, these services no longer constitute 'programmes' in the traditional sense".[49]

Duration of media copyrights

Following implementation of the Rental Right Directive in the UK, films have copyright until seventy years after the death of the later of its two authors (producer and director) to die. For sound recordings, the period is fifty years from the end of the year of manufacture or release; for broadcasts and cable programmes, fifty years from the end of the year of transmission; and for published editions twenty-five years from the end of the year of first publication.[50]

INFRINGEMENT

The discussion so far has established that a website is very likely to enjoy copyright protection in some aspect or another. In this section we turn to examine

---

[48] See also the definition of a programme as an "item" for the purposes of broadcasting in CDPA 1988, s 6(3).

[49] T Dreier, "The cable and satellite analogy", in Hugenholtz (ed), *The Future of Copyright*, 57–65 at 58.

[50] See CDPA 1988, ss 9–15.

what rights the operator of the website has as a result; or, putting it another way, what acts are prohibited to a user unless authorised by the copyright owner. However, it is also useful to consider the position if the operator of the website has infringed someone else's copyright in assembling the site.

Under the Copyright, Designs and Patents Act 1988 as amended there are now six major forms of primary infringement of the copyright in any protected work. These restricted acts for which a copyright licence must be sought if they are to be lawfully carried out may be listed as follows:[51]

- copying
- issuing copies of the work to the public
- renting or lending the work to the public
- performing, showing or playing the work in public
- broadcasting the work or including it in a cable programme service
- making an adaptation of the work

In addition, a person who authorises another to do any of the above acts himself infringes the copyright as well.[52] The acts of infringement may be in relation to the whole of the work or to any substantial part of it; and measuring the substance of what has been taken "depends much more on the quality than on the quantity of what he has taken".[53] It follows, of course, that if the act can be shown to have been in relation to an insubstantial part of a work there is no infringement.

A crucial characteristic of the primary infringements is that there is liability even though the infringer is unaware at the time of acting that he is infringing copyright. The lack of knowledge may mean that the infringer escapes damages liability, although he can of course be interdicted and compelled to account for the profits of his infringement.[54] This position contrasts with the secondary infringements, under which, broadly speaking, there is liability for commercial dealing in articles which the dealer knows or ought to know are infringing copies of a copyright work. There is also secondary liability of this kind for those who provide the means for making infringing copies, or permit the use of premises, or provide apparatus, for infringing performances.[55]

What effect do these various forms of infringement have in relation to activities on the Internet?

---

[51] CDPA 1988 s 16(1).

[52] CDPA 1988 s 16(2).

[53] CDPA 1988 s 16(3)(a); *Ladbroke (Football) Ltd v William Hill (Football) Ltd* [1964] 1 WLR 273 at 276, HL, per Lord Reid.

[54] CDPA 1988 s 97(1); see also s 96(2). If primary infringement is committed knowingly, then additional damages may be recoverable under s 97(2). On this remedy see most recently *Redrow Homes Ltd v Bett Brothers plc*, 14 March 1997, Second Division, reversing Lord Johnston in the Outer House (1996 SLT 1254). It is understood that this case has been appealed to the House of Lords.

[55] CDPA 1988, ss 22–27.

Copying

The 1988 Act tells us that copying in relation to literary, dramatic, musical and artistic works means reproduction of the work in any material form, and includes storage of the work in any medium by electronic means.[56] It is also provided that copying in relation to any category of work (i.e. this time extending to the media copyright works) includes the making of copies which are transient or incidental to some other use of the work.[57] This is generally accepted as covering the loading of software into a computer's RAM. The Database Directive also provides that temporary reproduction is infringement of any copyright that a database may have.[58] The UK definition of reproduction can therefore be fairly readily extended to the browser on the Internet whenever she comes upon a new webpage. There seems to be no doubt, therefore, that when a user accesses a website she is committing an infringement of any copyright there may be in that site unless she has some form of licence for that act.[59] It has been said that this is akin to making it infringement of copyright to read a book, but it appears to be also the law in the USA, although apparently not clearly so in some of the countries of continental Europe.[60] Since it leads to the production of a fixed and not temporary copy, downloading material from a website, whether in digital form to one's own computer or floppy disk, or as hard copy by way of a printout, is more readily recognised in most legal systems as an infringing reproduction. Bearing in mind that a website may be a published edition of a copyright work, with an independent copyright in its typographical arrangement,[61] copying here will mean the making of a facsimile copy of the arrangement,[62] which could probably extend without too much difficulty to the printout although the main target of the provision is reprography, or photocopying. Finally, recalling the *Shetland Times* decision that a website item can be a cable programme, copying in relation to such a work includes making a photograph of the whole or any substantial part of any image forming part of the programme.[63]

The concept of copying implies a causal connection between two works, with the later being derived from the earlier. Independent production of the same or a similar work is therefore not an infringement; copyright is not a

[56] CDPA 1988 s 17(2).

[57] CDPA 1988 s 17(6).

[58] Parliament and Council Directive 96/9/EC, article 5(a). Note also the new *sui generis* right to prevent unauthorised extraction from a database regardless of its copyright status, which includes temporary transfer of all or part of the contents to another medium (article 7(2)(a)).

[59] Such a licence may of course be readily implied: see further below, 88–89.

[60] See e.g. *Mai Systems Corporation v Peak Computer Inc* 991 F 2d 511 (9th Cir 1993), cert dismissed, 114 S Ct 671 (1994) for the USA; and for comment on the lack of clarity in Europe see P Bernt Hugenholtz, "Adapting copyright to the information superhighway", in idem, *The Future of Copyright*, 81–102 at 88–89.

[61] See above, 75.

[62] CDPA 1988 s 17(5).

[63] CDPA 1988 s 17(4). For the definition of a photograph, see s 4(2).

monopoly in a particular form of expression. But a court which is shown similarity between two works and that the creator of the second had access to the first is likely to think that there is a prima facie case of copying.[64] There has also been recognition of the possibility of unconscious copying of a work to which one had been previously exposed.[65] This leads on to one of the major issues in modern copyright. Obviously when there is exact copying, as in the lifting of headlines in the *Shetland Times* case, or the placing of another's poetry or computer games on one's website, there is infringement on this ground; but suppose the copying is not precise? Or suppose, in the case of digital works, that the underlying expression is distinct but that the output looks or sounds the same? It is commonly said that copyright protects the form of expression rather than the ideas expressed; but it is also clear that, since taking "a substantial part" of a work is not allowed, there can be infringement even though the literal form of expression is different.[66] Thus, for example, the substance of a play may be the characterisation and sequence of incidents and events rather than the exact words used, and this can be protected by copyright.[67] The problem comes up most in modern conditions with regard to software and databases,[68] and may well emerge as an issue between websites with regard to their overall design and structure as well as their specific content.

Issuing copies of the work to the public

Section 18 of the 1988 Act in effect defines issuing to the public as putting copies into circulation for the first time.[69] It is sometimes described as the right of first sale. Only the copyright owner or his licensee can put a new reproduction of the work on the market. The right is exhausted by the initial sale, however; the second-hand bookseller does not require copyright licences in order to carry on business.

The "on demand" transmission characteristic of the Internet does not look much like the issue of copies to the public, although it might be seen as a form of "circulation". This is because section 18, unlike section 17 which deals with copying, makes no reference to the notion of a "transient copy"; the copies required for the purposes of section 18 may therefore be limited to those which are non-transient, which would go beyond mere "on demand" transmission. If so, it would then follow that the user who accesses material and passes it on to another is not guilty of infringement under this section so long

---

[64] *Stair Memorial Encyclopaedia*, vol 18, para 1046.
[65] *Francis Day & Hunter Ltd v Bron* [1963] 1 Ch 587.
[66] Note that copying is reproduction "in any material form", i.e. not necessarily in the same medium as the original work (s 17(2)); and that in relation to artistic work in 2D it includes 3D reproduction, and vice versa (s 17(3)).
[67] *Rees v Melville* [1914] MCC 168.
[68] See e.g. Cornish, *Intellectual Property*, 446–450.
[69] CDPA 1988 s 18.

as the transmission is electronic. But if these difficulties can be overcome and initial accession be described as the issue of a copy to a member of the public, the question still arises whether the principle of exhaustion applies so that what a party accessing a website does subsequently by way of further electronic transmission is within her rights just as she would be free to sell on the second-hand market a book which she had been the first to acquire from the publisher.[70]

Rental or lending of a work to the public

Rental is making a copy of a work available for use, on terms that it will or may be returned, for direct or indirect economic or commercial advantage.[71] The familiar example is the video or computer game rental, but following the Rental Right Directive of 1992[72] most forms of copyright work are now subject to this right. Lending right, an innovation of the Directive, is similarly defined, save that the restricted act is one performed otherwise than for direct or indirect economic or commercial advantage, and is carried out through an establishment which is accessible to the public.[73] Thus a public library's lending activities now require a copyright licence unless the book lent is within the Public Lending Right scheme set up in 1979.[74] Rental and lending do not cover making copies available for the purpose of performance, showing, playing or exhibiting in public, or for the purpose of on-the-spot reference use.[75] Are rental and lending rights applicable to Internet activities?[76] There are again difficulties with the concept of a copy, which is what must be made available, and this is underlined by the need for an expectation that the copy will be returned. This is difficult to square with the ordinary usages of the Internet. For rental some sort of economic or commercial advantage is necessary, while for lending there must be an establishment accessible to the public. It is less difficult, but still not easy, to see these in normal Internet services. Finally the browser or surfer on the Internet may be making "on-the-spot reference use" of the service, which would mean that the provider was not engaging in rental or lending activities.

As a footnote, it may be observed that the Database Directive provides for a *sui generis* right to prevent "re-utilisation" of the whole or part of the contents of a database, defining this as any form of making available to the public by dis-

---

[70] See further Hugenholtz, "Adapting Copyright", 95–98.
[71] CDPA 1988 s 18A(2)(a).
[72] Council Directive 92/100/EEC.
[73] CDPA 1988 s 18A(2)(b).
[74] CDPA 1988, s 40A. Note however that the library of an educational establishment is generally exempted from lending right: CDPA 1988 s 36A.
[75] CDPA 1988 s 18A(3).
[76] For discussion see J Reinbothe and S von Lewinski, *The EC Directive on Rental and Lending Rights and on Piracy* (1993), 41–42. Cf Hugenholtz, "Adapting copyright", 90.

tribution of copies, by renting, or by on-line or other forms of transmission. Public lending is excluded, and first sale of a copy of the database within the Community exhausts the right to control resale within the Community.[77]

Public performance, showing or playing

The public performance right is restricted to literary, dramatic and musical works, and is particularly important for the exploitation of music and drama for obvious reasons. As discussed earlier in this paper, there is no reason why the script or score of a dramatic or musical work should not appear on a website, but more typically a webpage will incorporate a literary work. For the purposes of the 1988 Act, a performance covers any mode of visual or acoustic presentation, including by means of a cable programme.[78] There is nothing in this language to prevent an unauthorised display on a computer screen of the text of a literary work being a "performance" of that work, provided that it takes place "in public".[79] In the case of sound recordings, films, broadcasts and cable programmes, the equivalent form of infringement is playing or showing the work in public.[80]

What will prevent this form of infringement being of much relevance to the Internet, at least in its present pattern of usage, is the fact that most displays of material do not take place in public. But it is important to be aware that the definition of "public" for this particular copyright purpose is quite wide. "To be in public a performance does not have to be to a paying audience or by paid performers."[81] There has to be an audience for the performance, and the critical question is the relation between the copyright owner and that audience, "emphasising the primacy of the owner's entitlement to an economic return from his proprietary rights".[82] Traditionally the audience has been grouped together in some place where members of the public may gather, such as a theatre, a club, a shop or a place of work. But it is no longer clear whether a gathering in one place is a necessary condition for performance in public. Thus in recent times, it has been held in Australia that playing recorded music "on hold" to users of mobile telephones was "in public" even though the distribution of the material was not necessarily, or even very often, simultaneous for each member of the audience.[83] The Spanish Supreme Court has also held that non-simultaneous transmissions of copyright material to

---

[77] Parliament and Council Directive 96/9/EC, article 7(2)(b).

[78] CDPA 1988, s 19(2)(b).

[79] As might also occur with an overhead projection machine which displays documents laid on its glass paten.

[80] CDPA 1988, s 19(3).

[81] Cornish, *Intellectual Property*, 376.

[82] Ibid.

[83] *Australasian Performing Right Association Ltd v Telstra Corporation Ltd* 23 August 1995, Federal Court of Australia [1997] 28 IIC 136.

different persons in individual hotel bedrooms requires copyright licences.[84] The impact of decisions like these is most likely to be felt, not by the individual user accessing a website from a personal computer, but by the website operator who has incorporated other people's copyright material on his site, and could therefore be seen as performing or playing or showing that material. The fact that the members of the audience would be quite unaware of each other, and joining and leaving the audience at various times, would not seem to be relevant. There does appear to be a statutory defence in section 19(4), however:

> Where copyright in a work is infringed by its being performed, played or shown in public by means of apparatus for receiving visual images or sounds conveyed by electronic means (computer on modem or network?), the person by whom the visual images or sounds are sent . . . shall not be regarded as responsible for the infringement.

Broadcasting or inclusion in a cable programme service

Neither accessing a website nor incorporation of other people's copyright material thereon can constitute broadcasting, since as already noted broadcasting is a wireless technology.[85] But "inclusion in a cable programme service" was the second basis for the interim interdict in the *Shetland Times* case. A question which may be asked, however, is whether enabling a user of one website to link to another site means that the second is "included" within the other, or whether there are simply two connected but otherwise independent sites, the appropriate analogy being perhaps with footnotes or bibliographies or "further reading" lists in a printed text.

Adaptation

This form of infringement applies only to literary, dramatic and musical works. Examples of adaptations are translations in relation to literary works; dramatisations of non-dramatic works; arrangements or transcriptions of musical works; and arrangements, alterations or translations of computer programs.[86] It is perhaps with regard to this last that this form of infringement is most relevant to the Internet and website operators in particular.

---

[84] *SGAE v Hotel Blanco DonJ.SA*, 11 March 1996, [1997] 1 EIPR D-21. Interestingly Spain is one of the few countries prior to the implementation of the Database Directive with express provision that "public *access* to computer databases by means of telecommunication" is infringement where the database incorporates or constitutes a protected work.

[85] See above, 76.

[86] CDPA 1988 s 21(3).

Authorisation

Authorisation of another to infringe is itself infringement.[87] The courts have defined authorisation as meaning sanctioning, approving, or countenancing, where there is authority or control over those who actually infringe.[88] This form of liability has obvious importance for the commercial service providers, universities, and other bodies which set up the facilities on which infringing Internet activity takes place. Can such bodies be liable for infringing use of the facilities as authorising it to take place? The general answer is probably in the negative so far as the UK is concerned. Commercial libraries renting out sound recordings and manufacturers of double-headed audio tape decks have been held not liable despite the fact that their services and products rendered infringement easy and probable.[89] Two crucial factors in these cases were that lawful activity was possible with the facilities provided, and that the defendants had given express warnings to customers against use for infringing copying. By contrast, a university which provided photocopying facilities for staff and students in its library was found to have authorised infringement because it had taken no steps to deter such activity.[90] The appropriate action for those who provide Internet facilities therefore appears to be ensuring that users are made aware of the existence of copyright and warned against its abuse, whether in putting material on to the service or downloading it.

Situations in which service providers and site operators might be liable for authorisation of infringement may appear from consideration of the substantial body of US cases which focus upon the equivalent concept of contributory infringement. The decisions do not appear favourable to service providers and bulletin board operators. In *Religious Technology Center v Netcom On-Line Communication Service*,[91] for example, it was held that a service provider could be liable as a contributory infringer if it knew or ought to have known that infringement was taking place on its system, and if simple steps to prevent this were not taken. But the court did provide some comfort for providers and operators in that the claim of primary infringement had to be reasonably verifiable by them before it could be held that they had failed to act. More recently, in *Sega Enterprises Ltd v Maphia*[92] and *Sega Enterprises v Sabella*[93] there have been specific findings of contributory infringement against bulletin board operators on the basis of knowledge of and participation in the prim-

---

[87] CDPA s 16(2).

[88] *Stair Memorial Encyclopaedia*, vol 18 para 1067.

[89] *CBS Inc v Ames Records and Tapes Ltd* [1982] Ch 91; *CBS Songs Ltd v Amstrad Consumer Electronics plc* [1988] AC 1013.

[90] *Moorhouse v University of New South Wales* [1976] RPC 151 High Court of Australia.

[91] 907 F Supp 1361 (ND Cal, 1995).

[92] US District Court for the District of Northern California, 16 December 1996 (http://www.bna.com/e-law/cases/sega2.html)

[93] US District Court for the District of Northern California, 18 December 1995 (http://www.bna.com/e-law/cases/sega1.html)

ary infringing activities (copying video games) by provision of facilities, solic-
itation of unauthorised uploading by subscribers, the provision of "road
maps" on the bulletin board to identify games available for downloading, and
the sale of copiers to facilitate the playing of the downloaded games. Despite
the caution with which the British courts have handled this particular form of
infringement, there can be little doubt that, confronted with similar facts, they
would find authorisation of infringement to have taken place.

Secondary infringement

Two comments may be made about the "secondary infringements" which
were briefly summarised at the beginning of this section.[94] Infringement by
dealing in infringing copies would seem to require hard rather than electronic
copies.[95] Infringement by providing either premises or apparatus for infringing performances might have implications for businesses such as "cyber
cafes", if it can be said that display on the Internet is an infringing public performance of a work.[96] Peter Wienand has also drawn attention to the importance of section 24(2) of the 1988 Act:[97]

> [The] Act provides that it is also an act of secondary infringement to transmit a
> work "by means of a telecommunication system (otherwise than by broadcasting or
> inclusion in a cable programme service), knowing or having reason to believe that
> infringing copies of the work will be made by means of the reception of the trans-
> mission in the United Kingdom *or elsewhere*" [emphasis supplied]. Although this
> requires a belief that the reception will result in infringing copies, this is not difficult
> to establish if . . . electronically (albeit) transiently stored copies are infringements.
> This could mean that unauthorised senders of material via the Internet will be
> infringing copyright unless they could convincingly argue that they did not believe
> that (infringing) copies would result.

DEFENCES

Fair dealing

The Copyright, Designs and Patents Act 1988 makes extensive and detailed
provision by which various specified acts which would otherwise fall within
the scope of the infringement rules are made lawful.[98] Such acts therefore do
not require the licence of the copyright owner. The UK Act contrasts with US
law, which provides a general "fair use" defence covering purposes "such as"

---

[94] See above, 82–83.
[95] CDPA 1988, s 27.
[96] See above, 82–4.
[97] Wienand, "Legal Implications of Electronic Data Exchange", 85.
[98] CDPA 1988, ss 28–76.

criticism, comment, teaching, scholarship and research, and indicating that factors to be taken into account "include" such matters as whether the use is of a commercial nature or for nonprofit educational purposes, the amount and substantiality of the portion used in relation to the whole work, and the effect of the use upon the market or value of the copyright work.[99] There is also a contrast with Continental laws, which tend to exclude private copying from the scope of copyright.[100]

Probably the most obviously significant permitted act for users of websites under the 1988 Act is the provision that fair dealing with a literary, dramatic, musical or artistic work (but not computer programs or media works) which is for the purposes of research or private study does not infringe its copyright. The exemption would appear clearly applicable to the user of a website making hard or electronic copies of the material she finds there; but how much can be taken? Parliament has resisted publishing lobbies seeking a quantifiable measure of how much of a work may be copied or used under this exemption, and it remains arguable that in some circumstances the whole of a work may be taken. Can the operator of a website use the research and private study exemption to justify putting up on her site the copyright works of others? In the French cases about the unauthorised inclusion of the poetry of Raymond Queneau on websites, it was held that a website unprotected by security devices and open to any visitor was in the public domain and that the copying could not be justified by the general exemption in French law for private copying.[101] UK law has no general saving for private copying, and it seems likely that a British court would reach the same conclusion as the French one, albeit by the route that the private study exemption applies only to one's own study and not to making private study possible for third parties.[102] Admittedly in the UK cases the copier was supplying the copied material in the course of business, while a website producer might well not be earning any financial return from her activities; but the court would likely be concerned about the probable damage to the earnings of the copyright owner and so deem the activity unfair.

Fair dealing for purposes of criticism or review also exempts from charges of copyright infringement.[103] In an American case about posting the published and unpublished works of L Ron Hubbard on a bulletin board, the party who made the posting was held unentitled to a fair use defence although he had added to the texts some criticisms of Hubbard's doctrines, in consequence of

[99] Copyright Act 1976, s 107.

[100] See e.g. the French Intellectual Property Code of 1 July 1992, articles L122-5, L211-3 and L212-10, and German Copyright Act 1965, article 53. Observe that a concomitant of the right of private copying in these countries is the levies on blank audio cassettes and reprography. For a brief account of French and German law in this area, see S M Stewart, *International Copyright and Neighbouring Rights*, 2nd edn, vol 1 (1989), paras 14.10 and 15.08-15.09.

[101] French Intellectual Property Code of 1 July 1992, article L122-5.

[102] *University of London Press Ltd v University Tutorial Press Ltd* [1916] 2 Ch 601; *Sillitoe v McGraw-Hill Book Co (UK) Ltd* [1983] FSR 545.

[103] CDPA 1988 s 30.

the very small amount of commentary compared to the quantity of copied text.[104] There is a parallel case in the UK, also involving the unauthorised publication of the works of L Ron Hubbard with some critical commentary, but in traditional rather than electronic media. The Court of Appeal also found that the fair dealing defence was inapplicable, for reasons anticipating those of the American court.[105]

The limited scope of the permitted acts bear particularly harshly upon activities within educational establishments.[106] It is of some interest, therefore, that Sir Ron Dearing's 1997 report on the future of higher education in the UK, which argues strongly for greatly expanding the use of information technology in the sector, has commented that "there must be provision for the free and immediate use by teachers and researchers of copyright digital information".[107] The Report recommends a review of copyright legislation to facilitate this. Such a sweeping exemption would run counter to the British tradition in this area, but would find support in, for example, US and German legislation.

The 1988 Act also contains very detailed provisions exempting certain activities of libraries and archives from the scope of copyright infringement. Speaking very broadly, these provisions enable libraries and archives prescribed by the Secretary of State to supply readers with a single copy of copyright material for the purposes of private study or research, provided that the reader pays a sum not less than the cost attributable to producing the copy.[108] No website operator has yet been designated by the Secretary of State for these purposes, and it seems clear that library-like or archival activities with copyright material by such an operator will fall outside the scope of fair dealing.[109] It would certainly not be possible for an operator to claim fair dealing in making copies in advance of a specific commission, or in retaining them until a commission was given. But if it is right that a website is a cable progamme service and a webpage a cable programme as an item within the service, as held in the *Shetland Times* case, then there may be room to plead the "time-shifting" exemption which is specifically allowed under the 1988 Act for private recording of broadcast or cable material to enable it to be viewed

---

[104] *Religious Technology Center v Lerma*, US District Court for the Eastern District of Virginia, 4 October 1996 (http://www.bna.com/e-law/cases/lerma.html). In similar circumstances in *Religious Technology Center v Netcom On-Line Communication Service* 907 F Supp 1361 (ND Cal, 1995), however, the court held that Netcom, a service provider, might have a valid fair use defence.

[105] *Hubbard v Vosper* [1972] 2 QB 84.

[106] See apart from sections already cited CDPA 1988 ss 32-36; Cornish, *Intellectual Property*, 433–441.

[107] National Committee of Inquiry into Higher Education (Chairman Sir Ron Dearing), *Higher Education in the Learning Society* (1997), para 13.34; and see Recommendation 43.

[108] CDPA ss 37–44; Copyright (Librarians and Archivists) (Copying of Copyright Material) Regulations 1989, SI 1989/1212.

[109] Compare the American case *American Geophysical Union v Texaco Inc* 802 F Supp 1 (SDNY, 1992) affd 60 F 3d 913 (2nd Cir 1994), holding that archival copying of scientific journals for internal use by a for-profit research laboratory was not fair use.

at a more convenient time.[110] This would seem most likely to benefit the user of the webpage.

Implied licence

There is no requirement in UK copyright legislation that non-exclusive licences should be in writing. "Express consent [of the copyright owner] is not necesary and a licence may be implied from the dealings between the parties."[111] Given the nature of the Internet, it seems highly probable that a person who puts material on a website is consenting to its being accessed by users of the system, so nullifying the infringement by transient reproduction which would otherwise arise under UK law. There are also questions about whether such an implied licence legitimises access by means of hypertext links, as in *The Shetland Times* case, or through the use of search engines. In particular, does the operator of a website impliedly licence the producers of search engine databases to add her site to that database, thus making it easier for users to find? In *British Leyland v Armstrong Patents Co Ltd*[112] the issue was the right of the defendants to mass-produce and supply spare parts for cars, the design of which was (as the law then stood) the copyright of the plaintiff car manufacturers. When the case began, owners of cars and other goods were thought to have an implied licence to infringe this copyright for the purpose of repairing their property. The defendants argued that this licence extended to their activities, to enable owners to exercise their rights efficiently. The argument that the implied licence could stretch so far was rejected both at first instance and in the Court of Appeal,[113] because the defendants manufactured the parts before receiving any particular commission from customers. Such reasoning would seem clearly applicable also to the work of the creators of the search engine.

Returning to the user's implied licence, can it go beyond access to cover other otherwise infringing acts, such as printing out or downloading material? This is more debatable, although again well-established practice might mean that, in the absence of express prohibition or security measures by the website operator, such activities should normally be treated as authorised. A recent Australian case, *Trumpet Software Pty Ltd v OzEmail Pty Ltd*,[114] shows how far a court may be prepared to go with the concept of an implied licence. The defendants were held entitled to bundle the plaintiffs' software with their own and distribute it commercially over the Internet against the plaintiffs'

---

[110] CDPA 1988, s 70.

[111] Laddie, Prescott and Vitoria, para 14.12.

[112] [1986] RPC 279.

[113] The House of Lords criticised the use of the concept of implied licence to justify repair by the owner, and took repair to be a right which needed no licence of any kind from the copyright owner.

[114] [1996] 18(12) EIPR 69. See further Waelde, "Intellectual property and the Internet", 69–70.

wishes, because the software had been originally marketed as "shareware", that is, as available for free use and reproduction. This has obvious significance for the Internet because so many of those putting material up believe it to be a community rather than an area of sharply defined and fenced property rights. But the Australian court did draw limitations upon the implied licence, holding that the redistribution was only to be of the entire software, without any adjustment to the original product.

Public policy and public interest; no derogation from grant

Going beyond the confines of the copyright legislation, the judges have created at least three limitations upon copyright.[115] One is the public policy concept that certain types of work—pornography or material published in breach of a lifelong obligation of secrecy, for example—are undeserving of the protection of copyright.[116] This could obviously cover much material on the Internet. A second limitation is one which allows otherwise infringing acts on the grounds that they are in the public interest.[117] The scope of this defence remains uncertain, but its most obvious application is in relation to the unauthorised publication of information and material generated but kept secret by public authorities. If the authority's motivation in preventing publication is improper—for example, to conceal the failings of its officials—then an unauthorised publication may be justified.[118] A possible test case may be provided by the dispute which broke out in 1997 between Nottinghamshire County Council and three journalists who put on the Internet the previously unpublished report of an investigation in 1989 into the Council's handling of a major child abuse case involving incest and Satanism. The Council obtained a temporary injunction against the unauthorised publication in June 1997, and full discussion of the issues will doubtless take place if and when a full hearing occurs.[119]

Finally, in the *British Leyland* case[120] mentioned in the previous section, the House of Lords declared that a copyright owner could be deprived of his rights where their exercise was in "derogation from grant". The context, as already noted, was the manufacture and supply to consumers of spare parts for cars, to which the car manufacturers took objection by means of copyright. The House found that car owners had a right to repair their vehicles, and that the car manufacturers could not exercise their copyright so as to pre-

---

[115] These exceptions are preserved by CDPA 1988, s 171(3).

[116] See e.g. *Glyn v Weston Feature Film Co* [1916] 1 Ch 261; *Attorney-General v Guardian Newspapers Ltd (No 2)* [1990] 1 AC 109.

[117] *Beloff v Pressdram* [1973] RPC 765.

[118] See in particular the breach of confidence case, *Lion Laboratories Ltd v Evans* [1985] QB 526, in support of this broad formulation.

[119] Y Akdeniz, "Copyright and the Internet", (1997) 147 *New Law Journal* 965-966.

[120] [1986] AC 577 gives the House of Lords' speeches only.

vent third parties enabling the owners to exercise their rights as cheaply as possible. This was founded on the general legal principle of "no derogation from grant", established in the context of leases, sales of goodwill and easements or servitudes. It had never been previously applied to copyright, and the reasoning of the House on the point is unsatisfactory.[121] The Privy Council has recently indicated that the principle should be interpreted very narrowly in copyright law.[122] Nonetheless, it is still applicable, and may find some application in the context of the Internet, perhaps in relation to the questions about activities such as downloading and the construction and deployment of search engines mentioned above in the comments on implied licences.

INTERNATIONAL REFORM

The foregoing survey of the application of UK copyright to the Internet has shown some of the difficulties with which the law is now faced, and the occasional comparative reference has shown that they are also confronted in other legal systems. Given the global reach of the Internet, and its probable social and commercial significance as the network matures into the information superhighway, it has seemed necessary to take international action to enable copyright law to respond and adapt in a reasonably uniform and harmonised way around the world. The USA took the initiative with a report in 1995 by its Information Infrastructure Task Force entitled *Intellectual Property and the National Information Infrastructure*. The European Union, concerned to harmonise the diverse copyright laws of its Member States, followed suit with Green Papers in 1995 and 1996.[123] 1996 also saw the completion, under the auspices of the World Intellectual Property Organisation, of a Copyright Treaty additional to the Berne Convention, which is specifically aimed at some of the most troublesome issues.[124]

Some of the treaty is relatively uncontroversial. The 1996 Treaty makes explicit, as Berne does not, that copyright protection is limited to expression and does not cover ideas and other abstractions as such (Article 2). Computer programs receive protection as literary works (Article 4). Databases which by selection and arrangement of their contents constitute intellectual creations are also to be protected (Article 5). Authors are given the exclusive right of

---

[121] See H L MacQueen, *Copyright, Competition and Industrial Design*, 2nd edn, 3(2) Hume Papers on Public Policy (1995), 45–47.

[122] *Canon Kabushiki Kaisha v Green Cartridge Co (Hong Kong) Ltd*, The Times,1 May 1997.

[123] *Copyright and Related Rights in the Information Society*, COM (95) 382 final; *Follow-Up to the Green Paper on Copyright and Related Rights in the Information Society*, COM (96) 568 final. For comment on the 1995 Green Paper, see C Waelde, (1996) 1 *Scottish Law and Practice Quarterly* 305–314.

[124] For a general comment see T C Vinje, "The new WIPO Copyright Treaty: a happy result in Geneva", [1997] 5 EIPR 230–236.

authorising the making available to the public of copies of their works through sale or other transfer of ownership (Article 6); "making available" and "other transfer of ownership" may reach the supply of material through the Internet. But it is left to the Contracting Parties to determine when this right is exhausted by first sale or otherwise. Commercial rental of computer programs, films and works embodied in sound recordings is also recognised as within the scope of copyright (Article 7).

However, there are some more difficult provisions and some significant absences. Article 8 provides for a new "right of communication to the public" by wire or wireless means. This right includes making work available to the public in such a way that members of the public may access these works from a place and at a time individually chosen by them; i.e. by way of transmission on the Internet. There was also a proposal for an Article stating explicitly that the right of reproduction included temporary or transient reproduction, as is already the position in the UK, but this was dropped after much controversy, although it was agreed that the present Berne provision (Article 9(1)) does not cover such reproduction.[125] However, Article 10 succeeds in setting the scene for a more restrictive approach to user rights or limitations on the scope of copyright. Article 9(2) of Berne states that reproduction may be allowed "in certain special cases, provided that such exploitation does not conflict with a normal exploitation of the work and does not unreasonably prejudice the legitimate interests of the author". For some reason, Article 10 of the WIPO Treaty repeats this formula no less than twice, but, significantly, where Berne talks of "permitting" such acts, the Article speaks of "confining" them. The scene is thereby set for the elimination or whittling down of user rights and the assertion of producer control over the use of the Internet. This is also apparent in other Articles, which require Contracting Parties to provide a legal framework to protect technological means of control over use such as copy protection and encryption against circumvention by third parties (Articles 11 and 12), and do not allow any reservations to the Treaty (Article 22).

The new Treaty provides important background to the efforts of the European Union to find its own solutions to the problems. A Directive, a draft of which was expected at the time of writing to be published in October 1997, will probably cover the following areas:

- harmonisation of the reproduction right, including limitations thereupon; areas of concern will once again be temporary reproduction rights, and also perhaps private reproduction rights;
- creation of a "communication to the public" right, to meet the special problems of "on-demand" digital transmissions;
- legal protection of the integrity of technical identification and protection schemes;

---

[125] See Vinje, "The new WIPO Copyright Treaty", 230–234; Waelde, "Intellectual property and the Internet", 66–69.

• harmonisation of distribution rights so that only first sale in the Community by or with the consent of the right-holder exhausts the distribution right.

Further possibilities for action are digital broadcasting, levies on the technology which facilitates private copying if this becomes generally allowable, questions of applicable law, law enforcement mechanisms, management of rights at Community level, and harmonisation of moral rights. This last arises because it is thought that in a digital world an author's work can be multiplied infinitely and also manipulated infinitely; some kind of protection should therefore be available to assert the author's rights to be identified and to have the integrity of his work respected.

In all this, it is evident that the scope and reach of copyright are likely to be considerably extended over the next few years. For many, this will be a matter of regret. The aim is clearly to establish as strong a regime of protection as possible for authors, providing a situation where publication on the Internet can realise its full economic potential. In some sense the divergent Anglo-American and Continental approaches to copyright are drawing together to ensure that the author gets recognition and reward on the Internet as elsewhere. As a result, copyright is moving ever further from controlling the existence of copies to controlling the use made of material, and in this there is a danger of overlooking the public interest in the dissemination of ideas, information, instruction and entertainment without undue burden, and in the rights of free expression and privacy. Yet the uneasy may take comfort. Laws can be written in the most draconian terms, but the critical question is whether they can be enforced. It is all very well being able to say that the author has a copyright in the UK, but what good is that against an infringement in Eastern Europe or Asia? The problem of enforcement of rights is what should be taking up the attention of reformers who want to realise and maximise the commercial potential of the Internet. The new laws are being strongly expressed to act as a symbol of deterrence, an approach which may in fact reflect the real weakness of the position in which commercial interests now find themselves. Much depends on how the technology develops, but one possibility is clearly that the old problem with which copyright is designed to deal—market failure to make the production of ideas and information worthwhile—could begin to disappear. The technology which creates the Internet may one day also mean that an author can make her material available while at the same time ensuring that every user is recorded and makes payment directly to her for the privilege, the whole transaction being triggered automatically in the system by the user's accession of the material. Contract, in other words, could replace copyright.[126] But a world like that appears to be, alas, still some way off.

---

[126] Although the probable role of collecting societies in such a world might in turn raise doubts about the real benefit to the individual author.

PART 3
Electronic Commerce

6

Contract Formation on the Internet
Shattering a few myths

LARS DAVIES[1]

INTRODUCTION

The important topic of contracting across the Internet has generated a great deal of debate. Remarkably perhaps, the debate has not really addressed the fundamental issue of whether or not contracts can be formed on the Internet but rather has used extant contracts as a starting point. Though this can be a valid step to take when the structure or form of a contract is known the ensuing discussion can gain much more if the fundamental questions of how, when and why are dealt with rather than left out or avoided altogether. This is especially so when attempting to look at contract formation in the wider context of the Internet.

Why does contract formation on the Internet merit treatment as a discrete subject in its own right? The answers to this often asked question are twofold. Firstly the development of commercial activity on the Internet requires some investigation into contracting across this communications medium. From an obscure academic beginning, the Internet has developed into something of a global communications environment and businesses and other commercial entities are attempting to develop new business models to exploit the potential that they believe the Internet holds as an international trading medium. One of the requirements for these business models to be viable is a reliable and enforceable method of contracting.

Secondly, and much more importantly, the workings of the Internet can and do pose many problems when looking at contract formation. The workings define the very nature of the Internet and consequently govern the mechanisms of contract formation. Consequently it is impossible to deal adequately with this topic without first having a basic understanding of what the Internet is and how it works. Indeed the workings of the Internet must govern any

This document is designed to provide a general guide to the relevant law. It does not purport to be comprehensive in any way and is not intended to provide legal advice of any nature.

[1] Lars Davies, Research Fellow, Information Technology Law Unit, Centre for Commercial Law Studies, Queen Mary and Westfield College, University of London.

analysis of contract formation and without a basic understanding all such analysis would be fundamentally flawed. Worse even, the outcome of the analysis would almost invariably be wrong.[2]

Major issues which should always be kept in mind are where is the contract formed and which laws and jurisdiction apply? If the postal rule applies then part of the answer to the first issue is very simple; the contract is formed at the location from where the acceptance was sent.[3] If it does not then the analysis of the contract formation is more involved.[4]

WHAT IS THE POSTAL RULE?

The postal rule, which is an exception to the general rule that an acceptance is only effective when it is received by the offeror, is a strange beast which seems to exist mainly in common law jurisdictions and refers to an implied, and rebuttable rule of contract formation. The rule applies only when the parties to an agreement do not communicate with each other by way of instantaneous communications such as by telephone but instead use a non-instantaneous method of communications such as the post. The rule, put simply, states that an acceptance is effective once it is posted, rather than when it is actually received. The essence is that the acceptor has entrusted his communication to a third party or put the communication beyond his control.[5] The effect is that if the rule applies then a contract is formed when the acceptance is sent regardless of whether the offeror receives the message or not. This may seem somewhat unfair but the rule is simply based on a pragmatic weighting up of the risks entailed in contracting in this manner[6] and provides a solution to a difficult problem.[7] In any case the offeror can always negate

---

[2] Getting the correct answer by an incorrect analysis is almsot as bad as getting the wrong answer by the wrong means. Getting the wrong answer from the right analysis shows a little understanding of the underlying issues.

[3] Determining this actual location may be an altogether different and more involved problem as is discussed later. The postal rule, if it applies, simply tells you what to look for; namely the location from where the acceptance was sent.

[4] This is wet towel around the head work. It also involves drinking plenty of coffee.

[5] *Household Fire Insurance v Grant* (1879) 4 Ex. D. 216, 48 L. J. Ex. 577, 41 L. J. 298. As per Thesiger L.J.:

"The acceptor, in posting the letter, has . . . put it out of his control and done an extraneous act which clenches the matter, and shows beyond all doubt that each side is bound."

[6] *Household Fire Insurance v Grant.* As per Thesiger L.J.:

"There is no doubt that the implication of a complete, final, and absolutely binding contract being formed, as soon as the acceptance of an offer is posted, may in some cases lead to inconvenience and hardship. But such there must be at times in every view of the law. It is impossible in transactions which pass between parties at a distance, and have to be carried on through the medium of correspondence, to adjust conflicting rights between innocent parties, so as to make the consequences of mistake on the part of a mutual agent fall equally on the shoulders of both."

[7] *Brinkibon Ltd v Stahag Stahl und Stahlwarenhandelgesellscaft* [1983] 2 A.C. 34; [1982] 2 W.L.R. 164; [1982] 1 All E.R. 293.

the rule by requiring that he receives the acceptance for it to become effective. What is important to realise, however, is that the postal rule is not a magic bullet that solves all ills and the rule will only apply in some limited circumstances.

LAWS AND JURISDICTION

The place at which the contract is formed is merely one question. The other issues of choice of law and jurisdiction hang on the answer to that question for an obvious reason as will be seen.

The general rule is that parties are free to agree the laws and the jurisdiction[8] which they wish to govern the contract. They do this to ensure that they will know the laws which govern the contract and also the rules and procedure of the courts which may need to determine any dispute that arises as a consequence of the contract. However, the fact that the parties can chose the law or jurisdiction does not necessarily mean that the choice is valid or enforceable and this is why the location of the contract formation has a bearing on this matter. The contractual terms which purport to define the law and jurisdiction must be valid and the validity is determined by the laws of the jurisdiction in which the contract is formed regardless of any term within the contract itself. This point is often forgotten but it is vital. Every jurisdiction has rules which govern the freedom of parties to choose the law or jurisdiction[9] of a contract and it is these rules which will determine whether or not the terms or choices themselves are valid.[10]

[8] These are two separate issues. Parties can choose a jurisdiction without choosing a law or choose a law without choosing a jurisdiction but this is rare and can be dangerous.

[9] The Brussels Convention is one such example. This applies to Member States of the European Community and governs the choice of law for civil and commercial matters within the EC. Put very simply the Convention operates in one of three ways. The basic rule, in Schedule 1 of the Convention, is that the defendant must be sued in his local court, with the meaning of the word 'local' dependent on whether the defendant is an individual or a company. For a few matters, the Convention stipulates an exclusive jurisdiction which cannot be altered by contract. For many other matters the Convention implies a choice of law and jurisdiction where no explicit choice to the contrary exists, and this means that for that class of contract the parties can agree to contract out of the Convention; that is they can override the Convention but must do so explicitly. An example are the rules governing contracts. Here the general rule is that the relevant jurisdiction is that in which the contract is to be performed. If there are many jurisdictions where the contract is performed, then the relevant jurisdiction is that in which the dispute arises. If, however the contract could be performed in several different jurisdictions as opposed to being required to be performed in those jurisdictions then the situation is amusing. The way in which the Convention is interpreted differs in different jurisdictions within the EC. The English Courts hold that there is a choice of jurisdictions, namely those where the contract could be performed, and it is for those jurisdictions to seize jurisdiction. The Scottish Courts hold that the relevant jurisdictions are those in which the contract was performed. A subtle difference, perhaps, but an important one. It should come as no surprise whatsoever that good commercial contracts will get out of the general rules surrounding contracts as quickly as possible. After all why deal with it when you can get rid of it? A good principle for commercial lawyers.

[10] This may strike some as being a bit strange and they would be correct. For example the choice may be valid but the term in which that choice is made may itself be invalid. In this case

WHAT IS THE INTERNET AND HOW DOES IT WORK?[11]

So what is the Internet? The first and perhaps most important thing to know about the Internet is that it does not actually exist. There is no such thing as the Internet. This statement may seem a little strange given the vast publicity that the 'Internet' has received over the past couple of years but it stands examination nevertheless. What does exist is a developing group of national and international, private and public computer networks which can and do connect to and communicate with each other, and it is these networks, when taken together, which form the thing which people often refer to excitedly as the 'Internet'. There is, therefore, no single entity which owns or controls the Internet. Instead any ownership and control[12] which may exist vests in each of the discrete networks that make up the patchwork that is the Internet.

What then makes the Internet work? The answer[13] to this question further complicates the legal analysis of contract formation and it is here that the true nature of the Internet starts to become apparent.

The Internet consists then of interconnected networks which talk to each other. These networks need not be of the same type and so in order to allow them to communicate with each other they must use a common method of communication, a lingua franca. The networks and computers that attach to these networks use a set of protocols, the Transmission Control Protocol/ Internet Protocol, commonly referred to by the shorthand TCP/IP.[14] The term is slightly misleading as the set consists of a suite of protocols rather than just these two but these are the main protocols in the set.

---

the whole term falls apart and the choice disappears into the great courtroom in the sky. Equally the term may be valid but the choice of law invalid. The term survives but is completely ineffective. Both scenarios can be annoying at best and very expensive at worst. They do, however, provide great sources of amusement for lectures.

[11] This article can give no more than a brief outline of the workings of the Internet. For a more detailed description of how the Internet works, see Krol, *The Whole Internet User's Guide & Catalog*, O'Reilly & Associates, Sebastopol CA, 2nd ed., 1994; and Wiggins, *The Internet for Everyone*, McGraw-Hill, New York, 1994.

[12] Control of the networks is completely distinct from other controls over the use of some of the services that are provided over the networks, such as DNS or the Domain Name System. With DNS, control is not attached to the individual networks but to the individual domain at various levels. These may in some circumstances be synonymous with individual networks but that is purely coincidental. For all purposes, the controls are discrete and several and should be regarded as such.

[13] A basic understanding of the technical issues is all that is required here. A more in depth explanation usually instills fear and trepidation. Mongolian Tribal Law can suddenly become overly fascinating and all absorbing as a result.

[14] For a full explnation of how TCP/IP works, see Bearpark, *Protocols for Application Communication*, McGraw-Hill, London 1995; Washburn & Evans, *TCP/IP Running a Successful Network*, Addison-Wesley, Wokingham, 1993; Hunt. *TCP/IP Network Administration*, O'Reilly & Associates, 1993.

LOTS AND LOTS OF LITTLE BITS

Computers store and handle digital data as strings of bits or zeros and ones. Each of these strings can also be regarded as a binary number, a number represented by zeros and ones, albeit a rather large number. The protocols allow computers to communicate and transmit digital data using two techniques. The protocols slice the data into very small packets or parcels of data. These packets are then transmitted across the Internet to the receiving computer which reassembles the packets into an exact copy of the data that was sent. In effect the data is copied from one computer to another. These packets can arrive at the receiving computer in any order. Some of the more complex protocols allow the computer to reassemble the packets in the correct order and request the sending computer to retransmit any packets that are missing, but the basic protocols simply send and receive data without any error correction.

Secondly the protocols handle the addressing mechanism which the computers use to find and contact each other. At present the protocols use a set of unique 32-bit numbers to give each computer an address. All that the computers see are these 32-bit numbers. The numbers do not signify any geographical or jurisdictional location, they simply indicate the network to which the computer is attached. The final feature of the protocols is that the actual path of communication is, for the most part, completely irrelevant. Each individual packet of data can take a completely independent path to that of the others. All that the protocols are concerned with is whether the computers can see each other and whether data can be transmitted between them.

The third thing that must be kept in mind is that contrary to popular belief the Internet does and provides absolutely nothing. Just as with any computer users have to do something with the wretched thing to make it do anything. Switch the thing on and leave it and all you have is an expensive, and not very efficient heating system. An electricity consuming lump of fried sand. The Internet does not provide any data or information, nor does it access computers or provide services. It is users who do all of these things and more. The Internet is simply a communications system over which users can provide these services and over which they can carry out these activities. It is these services, such as electronic mail, news, and the world wide web that users see when using the Internet. The two services that users are likely to use to enter into agreements are electronic mail and world wide web.

CLIENTS AND SERVERS

Computers that are connected on the Internet are often confusingly described as clients, or servers. This distinction does not indicate the size of the computers nor indeed does it necessarily distinguish between different computers. Rather it indicates the function of computer code on the computer. A server generally runs programs which are used to provide services or serve up data on request, whilst a client is simply a piece of computer code on a computer which can access the services provided by the server. Even more confusing is the fact that a computer can serve both roles. Indeed one of the attractions of the Internet is that any computer that is attached can offer services and so be classed as a server. The safest way to think about this is to say that a computer is acting as a server if it is providing a service, and a client when it access any server, even itself. Computers can be a little schizophrenic.

ELECTRONIC MAIL

Electronic mail makes up by far the greatest part of traffic on the Internet. A user simply uses an electronic mail client program to create a message, addresses the message to the recipient and then sends it on its way. That is what the user sees. What actually happens is a tad more complex. The client program first transmits the message to the sender's mail server. This is a program that can run either on the same computer as the client program or on an entirely different computer which can be anywhere on the Internet. The sender's mail server then sends the message to the recipient's mail server. The recipient uses his client program to access any mail stored by his mail server. Again this server can run on the recipient's computer or on another computer. It does not matter in the slightest where the mail servers are running. The electronic mail may be sent directly to the recipient's server, or it may travel via several different servers before reaching the recipient. The servers may also store, or queue, the message for a time before sending it on its way.

Two common misconceptions, which are often dispelled after a few days of attempted use, are that electronic mail provides an instantaneous method of transmitting messages between computers and that it is a robust and totally reliable means of communication.[15] It is neither. An important consideration to bear in mind is that some electronic mail clients operate in the background and will automatically retrieve new messages, whilst others are passive and wait for a user to access his mailbox. The sender therefore cannot be sure when the addressee receives or reads the message. Some systems allow the sender to require the recipient's client program to send the sender a receipt when the user accesses and reads his mail. Unfortunately the receipt is sent as electronic mail. This thus suffers from the same problems as normal electronic mail and so provides no more reliability than normal.[16] However, if a receipt is received then the user can usually be sure that the recipient, or his system,

[15] See Stoll, *Silicon Snake Oil: Second Thoughts on the Information Highway*, Macmillan, London 1995, Chapter 10 for a humorous comparison betweeen electronic mail and the US postal service. The book also acts as a good antidote to Net fever, an over-exuberant belief in the Internet.
[16] This does, however, use up network bandwidth and fill mailboxes with unwanted messages. It can also have the amusing effect of crashing a few aging mail servers.

has accessed the mail. Whether or not he actually reads the message is another question altogether. Some client programs use mail filters to filter mail and file it into different mailboxes. The result is that the system may state that the user has accessed his mail. It does not mean that the user has read the messages.

WORLD WIDE WEB

The World Wide Web is perhaps the most famous service[17] on the Internet at present. The service uses two technologies, the HTTP or HyperText Transfer Protocol and HTML or HyperText Markup Language. These two technologies are separate and distinct. HTTP is a protocol that allows client programs, often known as Web Browsers, to call up and request documents and other resources provided by a web server. HTML is simply a text markup language which tells a browser how to display the various elements of a page of hypertext. Hypertext is simply the term used to describe a 'page' of information which can contain media types other than text, such as graphics, images, sound, moving video and so on. It can also contain links or pointers to other pages or files. The user navigates around the pages by simply clicking on these links.

The user uses his Web Browser to request a particular page from a Web Server, which, if it holds the page, transmits it to the user. The page may contain links to other media types. These will also be called automatically by the browser and the whole page assembled and displayed in all its beauty.[18] One feature of this technology is that the various constituent parts of a page can be held on different servers anywhere on the Internet. The browser does not care where they are so long as it can access and download the relevant data. The user is usually blissfully unaware of the drama that underlies his request. All he sees is the page slowly forming before his eyes.

The hypertext links in a page of HTML can also refer to different services and protocols. Thus users can construct pages that allow other users to send them electronic mail and this is one of the ways in which commercial web sites can create pages to offer goods and services to users. The user clicks on the relevant link to send electronic mail to the relevant recipient, business or otherwise.

Advanced versions of HTML, HTML versions 2 and above, allow users to create much more interactive pages such as input forms. When a client program accesses such a page his browser displays a page which contains a form which he can then fill in. The user can enter information into the form and use his browser to transmit the data back to the server where it can then be

---

[17] A common misconception is that the World Wide Web is a network and this is perhaps due to its name. It is not. It is only a service, albeit a rather famous service.

[18] Either that or the browser will crash his system.

processed and acted upon, or sent on to another server to be processed. The data can be manually processed by a computer operator who receives the information but it is much more usual to process the date automatically. This is done using Common Gateway Interface or CGI programs or scripts running on a server which will process the data and respond by carrying out predetermined functions such as transmitting newly created pages to the user, or sending electronic mail to another party such as a commercial vendor, where the message may or may not be processed automatically.

HOW DO USERS CONNECT?

Users can connect to the Internet in one of two ways. The most direct way is for users to connect to the Internet via an Internet Service Provider. This gives the user a direct connection, a vanilla connection, to the Internet. The user's computer may itself be connected to the Internet, or may be part of a network that is connected to the Internet. It does not matter. What matters is the direct connection. The Internet Service Provider may also operate servers which are either publicly accessible, or accessible only to its subscribers, the users who connect via its links, but its business is essentially one of connecting computers and networks to the Internet and nothing more.

Users may also connect via On-Line Service Providers. Here the scenario is completely different. The user does not connect directly to the Internet but instead connects to a separate system. The system operator offers its users various services such as electronic mail, discussion groups and so on. One of these services may be a connection to the Internet. However, unlike the situation with the Internet Service Provider the user here connects through the On-Line Service Provider's system and not via a direct link and this difference can have interesting effects for contract formation.

CONTRACT FORMATION SCENARIOS

The patchwork of networks that makes up the Internet allows users and computers to communicate with each other regardless of distance or national borders in a very simple and yet very powerful and flexible manner and it is this, together with the power and flexibility of the computers making up the networks, which makes the Internet very attractive to business and commercial interests. The ease and flexibility of communications on the Internet allows users to enter into agreements with the greatest of ease. Time difference and geographical location do not present a problem. The issue is not whether or not the users enter into agreements. The real issue is whether or not these agreements can constitute contracts.

The borderless nature of the Internet creates several legal issues for commercial transactions which occur over or in some way involve use of the Internet. If a transaction takes place between computers or users in different jurisdictions then the question arises as to which laws govern the transaction. This is compounded by the problem that the involvement of different jurisdictions is not immediately apparent. Another question which must be asked is where was the contract formed, or even was a contract formed at all? Does the jurisdiction in which any agreement was entered into recognise that agreement as a legally valid contract?

The borderless nature of the Internet is not the only concern. The nature of the communication used in entering any agreement is itself a great source of problems that must be addressed.

The questions that are usually asked are what *law* applies to contracts formed on the Internet, which courts have *jurisdiction*, and what *terms* apply? The most important question however, and one which is rarely asked, is whether or not a contract was actually formed, and if so *where* that contract was formed and *when*.[19] Until these are answered it makes no sense to even attempt to ask what laws apply as the answers will depend on those given to the first three questions. If contracts were not formed then any discussion on which laws apply is completely irrelevant and a complete waste of time. Only if contracts were formed can any meaningful discussion take place. An obvious point, perhaps, but one which is often missed.

The analysis to determine whether a contract has been formed has two distinct but interrelated parts; the topography or structure of the network connection between the communicating computers and the services used for communicating. The Internet is such an incredibly flexible and powerful communications system that it is impractical to examine every possible topography. However, not all is lost as virtually all communication on the Internet takes the form of a combination of one or more of five basic scenarios. A good approach is therefore to attempt to examine these five scenarios; they could be regarded as constituting a basic set of building blocks; networking using lego bricks perhaps.

The five basic scenarios are as follows: simple communications between two computers, communications carried out on a common server, communications via intermediate servers, multiple intermediate servers and networks, and the virtual market place.

i) Simple communications between two computers

In this scenario users, that is the customers and the suppliers, simply receive and action all messages on their own computers or on computers to which

---

[19] This may seem a tad trite but it is vital. It is of no use whatsoever to suggest that somewhere in the soup of electronic communications that make up a series of messages a contract was formed but it is not known exactly where or when; just that a contract was some how formed. In order for there to be a contract the exact instant when it came into existence must be identifiable, and not merely be a vague and nebulous occurrence; a point often lost on law students.

they have physical access. The usual form for messages in this scenario is electronic mail, but they can also comprise of web pages downloaded from the users' computers. The scenario is very simple to look at as there are no third parties who are actively involved in the communications and the communications are under the control of the users themselves.[20] The messages may, and indeed will often travel via several servers but these will simply forward the messages. They have no other function whatsoever.

Given the simplicity of the topography it is easy to see that the general principles of contract formation apply, namely that the contract is formed when the offeror receives the acceptance. In this scenario the contract is formed where the offeror is located and so comes under that jurisdiction unless special rules apply. The postal rule cannot apply in this scenario as the users have not entrusted their communications to a trusted third party. No third party is involved.

One problem for the unwary is that contracts formed under this scenario could easily be formed when the parties use computers on a temporary basis, such as in the so-called Cyber Cafes; meeting places where users can rent computer access for a short time. This does not present too much of a problem where the users access these computers in their own jurisdictions. Where they use these computers in other jurisdictions they may find that their agreements come under the laws of those other jurisdictions. This can result in special rules applying to the contract, or in some circumstances, that any agreement entered into is held not to constitute a contract.

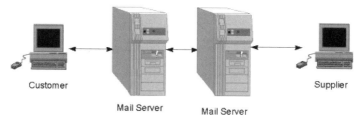

Parties communicating by electronic mail

Parties communicating via the World Wide Web

[20] This is similar to the situation that exists with standard telephone communications. The telephone networks are controlled by the telephone companies but the users, and only the users, control the actual communication between themselves.

Parties communicating via the World Wide Web

ii) *Communications carried out on a common server*

This scenario is somewhat deceptive and can, and often does, lull the parties into a false sense of security. Here the parties may or may not be in different jurisdictions but they communicate with each other using a common server, such as where all the parties are users of a single On-Line Service Provider's system,[21] such as CompuServe. All communications take place on this server. Any electronic mail is created,[22] stored, sent, delivered and processed on the server as are any web pages and scripts. This has several consequences for the parties. Firstly the parties have trusted their communications to a third party, the server operator, and so it could be argued that the postal rule applies here and any contract is formed when the acceptance is sent by a user to the offeror. Secondly, and perhaps more importantly, if a contract is formed then it comes into being not in the place where the offeror, or if the postal rule applies the sender, is located, but rather *in the server itself*. The relevant jurisdiction is thus that of the server, and not necessarily that of the users.

One of the most common problems with this scenario is that the users may be completely unaware of the jurisdictional question and may assume that any contracts they enter into are subject to another jurisdiction, such as their own. This is especially so where two or more users in the same jurisdiction, for example England, contract with each other via a server located in a third jurisdiction for example Germany. Users may attempt to circumvent the problem by incorporating a choice of jurisdiction and choice of law clause. However, the primary jurisdiction is that of the server, and all questions as to validity of contract or validity of the clauses are initially subject to that jurisdiction.

iii) *Communication via intermediate servers*

In terms of the jurisdictional problems this scenario is similar to that of the common server, the difference being that there are now at least two servers involved in handling and processing the messages. Here the users connect to *different* servers, on which they create and process messages. They then send these messages on to other users. These other users may also access their mail,

---

[21] This scenario is quite different to a user who accesses such a server to interact with some of its services but who is actually connected to the Internet through an Internet Service Provider. The question is then a matter of where does he create and receive messages. If he is using terminal software which allows him to create the message on the server then he could be said to be using the common server.

[22] The users may create and store the messages on the server itself, or they may use software which allows them to create messages and read messages off-line. That is they create and read messages on their own computers. However, none of the messages can be sent or downloaded until the user connects to the server; the software simply acts as a proxy. Without that software the user would still have to create the messages on the server.

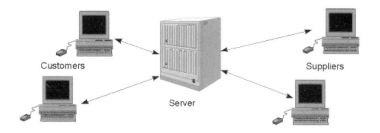

Parties communicating via a common server

not on their own computers, but on other servers. The similarity with the common server scenario then is that these servers may be located in jurisdictions different to those of the users.

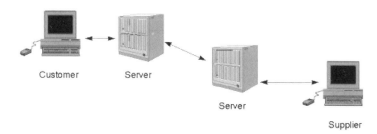

Parties communicating via intermediate servers

This scenario frequently occurs when dealing with the World Wide Web. A user may access and interact with a web server in one location. The result of this interaction may be that the server sends information to another server in either the same or another location. The second server then processes the information and can either interact directly with the user, so displacing the first server, or send information back to the first server, which then interacts with the user.

One obvious question which arises is where is a contract formed if at all? If the postal rule applies then the contract is formed on the computer from where the acceptance was sent. If the postal rule does *not* apply, then the con-

---

[23] *Thornton v Shoe Lane Parking Ltd* [1971] 2 Q.B. 163;[1971] 2 W.L.R. 585; [1971] 1 All E.R. 686 contains an example of a machine actioning a contract, the machine being a car park ticket vending machine. In that case Lord Denning M.R. stated that:

" the offer is made when the proprietor of the machine holds it out as being ready to receive the money. The acceptance takes place when the customer puts his money into the slot."

Using an analogous argument the offeror in these scenarios can be said to make the offer when he indicates that the computer is ready to receive the acceptance from the acceptor. The computer is not the contracting party but merely acting as a means of communication, and possibly as an agent, for the parties or, at the very least, the offeror.

tract is formed on the computer which actioned the acceptance;[23] this is not necessarily that of the offeror, especially if the message is actioned automatically. The answer thus depends on whether the postal rule applies, which message constituted an offer and which an acceptance, and the functions of the servers. Which computer actioned the acceptance, the first or the second? Which computer sent the acceptance?

iv) Multiple intermediate servers and networks

This scenario is in reality an extension of the one mentioned above where messages are relayed to and actioned on several different servers. Again the main problems that arise are jurisdictional. An example, and one which is extreme, is where a message is relayed to a network operated by a commercial entity. The network may include servers that are situated in different jurisdictions and the message may be relayed to any one or several of these servers before it is actioned. The question again is in which jurisdiction is the contract formed. The answer may not be immediately apparent and again the functions of the messages are important.

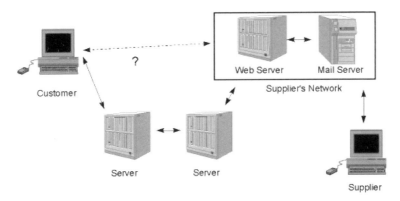

Parties communicating via multiple intermediate servers and networks.

v) Virtual market place

The virtual market place is a strange creature indeed. These market places, almost all of which take the form of World Wide Web sites, are sited on servers which host pages or services offered by several commercial concerns so in effect they represent a form of market place where individual vendors or businesses have pages of information which users or customers can access. From the users' perspective they interact with that server and that server alone. However the interest is not so much in what the user sees as what actually takes place behind the scenes.

Depending on how the server is set up some or all of the processing that is triggered by the interaction between the user and the server may take place in the server itself. The server may also send information out to some or all of the vendors' sites where it is actioned. The problem is determining when and where exactly a contract is formed if at all. Does the server act in the capacity of agent for the commercial vendors and process the information to the extent that the contracts are formed on the server, or does it simply pre-process the information into a useable form before forwarding it on to the vendor for further processing where the contract is formed? Where is the acceptance received and acted upon? The question that must be asked is what is the function of each message. Are the messages to the vendors simply conveying the acceptance, or offer as the case may be, or have the parties already entered into a contract in which case are the messages simply a request to deliver the goods or services to a particular location at a particular time?

Another question, which is especially important in this scenario, is who are the parties contracting with? Do the users contract with the operator of the market place or the individual vendors themselves?[24] Perhaps the structure of the market place is more complex whereby for some transactions the users contract with the operator whilst in other circumstances the users contract with the vendors themselves. This problem leads directly to the vexed issues of governing laws and jurisdictions for the various transactions.

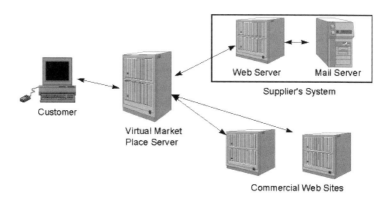

The Virtual Market Place

LEGAL ISSUES ARISING FROM COMMUNICATION

The scenarios themselves go some way to illustrate the different topographies that parties can use to communicate with each other and enter into agreements between themselves. The communications used also have a large effect

---

[24] The answer may not be immediately apparent to the users or even the operators of the virtual market places.

on the analysis of the trinity of if, where, and when.[25] The communications can be separated into two distinct types; direct communication between the parties and indirect communication between the parties. These distinctions do not refer to communications which are instantaneous and those which are not; most communication across the Internet incurs some delay albeit small. Rather it refers to communications which are transmitted directly to the parties and those which are not.[26]

DIRECT COMMUNICATIONS

When examining direct communications, two possible options exist for rules relating to contract formation, namely that the standard rules relating to instantaneous communications apply, or that the postal rule applies.

As previously stated the Internet does not always facilitate instantaneous communications. The speed can range from very very fast indeed, or virtually instantaneous, to it must be quicker to copy the data on to a disk and swim across the Atlantic with it. Distance between computers has very little to do with the speed difference and often links from afar can be much quicker that links to the next street. What matters is the work load on a server, computer, or network at the time it is accessed.

An Internet link does, however, have some similarity to a telephone or telex link. Although there is no direct physical link between the users, the link has much more in common with telegraphy than with the post, and one user can usually determine if the other has received his message or not within a fairly short time. This may be indicated by the reception of a partial message, or not receiving a response where an automated response would be expected. Even if no such response were expected it would still be up to the party communicating the message to ensure that the other received it.[27] The offer must be received by the offeree and the acceptance must be received by the offeror in order for the messages to be effective. In these circumstances under English Law the contract will not be formed until the acceptance is received by the offeror as a whole and this will determine the jurisdiction under which the contract is formed.[28] A partial reception will not usually suffice[29] unless the

---

[25] Legal questions often come in threes.

[26] A set of communications between parties can consist of both direct and indirect communications.

[27] *Entores Ltd v Miles Far East Corporation* [1955] 2 Q.B. 327; [1955] 2 All E.R. 493; [1955] 1 Lloyd's Rep. 511. As per Parker LJ when discussing the case of communication via telex:

"... though the dispatch and receipt of a message is not completely instantaneous, the parties are to all intents and purposes in each other's presence just as if they were in telephonic communication, and I can see no reason for departing from the general rule that there is no binding contract until notice of the acceptance is received by the offeror."

[28] *Brinkibon Ltd v Stahag Stahl und Stahlwarenhandelgesellscaft.*

receiver has acted upon the partial reception as if it were a full acceptance, in which case it is effective.

This does not deal fully with the issue of when the contract was actually formed. Messages transmitted to World Wide Web browsers are usually displayed shortly after they are received by the user's browser. However, it is possible to write short programs or scripts that will interact with Web servers and keep for later viewing any information sent as a result. Likewise electronic mail is first sent to and stored on a mail server before the user can access it. When are these messages received? Are they received for the purpose of contract formation when the message is received by the server or script, or when the user actually accesses them and reads them?[30]

The above analysis may hold where the parties have not entrusted their communications to a third party. Where the parties do entrust their communications to a third party, such as when they communicate via a single common server then one possibility is that the postal rule[31] will apply to the communications.[32] This would mean that any acceptance would be effective

---

[29] The arguments here are akin to those given by Denning L.J. in *Entores v Miles Far East Corporation*. Take the example given of two parties communicating across a river or courtyard whose words are drowned out by an aircraft. The words of acceptance must be repeated to ensure that they are heard for there to be a binding contract. Likewise the example given of a break in a telephone conversation or a telex transmission, where normally the message should be repeated and received by the offeror before the contract is formed. These are analogous to a break in communications across the open Internet. Here the users would most likely become aware of the break, that their messages had gone to the great hard disk that can never be found and so would need to repeat the communication, resend the acceptance, before a contract could be formed. Just as words can be blown away in the wind and telephone lines blown down by the wind, so on the Internet bits can disappear into the great bit bucket in the sky. The analogy is good as lightning storms can play havoc with the Internet. The aftermath can be fun to watch.

[30] The point in question is unclear and undecided. However, in some jurisdictions the message will be deemed to be delivered once it is made available for the recipient, such as when a message is delivered into the recipient's mailbox, regardless of whether or not he has accessed it. In Scots law, on the special facts in *Burnley v Alford* 1919 2 SLT 123, an offer was held recalled when the recall would in the normal course have reached the offeree but did not do so because there was no one at the address. Article 1335 of the Italian Civil Code stipulates that an acceptance is effective once it has reaches the offeror's premises so long as he is then likely to receive it. The question obviously arises as to whether an electronic mailbox, regardless if its actual geographic location, constitutes part of the offeror's premises. In the US the cases of United Leasing 656 P.2d 1250 and *Kendel v Pontious* 261 So.2d 167 hold that an offer is accepted if reasonable efforts were used to communicate the acceptance; Restatement (2nd) of Contracts § 56 comments a & b.

[31] *Adams v Lindsell* (1818) 1 B & A 681; *Household Fire Insurance v Grant; Dunlop v Higgins* 1 H.L. 381. An interesting adjunct to this rule is that though an acceptance is effective once it is posted a message revoking an offer is not effective until it is received by the recipient; *Byrne & Co v Van Tienhoven & Co* (1880) 5 C.P.D. 344; 49 L.J.C.P. 316; 42 L.T. 371., and for Scotland see *Thomson v James* (1855) 18 D. 1. The Scottish Law Commission has proposed the abolition of the postal rule in Scotland, Scottish Law Commission Memo. No 36, *Constitution and Proof of Voluntary Obligations: Formation of Contract.*

[32] Though there are strong arguments for supposing that the postal rule may apply in these circumstances it is not possible to specify a closed set of rules that will apply to all situations. As Lord Wilberforce states in *Brinkibon Ltd v Stahag Stahl und Stahlwarenhandelsgesellscaft*:

"No universal rule can cover all such cases; they must be resolved by reference to the intentions of the parties, by sound business practice and in some cases by a judgment where the risks . . . should lie"

the moment a user sends the message and not when it is received by the offeror.

This would seem to follow from an analysis of the operation of a common server whereby the communications take place in a system over which the server operator has a great deal of control.[33] Users sending a message into the server would be fairly sure of the message arriving at the recipient's mailbox, unlike mail sent into the Internet in general over which no operator has absolute control.[34] Two possible justifications exist for this idea. The first, and one of the explanations often used to justify the rule, is that such a rule would provide the most convenient answer to a difficult problem.[35] The second justification rests on an analogy with postal communications. Using the analogy the offeror entrusts his communications to an independent third party and impliedly allows the acceptor to do likewise. Consequently once the offeror and acceptor have carried out all the necessary procedures to effect communications, the messages are deemed to be transmitted regardless of whether or not they arrive.[36] The offeror can of course always state that no acceptance will take effect until he actually receives the message and so obviate the postal rule. Using this argument any message would take effect once the sender sends it from his mailbox into the system, that is once the system takes control of the transmission and delivery of the message.

The postal rule, if it does operate, can only do so when the parties are actually connected to the servers. Users of such systems often have software that

There are also some doubts about the absoluteness of the postal rule in Scotland—see *Sloans Dairies v Glasgow Corp* 1977 SC 223; 1976 SLT 147 per Lord Dunpark.

[33] The system stores the mail and forwards it on to the correct mailbox. The system controls the entire process from the initial transmission by the sender, through the sorting through the system, to the delivery to the recipient.

[34] It is possible to set mail servers to deliver their mail by set routes through the Internet and in this situation it may be possible to argue that the postal rule should also apply here.

[35] As per Lord Brandon in *Brinkibon Ltd v Stahag Stahl und Stahlwarenhandelgesellscaft*:

"The cases on acceptance by letter and telegram constitute an exception to the general principle of the law of contract .... That reason of commercial expediency applies to cases where there is bound to be a substantial interval between the time when the acceptance is sent and the time when it is received. In such cases the exception to the general rule is more convenient, and makes on the whole for greater fairness, than the rule itself would do."

[36] As per Thesiger LJ in *Household Fire Insurance Co. v Grant*:

"There is no doubt that the implication of a complete, final, and absolutely binding contract being formed, as soon as the acceptance of an offer is posted, may in some cases lead to an inconvenience and hardship. But such there must be at times in every view of the law. It is impossible in transactions which pass between parties at a distance, and have to be carried on through the medium of correspondence, to adjust conflicting rights between innocent parties, so as to make the consequences of mistake on the part of a mutual agent fall equally upon the shoulders of both. At the same time I am not prepared to admit that the implication in question will lead to any great or general inconvenience or hardship. An offeror, if he chooses, may always make the formation of the contract which he proposes dependent upon the actual communication to himself of the acceptance."

In Scotland the situation is similar as per *Burnley v Alford* although the focus is on deemed communication rather than transmission.

allows them to create and read messages off line.[37] However the users have not entrusted their communications to the third party until they actually connect to the servers so the rule cannot take effect until the connection is established and the message transmitted from the users' computers to the servers.[38] The same argument holds where two or more parties use systems which, though operated by different operators, have created dedicated gateways to handle electronic mail between the systems.

The safest route for the offeror to take should now be obvious. First, the offeror should obviate the postal rule and stipulate that any acceptance will *only take effect once he receives the message*. Then he should perhaps also define what is meant by "receiving" to make sure that no misunderstandings occur.[39]

INDIRECT COMMUNICATIONS

This situation is absolutely horrid from a topological point of view. Here the users may initially communicate with a particular server but that server may then communicate with another server[40] and this second server may either process the messages and transmit them back to the original server and that original server interact with the users, or the second server may transmit the messages on to another server, and so on.[41] The postal rule will most likely not apply as the communications are not entrusted to a third party, and this will hold wherever the communications leave any closed system, such as a common server, and go out into the Internet. The questions to be asked are as before: namely if a contract is formed at all, and if so, where and when.[42] The trinity yet again.

[37] The software allows users to create any messages that they wish to send without needing to be connected to the server. The messages are only sent when the users actually connect to the server. The software may also allow users to download all of their messages in one go so that they may read them at some other time. The purpose of the software is to reduce the time that the users are connected to the servers. This not only reduces the overall workload of the server but also reduces the users' telecommunications costs.

[38] In the classic scenario of communication via the post the postal rule will not apply if a party does not post the letter correctly. See *Re London and Northern Bank, ex parte Jones* [1900] 1 Ch 220.

[39] For example what should happen if a message is delivered into the user's mailbox but, before the user can read it the computer crashed and destroys the message? Has the user received the message?

[40] The other servers referred to here would be operated and controlled by different server operators. If they are controlled by the same operator then, provided they have a reliable interlink they could probably be regarded as being part of the same system.

[41] See communications scenarios (iii), (iv) and (v) above.

[42] Where the topology of the communications is such that the parties and the contract are within the jurisdiction of England and Wales then the courts may well take a similar approach to that evidenced by Lord Wilberforce in *Brinkibon Ltd v Stahag Stahl und Stahlwaren-handelgesellscaft* and impose a workable solution to a difficult problem even though such a solution may well conflict with legal niceties. If the issues involve the question of differing jurisdiction then the courts will have to examine the issues with regard to the rules of the conflict of laws.

What is important to realise is that the communications topology must be examined before it is possible to determine the rules of contract formation.[43]

OFFER FOR SALE OR INVITATION TO TREAT

Offers for sale made to the world can prove to be somewhat inconvenient.[44] Revoking them can also prove a little difficult. It is, however, generally accepted that most Web pages or electronic mail messages that inform users of the availability of goods or services are akin to advertisements and so constitute invitations to treat.[45] Hence the user, when he replies to such an advertisement makes an offer to the commercial entity. The commercial entity must then send an acceptance to the user or do something which entails acceptance of the offer. This is the general picture when looking at consumer contracts on the Internet.

Nothing prevents users from entering into classic contracts where the initial message is an offer, rather than an invitation to treat. Here the standard pattern of communications take place; the offeror, either the user or commercial entity makes the initial offer and the offeree sends his acceptance.

INCORPORATING TERMS AND CONDITIONS

An issue which poses some serious problems is that of incorporating terms and conditions into contracts made over the Internet. The basic requirement is that the terms and conditions must be made known to the parties before they enter into an agreement and this is where the problems occur. The terms and conditions must be made known to the users before they accept the offer and enter into a contract. How then should this information be presented to the users?

One of the problems with contracting over the Internet is presenting this information to the users. The users must be given the *opportunity* to read and agree to the terms and conditions; whether they actually do or not is beside the point.

---

[43] *Brinkibon Ltd v Stahag Stahl und Stahlwarenhandelgesellscaft.* As per Lord Wilberforce where he speaks of telex communications:

"... the use of telex communication has been greatly expanded, and there are many variants on it. ... No universal rule can cover all such cases; they must be resolved by reference to the intentions of the parties, by sound business practice and in some cases by a judgment where the risks should lie."

[44] *Carlill v Carbolic Smoke Ball Co.* [1893] 1 Q.B. 256.

[45] *Pharmaceutical Society of Great Britain v Boots* [1953] 1 Q.B. 401; [1953] 2 W.L.R. 427; [1953] 1 All E.R. 482. *Gibson v Manchester City Council* [1979] 1 W.L.R. 294; [1979] 1 All E.R. 972.

It is a simple task to present the terms and conditions in electronic mail messages, and these should be present in any invitation to treat or, if the classic method is used, in the offer itself. If the first message is an invitation to treat then it is too late to put any terms or conditions in a message of acceptance; this will effectively be an counter offer and revoke the original offer made by the user. The terms must therefore be communicated in the invitation to treat.

The World Wide Web can present more of a problem. The structure of any site must be set so that the user has to at least see the terms before he has the chance to accept the offer, if the first message is an offer for sale, or before he can make an offer if the first message is an invitation to treat. Merely giving the user an opportunity to find the terms on the site will probably be insufficient. Likewise burying the terms in an information page would most probably fail. A well marked and prominent link to the terms and conditions would probably be sufficient, but better practice would be to give the user the opportunity to read the terms and conditions *before* he can go on to accept or make an offer, and to ensure that he cannot proceed without acknowledging that he has read the terms. It is then his problem if he does not actually read them.

CONTRACTS TO AGREE CONTRACT FORMATION RULES

Can users avoid the problems inherent in leaving the questions of where and when a contract is formed to be determined by the standard legal rules? One method is to set out the terms and conditions in the offer in an attempt to vary the standard rules. For example an offeror may state that an acceptance takes effect only when the offeror receives it, and that the contract will be subject to the laws of England and Wales. This method, however, runs into the problems inherent with incorporating terms and conditions into electronic contracts.

Another method is to enter into a contract to agree the terms on which the users will enter into future contracts. This type of contract can often take the form of a written contract[46] which will govern all future electronic contracts but could also be in an electronic form; this will entail all of the issues that arise with electronic contracts. Such a term is valid under English law[47] and

---

[46] This is a classic paper-based contract which is valid in the jurisdiction in which the contracts will be formed. It is pointless to have a contract to decide on the rules of contract formation which will stipulate a choice of law and jurisdiction if it is not valid in the first place.

[47] *Manchester Diocesan Council for Education v Commercial and General Investments Ltd* [1970] 1 W.L.R. 241; [1969] 3 All E.R. 1593 as per Lord Greene M.R.:

"An offeror may by the terms of his offer indicate that it may be accepted in a particular manner. . . . If an offeror stipulates by the terms of his offer that it may, or that it shall, be accepted in a particular manner a contract results as soon as the offeree does the stipulated act, whether it has come to the notice of the offeror or not."

See also *Holwell Securities Ltd v Hughes* [1974] 1 W.L.R. 155; [1974] 1 All E.R. 161.

is used in EDI agreements to ensure that the parties can determine when and where all electronic contracts are formed.

Agreements to predetermine the rules of contract formation could easily be used in a common server scenario whereby users must agree to the terms of the agreement before they may gain access to and use the server. They could also be used on Web-based systems where users are first presented with a screen of terms and conditions which they must read and agree to before they gain access to the rest of the system.

OVERRIDING TERMS AND CONDITIONS[48]

Where two or more commercial entities enter into agreements at arms' length then they can usually agree to whatever terms they so wish.[49] However, the position differs with other types of contract, such as consumer contracts. Consumer protection legislation, such as that commonly found within EU Member States,[50] often imposes limits on the terms and conditions that may be excluded or varied and these cannot be overridden by agreement. Any terms which attempt to override the legislation are automatically void. The position is somewhat different within the United States of America.

The Distance Selling Directive,[50a] in its early incantations, presented several problems for businesses that wished to sell goods or supply services to consumers, the problems principally being in the requirement to provide prior information about the contract to the consumer in written form. This would automatically negate some of the benefits of contracting over the Internet, namely the elimination or reduction of large amounts of paperwork. This has now changed to a requirement to provide the required information in any way appropriate to the means of communication,[51] a vast improvement on the previous versions. The directive also gives consumers the right, in certain circumstances, to withdraw from the contract within seven days from the date of performance of the contract[52] and requires that the consumer receive written confirmation[53] of the information previously supplied prior to the contract.[54]

---

[48] See further MacQueen, p. 130.

[49] See for instance *Manchester Diocesan Council for Education v Commercial and General Investments Ltd, supra,* n. 47.

[50] For example see the Unfair Terms Directive 93/13/EEC OJ L 95 April 21 1993. This is implemented within the United Kingdom by the Unfair Terms in Consumer Contracts Regulations 1994, SI 1994 No 3159.

[50a] 97/7/EC May 20 1997.

[51] Article 4(2).

[52] Article 6(1). The date from which the seven day period runs depends on whether the contract is for the sale of goods or the supply of services.

[53] Article 5(1).

[54] Articles 5 and 6 still pose problems for some Internet contracts. Where the contract is clearly for the sale of goods then no real issues arise as the information required by Article 5 can be supplied on delivery of the goods themselves (Article 6(1)). Where the contract is clearly for the

In order to determine whether or not overriding terms and conditions apply the jurisdiction of the contract formation must be determined. This stands even if the parties have attempted to predetermine the jurisdiction and governing law. Such an agreement can only be valid if the choice is not void within the actual jurisdiction of the contract itself.[55]

SIGNATURES

The last little component of a contract, and often that which is most overlooked in discussions of Internet contracting, is the signature, though it must be remembered that not all contracts require a signature to be valid.[56] This little, and often innocuous little beast can and will cause problems when looking at the question of the validity of an agreement as a contract. A question that is rarely asked is what is a signature?[57] This question, at least in the context of the common law, is totally and utterly meaningless.[58] The correct question should be, as with all legal documents, what is the function of the signature? The answer usually depends on the type of document in question[59]

---

supply of services then again no issues arises. Indeed Article 5(2) remove the requirement for written confirmation where the "service is to be performed through the use of a means of distant communication". However, the situation is not so clear cut when it comes to supplying information, computer code or software over the Internet. The Directive does not explicitly define these as either services or goods, though it does make mention of what could be regarded as shrink-wrapped software, that is software packages bought off the shelf or by mail order or whatever, in Article 6(3). The issue is that there is some confusion as to the status of computer code or software. Software or computer code which is stored and supplied on a physical medium such as a tape or disk would most probably be treated as a good, in the same way as a music tape, record or CD is treated as a good. The value is in the intangible information contained in the medium and not the medium itself. However, the confusion arises when looking at information, computer code or software that is supplied electronically over the Internet as a stream of bits. If this is held as a good, then Article 5(1) might present a problem, as the benefit of paperless transactions is reduced. If this is held as a service then Article 5(1) may not apply through Article 5(2). Some EC competition law cases seem to point to the electronic supply of computer code or software as being a supply of a service, but the courts have yet to decide the matter.

[55] As an example in the United Kingdom see section 27(2) of the Unfair Contract Terms Act 1977.

[56] Unilateral contracts such as that in *Carlill v Carbolic Smoke Ball Co.* need no signature, whilst others can be formed through the actions of the parties and need no document whatsoever. Oral contracts obviously need no signature. Some contracts, however, do need to be signed, though the issue then is the function of the signature. For instance does it need to identify the signatory or does it simply need to evidence an intention to be bound? Does the contract require a personal signature or not?

[57] The rarity of the question might be a cause for celebration but is instead an indication of the fact that the signature is a misunderstood entity.

[58] The statement that a signature is a squiggle that is usually illegible, or a stamp or whatever says what it may look like but does not actually answer the question in a meaningful way.

[59] Must the signature 'mark' the document, which suggests some physical imprint on the document, or must it simply indicate the signatory's intention to be bound by the agreement? Must the signature authenticate the signatory in any way? These questions and more need to be investigated. A consequence of this is that what satisfies the requirement for one type of document does not necessarily satisfy the requirement for another type of document. A good discussion of

and so what may be valid for a will may not necessarily be valid for a contract for the sale of land, or a guarantee or whatever. Any agreement entered into on the Internet will, if signed, necessarily be 'signed' electronically or digitally. For the agreement to be held as a valid contract that signature must be valid for that type of contract in the jurisdiction in which the contract is formed.

CONCLUSION

The best conclusion to be drawn from the limited discussion above is that viewed in the cold light of day contracting on the Internet is a complete mess. So long as jurisdiction is not an issue, such as where the parties are in the same jurisdiction as that in which they form any contract, then the legal issues are quite easy to determine using the laws of the relevant jurisdiction; namely have the parties entered into a legally binding contract, and if so where and when? However, where jurisdiction is an issue then the question of whether or not the parties have entered into a valid contract is one to be answered according to the law in which that contract was formed, the main problem being to determine exactly which jurisdiction is relevant in the first place.

It is dangerous to rely on the postal rule, or an analogy of that rule, when attempting to determine where and when the parties may have entered into a contract. Indeed the sensible course of action would be to obviate the rule in all circumstances. This is mainly due to the fact that the underlying communications topology may not be as first viewed and that as a result the rule could have unforeseen consequences or may not even be applicable. In addition, the jurisdictions in which the contracts may have been formed may not actually recognise the postal rule. The question may then become one of attempting to determine where the contracts may have been formed and then paring down until one remains. If more than one possibility remains then it may be a question for the courts to decide. The only course of action in such a case would be for one or other of the parties to move quickly and attempt to seize jurisdiction in the courts that would be most favourable to them.

The last problem concerns the terms and conditions which may or may not be incorporated into any contract which the parties may have entered into. This is a question of both the jurisdiction of contract formation and whether or not any terms have been validly incorporated into the contract. The laws of the jurisdiction in which the contracts are formed may imply certain terms and conditions unless specifically excluded, whilst other terms may only be varied under certain circumstances. Any non-implied terms must be specifically incorporated and this usually requires the terms to be brought to the attention of the acceptor before he enters into the contract.

some of the problems posed by electronic or digital signatures is contained in chapter 5, Chris Reed, *Digital Information Law* (Centre for Commercial Law Studies, 1996)

The last and most important issue to consider is whether or not the agreement into which the parties have entered is actually a valid contract under the relevant jurisdiction. Certain types of contract must be in a paper form and cannot be in an electronic form.[60] The jurisdiction of the agreement may be certain and the terms may be validly incorporated but if the jurisdiction does not allow contracts in an electronic form for the subject matter of the agreement then no valid contract exists and the exercise will have been a complete waste of time.

[60] See further, Lloyd. p. 138.

7

Software Transactions and Contract Law

HECTOR L MACQUEEN[1]

INTRODUCTION

Software is supplied in many ways. Mass-produced packages such as Microsoft Office and Lotus 1-2-3 can be purchased "off the shelf" or "over the counter" in a shop, or ordered from the supplier by post, fax, email or telephone. In this scenario the software will be carried on some physical or corporeal medium such as a floppy disk or a CD-Rom. Alternatively, software can be downloaded direct to a computer from the Internet or some other computer to which the first one is connected. Here the supply occurs without the involvement of any physical medium. Again, the software may be embedded on a chip forming part of the computer or other machine within which it operates. Or, finally, the customer may require a special or "bespoke" software system, designed specifically for personal or business needs, which will be installed directly on the computers and servers without necessarily having any prior independent existence on disks or CD-Roms (although the customer may eventually receive copies of the software in such form for "back-up" purposes). A variation on this may involve the supply of standard widely available packages in an individually modified or "customised" form adjusted to the particular needs of the end-user.

A further element arises in software transactions when the supplier is not also the manufacturer of the software. As its creator, the manufacturer will own the copyright in the software. Copyright enables the manufacturer to prevent others from copying the work, issuing it to the public, performing, showing or playing it in public, broadcasting it or including it in a cable programme service, or making an adaptation of it. For these purposes, copying includes storage of the work in any medium by electronic means and the making of copies which are transient or incidental to some other use of the work. It is therefore clear that the perfectly ordinary and normal activities of

[1] LLB (Hons), PhD, FRSE., Professor of Private Law, University of Edinburgh, and Director, The David Hume Institute, Edinburgh. Email address Hector.MacQueen@ed.ac.uk.

the end-user of software will infringe the manufacturer's copyright unless appropriate permissions are in place. While copyright law itself establishes some limits upon the manufacturer's rights, further permissions will have to be express or implied.[2] It is common for the manufacturer to provide express permissions. There are two main ways of doing this. One is the so-called "shrink-wrap" contract, in common use for "off the shelf" supply. Here the packaging for the disks or CD-Roms carrying the software is surrounded by a tightly-wrapped clear plastic film, through which is visible a document setting out the manufacturer's terms and conditions for non-infringement of copyright by the eventual purchaser. The document itself, or a prominent tag on the packaging, or a large seal for the wrapping material, will proclaim in bold characters that opening the wrapping will constitute acceptance of the manufacturer's terms and conditions. An alternative approach involves the process of loading software into a computer for the first time. The user will not be able to complete loading unless he or she signifies assent to the manufacturer's terms and conditions, a copy of which will be available for display on the screen should that be desired. The assent may be transmitted to the manufacturer by means of registration cards to be returned by post, or, if the end user is "on line" or has a modem, by electronic communication also occurring as part of the loading process.

This paper examines from the perspective of Scots law the legal nature of software transactions. A point of departure is provided by *Beta Computers (Europe) Ltd v Adobe Systems Ltd*,[3] a decision of Lord Penrose in the Outer House of the Court of Session which confronted issues about (1) the basic contractual analysis of the relationships arising between a manufacturer of software, a supplier and an end-user, and (2) the categorisation of the contracts concerned. The commentary on this case will lead on to some discussion of the implied obligations arising as a result of the process of categorisation, before I turn to consider typical express terms found in software contracts and the constraints upon contractual freedom which exist in this particular field.

CONTRACTS BETWEEN WHOM?

Following a telephone order Beta supplied Adobe with a software upgrade. The software was manufactured or authored by a third party called Informix. The disks had been delivered to Adobe with a shrink-wrap licence from Informix. Adobe never opened the packaging and sought to return the software to Beta without payment. Beta's action for payment was dismissed on the basis that either there was no contract; or that Adobe had a right to reject

---

[2] On copyright see further my paper in the present volume, p. 67.
[3] 1996 SLT 604; 1996 SCLR 587.

the software until the licence was accepted; or that Beta were in breach of an obligation to supply an unqualified right to use the software.

Lord Penrose favoured the view that there was no contract at all until such time as a party in the position of Adobe had opened and accepted the terms and conditions in the shrink-wrap licence. He rejected an analysis in terms of two contracts, one between Beta and Adobe being of supply, the other being a copyright licence from Informix to Adobe. In his view, the transaction was to be regarded as an *unum quid*, since the customer was not really concerned with the medium as such but access to the software and the ability to copy it legitimately. Moreover when completed it was a contract creating a *jus quae-situm tertio* (that is, a third party right, henceforth JQT) in favour of the author/manufacturer of the software, which was of course third party to the formation of the contract between Beta and Adobe. The licence was in the third party's favour and, in Lord Penrose's opinion, fulfilled all the requirements of a JQT. It is this aspect of the case which most English commentators to date regard as merely a tartan curiosity, since there is not yet any equivalent to the JQT in English law; but given that the Law Commission has proposed the introduction of third-party contractual rights in English law, and that most countries other than England are perfectly familiar with this juristic concept, its possible relevance to software transactions involving three parties is of some importance.[4]

There are some difficulties with the analysis by Lord Penrose, attractive in some respects though it may seem at first sight. First, is there really no contract at all until such time as the user tears open the packaging of the software? Again, much software is ordered by telephone, often with the use of credit card numbers to effect a payment. Has the customer got no right to delivery at this point so that the supplier can freely decide whether, when and where to do so? That would be the position on Lord Penrose's reasoning here. Again, even an enthusiast for the JQT such as the present writer finds it difficult to accept that the licence terms and conditions are an instance of the doctrine.[5] The licence is a grant by the third party of rights to the purchaser which otherwise would not exist. It does not create rights for the third party, and it is creation of third party rights by appropriate terms in the contract which is the essence of the JQT. The rights of the author/manufacturer, namely those which arise from his copyright, exist quite independently of the contract between the supplier and the purchaser, and indeed of any contract between the purchaser and the third party.[6]

---

[4] For the comparative position on third party rights in contract, see *International Encyclopaedia of Comparative Law*, vol 7, ch 13 (1994). For the proposed English reform, see *Privity of Contracts for the Benefit of Third Parties*, Law Com No 242 (1996).

[5] For a detailed account of the Scottish JQT by the present writer see *The Laws of Scotland: Stair Memorial Encyclopaedia*, vol 15 (1996), paras 824–852.

[6] See also J N Adams, "The Snark was a Boojum, You See", (1997) 1 *Edinburgh Law Review* 386–392 at 391.

The better view would be that there are indeed two contracts, one for the supply of the software between vendor and purchaser, and another, the copyright end-user licence between author/manufacturer and purchaser. The question of whether the "shrink-wrap" technique—and indeed the postal or "on-line" registration technique—achieves the latter contract so as to bind the end-user depends on the usual rules about offer, acceptance and incorporation of terms and conditions into contracts—knowledge at least of the existence of terms and conditions if not of their actual content, signature, course of dealing, and so on—such as are already familiar from cases about tickets and parking machines.[7]

SUPPLY OF GOODS, SUPPLY OF SERVICES, OR INTELLECTUAL PROPERTY LICENCE?

The supply of software thus clearly involves at least one contract as a general rule. But it is not nearly enough to make this really rather un-startling observation. The nature of the contract must be identified, to enable us to decide what its terms and conditions are. This is critical to deal with the problem of liability when the software proves defective in some respect, whether as the result of an error in its design or some unsuspected "bug" which emerges only once the software is in use. In certain types of contract the law will imply terms about supplier liability unless they are expressly excluded. Thus, for example, in contracts for the supply of goods, the Sale of Goods Act 1979[8] and the Supply of Goods and Services Act 1982[9] require the goods supplied to be of satisfactory quality. The liability, which covers fitness for purpose and extends to minor defects in the product supplied, is strict, that is, regardless of the fault or otherwise of the supplier, and would therefore be capable of applying in respect of the unsuspected bug mentioned above. A party supplying goods knows that this obligation will apply unless it can be written out, and accordingly a decision has to be taken about whether or not to deal with this issue in the contract. On the other hand, in Scots law the terms to be implied in contracts for the supply of services are far from well worked out; probably, however, the liability is for failure to take reasonable care in the circumstances,[10] which might mean no liability for the unsuspected bug. But the supplier wanting more certainty about liability will have to provide that so far as possible by appropriate express terms.

Is the supply of software a supply of goods? Goods are corporeal moveables. In a software transaction, given that there is a corporeal moveable present in the form of the disk or disks bearing the software, it might seem that

---

[7] For Scots law in this area see most recently *Stair Memorial Encyclopaedia*, vol 15, paras 702–710. See further Davies', p. 97.

[8] Section 14 as amended by the Sale and Supply of Goods Act 1994 s 1.

[9] Applied to Scotland by the Sale and Supply of Goods Act 1994 s 6 and Sch 1.

[10] W W McBryde, *The Law of Contract in Scotland* (1987), para 6.38.

the supply of goods legislation can apply. The case is even stronger where the software is supplied as an integral part of a machine such as a computer.[11] But if the software is the essential thing being purchased rather than the disk, which is purely a carrier or medium of no intrinsic value, does the transaction have another, possibly indeterminate, legal character? Further, as we have seen, in many transactions there is no physical embodiment of the software involved. In *Beta v Adobe* Lord Penrose took the view that when the software transaction became complete as a contract, its legal categorisation was *sui generis*; it was an innominate contract. The basis for this conclusion was that the customer was not really concerned with the medium as such but with access to the software and the ability to copy it legitimately. A further conclusion not stated in the opinion of Lord Penrose is that probably there were no terms about liability to be implied, at least in law.

The matter of categorisation has also been discussed in a number of English cases, not all of which seem to have been cited to Lord Penrose. Each concerned the liability of the supplier for defects in the software in a context where it had supplied a software system for the needs of a particular customer. The general conclusion emerging from these cases is that it is not necessary to decide whether the contract is for the supply of goods or services, since the liability will be the same in either case, namely that, while it is understood that the supplier will correct bugs, if the software proves persistently unsatisfactory, the customer can reject it.[12] The leading English case now is *St Albans City and District Council v International Computers Ltd*,[13] which arose from a contract entered by the parties in 1988. Under the contract ICL were to supply the Council with a computer system for the administration of the Community Charge, which was to be introduced in 1990. As the result of an error in the software supplied under the contract, the population of the Council's area was over-stated by 2,966, and in consequence the Council set the Community Charge for 1990/91 too low. The Community Charge receipts were accordingly £484,000 less than they should have been, while as a result of the relevant legislation they also had to pay out some extra £685,000 to the Hertfordshire County Council. In addition there was a loss of interest that would have been collected on the Community Charge receipts. The Council claimed this total loss of £1,315,000 from ICL as damages for breach of contract. ICL argued (1) that there was no breach of contract; (2) that there was no recoverable loss, pointing to the Council's recovery of revenue by a higher

---

[11] See *Toby Construction Products Pty Ltd v Computer Bar (Sales) Pty Ltd* [1983] 2 NSWR 48. Note that the distinction between a computer program as such and the hardware which it causes to function has proved very difficult to apply in the context of patent law: see W R Cornish, *Intellectual Property: Patents, Copyright, Trade Marks and Allied Rights*, 3rd edn (1996) paras 5.63–5.69. The most recent case is *Fujitsu Ltd's Application* [1996] RPC 511 (Laddie J).

[12] *Eurodynamic Systems v General Automation*, 6 September 1988, Steyn J; *Saphena Computing Ltd v Allied Collection Agencies Ltd* [1995] FSR 616; *The Salvage Association v Cap Financial Services Ltd* [1995] FSR 654; *Simpson Nash Wharton v Barco Graphics Ltd*, 1 July 1991.

[13] [1995] FSR 686 (Scott Baker J); [1996] 4 All ER 481 (CA).

Community Charge in 1991/92; and (3) that a clause in the contract expressly limited recoverable damage to a maximum of £100,000.

In what was technically an obiter passage[14] of a judgment entirely in favour of the Council at first instance, Scott Baker J also found that the contract for the supply of software was "probably" one for the supply of goods, thereby enabling the Council to bring in the relevant statutory implied terms. The Court of Appeal, although upholding most of the conclusions of Scott Baker J, differed somewhat on this particular point. Sir Iain Glidewell, with whom Nourse LJ expressly agreed, took the view that disks were goods for the purposes of applying the supply of goods legislation, while computer programs, of themselves, were not. Was a disk carrying a defective program (as distinct from a disk defective in itself) defective goods under the legislation? Sir Iain thought that the answer to this question was yes, but suggested that where, as in the case before the court, a program was transferred into a computer by a supplier rather than sold as a disk to be installed by the purchaser, there was no supply of goods. However in such a contract there might still be terms implied at common law, to the effect that the program was reasonably fit, that is capable of achieving its intended purpose.

This approach of distinguishing the "off the shelf" transaction from the "bespoke" supply of a system comes close to that now adopted in the USA under the Uniform Commercial Code.[15] The implication is that the *Beta* case was indeed one of supply of goods, at least as between Beta and Adobe, since it seems to have been about the supply of standard software on disk. So far as concerns downloading from or via the Internet, however, there is no supply of goods. Yet the distinction is not wholly satisfactory. It leaves the problem of the undistributed middle—for example, the supply of customised standard software—and it is largely dependent on the presence of a physical medium, a matter which is entirely fortuitous—as, for example, if the provider of a system hands over a set of back-up disks. As John Adams has argued, perhaps it would be better to approach the issue, not through established but perhaps inadequate legal categories, but by asking what the liabilities of the manufacturer and the supplier ought to be.[16] If we take the view that the contract is innominate, it may be that there are no standard terms to be implied in law; but that still leaves open the possibility of implying terms in fact, that is, considering the particular circumstances of the case and determining a term to be implied which gives business efficacy to the contract, or asking whether, had an officious bystander proposed the term to be implied to the parties during negotiations, they would both have suppressed him with a testy "Oh, of course!".[17] Implication of a term in fact may indeed be what was going on in a number of the English cases on the subject. Thus, for example,

---

[14] At 698–699.
[15] See J N Adams, *Atiyah's Sale of Goods*, 9th edn (1995), 48
[16] Adams, "Snark was a boojum, you see", passim.
[17] *Stair Memorial Encyclopaedia*, vol 15, paras 715–716.

in *Saphena Computing Ltd v Allied Collection Agencies Ltd*,[18] the arguments about an implied obligation of fitness for purpose were based upon business efficacy and the "officious bystander" test, the hallmarks of implication of fact rather than law, while Staughton LJ preferred to rest his conclusion in favour of the purchasers upon interpretation rather than implication.

The *Saphena* case is also interesting for the apparent judicial acceptance of the proposition that "it would not be breach of contract at all to deliver software with a defect in it".[19] At least in the context of a "bespoke" supply,

> software is not a commodity which is delivered once, only once, and once and for all, but one which will necessarily be accompanied by a degree of testing and modification. Naturally it could be expected that the supplier will carry out those tasks. He should have both the right and duty to do so. . . . No doubt there was a time limit for that purpose—a reasonable time is that which the law would ordinarily imply.[20]

This may be different from the basic law of supply of goods. There the presence of the defect will tend to be seen as a breach of contract, unless the goods with the defect are of the standard which a reasonable person would regard as satisfactory. It is open to debate whether the reasonable person expects bugs in software; certainly when in 1976 Lord President Emslie made the suggestion that the reasonable person expected a new car to have teething troubles,[21] the decision was greeted with an uproar which ultimately led to the reform of the Sale of Goods Act into its present wording on minor defects.[22] Again, in the law of supply of goods, the supplier is not entitled to insist upon an opportunity to cure the defect, although if the customer allows attempts at repair the right to terminate the contract for the breach is not thereby lost.[23] In the general law of contract, however, Lady Cosgrove has recently observed that "it is a basic principle of the law of contract that if one party is in breach, the innocent party is not entitled to treat the contract as rescinded [terminated] without giving the other party an opportunity to remedy the breach".[24] The authority she cites, *McBryde on Contract*, at page 329, does not in fact support her statement of the law, although at the passage cited Professor McBryde does think it "attractive" and one "which may develop in our law". It is certainly a principle which would seem well adapted to the problems of at least some software transactions.

Another difficult question may be distinguishing between a contract for the supply of software and the licence granted by the owner of the copyright to

---

[18] [1995] FSR 616 (3 May 1988, CA).

[19] [1995] FSR at 652 per Staughton LJ.

[20] [1995] FSR at 652-653 per Staughton LJ.

[21] *Millars of Falkirk v Turpie* 1976 SLT (Notes) 66.

[22] See H L MacQueen "The Sale and Supply of Goods Act 1994", (1995) 63 *Scottish Law Gazette* 5–9.

[23] Sale of Goods Act 1979, s 35(6) (added by Sale and Supply of Goods Act 1994 s 2(1)).

[24] *Strathclyde Regional Council v Border Engineering Contractors Ltd* 1997 SCLR 100 at 104D.

the end-user. While this is not an issue where the supplier and the copyright owner are the same person, there may be greater difficulties when they are separate, and the end-user has contracts with both, as perhaps was the position in the *Beta* case. To what extent can the terms that may be implied in one type of contract also be implied in another type of contract? Should the liability of the licensor for defects in the software march with that of the supplier? If so, is there a possibility of double recovery by the end-user for the same defect? The proper approach would seem to be that a copyright licence entails no implied obligation on the licensor to ensure that the product associated with the copyright is without defects, and that only the supplier can be so liable. But actually distinguishing a copyright licence from a supply contract may be difficult if, for example, that licence includes clauses about the provision of helplines, maintenance, repair and replacement of faulty software.

A tentative conclusion would be that, while there are some situations where the law of supply of goods is appropriately applied (for example, where software is embedded within a piece of hardware), the general principles of the law of contract and the implication of terms in fact may often serve equally well. But it is freely admitted that this is an uncertain base upon which to rest issues of liability, and it is clear that the well-advised party will eliminate as many of these uncertainties as possible by means of written contractual terms. It is to the content and regulation of such terms that I now turn.

SOME TYPICAL TERMS

(1) Copyright permissions

A term giving the end-user permission to use the software is commonly found in the copyright licence element of a software transaction. However, such a term might well be implied if it was not express, since the transfer would lack all efficacy if the software could not be used. But the use will have to be the appropriate end-use of the software; the copyright will be reinforced by express prohibitions against the making of copies, alteration, modification and adaptation of the software, and sometimes its use on more than one machine or on a set number of machines. Where the licensor's return for the licence is royalties, dependent upon the extent of the licensee's use, there may be an implied term that the licensee *will* use.[25]

(2) Warranties and undertakings

Warranties are statements of fact about the software, with untruth constituting breach of contract entitling the aggrieved party to contractual remedies.

[25] *North American & Continental Sales v Bepi Electronics Ltd* 1982 SLT 47.

The express provisions in contracts commonly relate to the physical condition of the disks or CD-Roms upon which the software is supplied, and to the state and completeness of the supporting documentation. Suppliers tend not to provide express warranties about the fitness for purpose of the software. This is perhaps surprising, since under the supply of goods legislation it is possible to displace the statutory implied terms, not by direct exclusion,[26] but by the inclusion of express terms inconsistent with them.[27] Thus, spelling out in some detail the quality of product and performance the end-user may expect can have the effect of eliminating the vagueness of the implied term requiring satisfactory quality. It may also be useful to include undertakings with regard to testing, the correction of defects, and user support for at least a period of time after the initial supply.

(3) Exclusion and limitation clauses

A rather blunter instrument for limiting the hazards of implied terms is the inclusion of clauses excluding liability for breach of contract, negligence or any loss howsoever arising, or limiting liability to some fixed sum. Although common, the efficacy of such clauses is debatable, since these are exactly the main target for the controls of the Unfair Contract Terms Act 1977 and the Unfair Terms in Consumer Contracts Regulations 1994, as will be discussed in more detail in a later section.

(4) Prohibitions on assignations and sub-licensing

It is very common for copyright licences to prohibit assignation or sub-licensing by the licensee. The effect of a prohibition on assignation in Scots law is to nullify any purported assignation made without the licensor's consent.[28] There seems no reason to doubt that the same applies to a prohibition on sub-licensing. The purpose of the clause is to enable the licensor to retain some control over who has access to its software. The prohibitions may cause difficulty, notably if the licensee is a company which becomes insolvent or is taken over, or is a member of a group of companies within which there is subsequent re-structuring without appropriate transfers of incorporeal rights. The prohibitions are sometimes qualified by provision that the licensor's consent to an assignation or a sub-licence will not be unreasonably with-held. It may be that, since the licensor is the owner of the copyright and so retains a fundamental interest in it, reasonableness here is to be measured in relation to his interests and that it would be for the licensee to show the unreasonableness.[29]

---

[26] See further below, 130–131.
[27] Sale of Goods Act 1979, s 55.
[28] *Stair Memorial Encyclopaedia*, vol 18 para 652; vol 15, para 860
[29] *Stair Memorial Encyclopaedia*, vol 15, para 861, and note the analogy with leases, for which see also ibid, para 860 note 1

(5) Insolvency

A copyright licence may or may not provide that upon the insolvency of either party the contract comes to an end. However, the copyright which was the basis of the licence does not cease to exist as a result of the licensor's insolvency. The Copyright Designs and Patents Act 1988[30] provides that a licence granted by a copyright owner is binding on every successor in title to his interest in the copyright, except a purchaser in good faith for valuable consideration and without notice (actual or constructive) of the licence The copyright is an asset in the licensor's insolvency and should therefore be realised by the liquidator or other insolvency officer; a critical question if the licence has not been terminated by the insolvency may be whether or not the purchaser has actual or constructive notice of the licence.

(6) Choice of law, jurisdiction and arbitration

Of particular importance in the cross-frontier world of the Internet may be those clauses in a software transaction declaring which law applies to the contract and in which forum disputes are to be resolved. While in general party autonomy is to be respected in these matters, it should be noted that choice of law clauses cannot be used to evade the controls of the Unfair Contract Terms Act 1977[31] or the Unfair Terms in Consumer Contracts Regulations 1994.[32]

CONSTRAINTS ON TERMS: UNFAIR TERMS REGULATION

Unfair terms in contracts are subject to controls under the Unfair Contract Terms Act 1977 (henceforth UCTA 1977) and the Unfair Terms in Consumer Contracts Regulations 1994 (UTCC 1994). Both apply to contracts for the supply of goods or services. The UCTA controls extend to consumer and commercial contracts, and the Act's definition of "consumer" is sufficiently wide that a company may be one when not acting in the course of its business.[33] In contrast the UTCC controls protect only consumers under standard form contracts, and only natural persons acting for purposes outside their business can be consumers.[34] UCTA declares void terms excluding or limiting liability for death or personal injury, or for breach of the terms implied by law in consumer contracts for the supply of goods, while the other terms in contracts

---

[30] Section 90(3).
[31] Section 27.
[32] Regulation 7.
[33] UCTA 1977, s 25(1). See e.g. *R & B Customs Brokers Ltd v United Dominions Trust Ltd* [1988] 1 WLR 321.
[34] UTCC 1994, regs 2 and 3

caught by the Act are subject to a test of fairness and reasonableness.[35] Again in contrast UTCC makes no clause in contracts within its scope absolutely void but subjects them all to a test of unfairness, defined as causing a significant imbalance in the parties' rights and obligations under the contract, contrary to the requirements of good faith and to the detriment of the consumer.[36]

In England and Wales some of the UCTA controls are inapplicable to "any contract so far as it relates to the creation or transfer of a right or interest in any patent, trade mark, copyright, registered design, technical or commercial information or other intellectual property, or relates to the termination of any such right or interest".[37] There is no equivalent provision in the Scottish part of the Act, which takes a different approach of listing those contracts to which it applies.[38] Contracts relating to intellectual property rights are not mentioned in this list. If UCTA is to apply, therefore, it seems necessary once again to bring software transactions within one or other of the categories of supply of goods and services. This is probably also true for the UTCC controls. The English courts seem however to have managed to do this despite the apparently express prohibition in UCTA, and no doubt the Scottish courts can follow suit.[39]

In *St Albans City and District Council v International Computers Ltd*[40] the Council claimed a loss of £1,315,000 from ICL as damages for breach of contract. ICL argued that a clause in the contract expressly limited recoverable damage to a maximum of £100,000. Scott Baker J found that this limitation clause could be set aside under the Unfair Contract Terms Act 1977.[41] The clause needed to meet the requirements of fairness and reasonableness under the Act. Although the contract was not a consumer contract, it was one on ICL's "written standard terms of business". The judge noted that there had been negotiations between the parties at which these terms had been gone through paragraph by paragraph and the Council had indicated its unhappiness with the limitation clause. But ICL had advised that the contract would not be available without the clause, and the Council was under severe time pressure to get a system in place; this pressure was exploited by ICL, and the Council had no realistic alternative.[42] Since the conditions were therefore effectively untouched during these negotiations, they remained written

---

[35] UCTA 1977, ss 16, 17, 20 and 21.

[36] UTCC 1994, regs 4 and 5.

[37] UCTA 1977, Sch 1, para 1(c).

[38] UCTA 1977, s 15 (as amended by Law Reform (Miscellaneous Provisions) (Scotland) Act 1990, ss 68, 74 and Sch 9).

[39] See in addition to the case discussed in the succeeding paragraphs *The Salvage Association v Cap Financial Services Ltd* [1995] FSR 654; also G Smith "Software contracts", in C Reed (ed), *Computer Law*, 3rd edn, (1996), 53–80 at 69.

[40] [1995] FSR 686 (Scott Baker J); [1996] 4 All ER 481 (CA).

[41] For another case on this point reaching a similar result see *The Salvage Association v Cap Financial Services Ltd* [1995] FSR 654.

[42] [1995] FSR at 695–696.

standard terms of business.[43] It was now for ICL to prove that the terms were fair and reasonable. Relevant considerations were (1) the circumstances known to the parties when the contract was made; (2) given that the clause was one of limitation, ICL's resources and the availability to them of insurance cover; (3) relative bargaining power; (4) whether the Council had received an inducement to agree the term, or had had alternatives; (5) the Council's knowledge of the term; (6) the practical consequences of a decision one way or the other. ICL had very substantial resources and product liability insurance to the value of £50 million worldwide. The Council's bargaining position had been weaker than ICL's; it had received no inducement to agree the term. Scott Baker J said further:[44]

> On whom is it better that a loss of this size should fall, a local authority or an international computer company? The latter is well able to insure (and in this case was insured) and pass on the premium cost to the customers. If the loss is to fall the other way it will ultimately be borne by the local population either by increased taxation or reduced services. I do not think it unreasonable that he who stands to make the profit (ICL) should carry the risk.

So far as concerned the Unfair Contract Terms Act 1977, the Court of Appeal confirmed (1) that the occurrence of negotiations did not prevent there being "written standard terms of business", and (2) that the judge's views on reasonableness should not be disturbed, applying Lord Bridge in *George Mitchell (Chesterhall) Ltd v Finney Lock Seeds Ltd*.[45]

What is the Scottish perspective on this application of the Unfair Contract Terms Act? The Scottish provisions are to much the same effect as the English ones discussed in the case. Thus under section 25 "business" includes "the activities of any ... local or public authority", so that the contract would not be a consumer contract here either. Under section 17, any term of a contract which is a standard form contract must be fair and reasonable to enable a party in breach of the contract to restrict its liability to the customer. A standard form contract is not defined by the 1977 Act, although the phrase "written standard terms of business" does appear in section 17(2). It has been held in the Court of Session that there may be a standard form contract even though some of the terms are negotiated for the particular contract;[46] so it would seem *a fortiori* when there are negotiations but no adaptation of any term in consequence. The Scottish provisions about the reasonableness of limitation clauses and the burden of proof are to be found in section 24 of the 1977 Act. It therefore seems reasonable to treat the *St Albans* case as authoritative in Scotland on the 1977 Act, albeit that in decisions on reasonableness each case will turn largely on its own facts. The main significance of the

---

[43] Ibid at 706.
[44] Ibid at 711.
[45] [1983] 2 AC 803 at 816.
[46] *McCrone v Boots Farm Sales* 1981 SC 68; *Border Harvesters Ltd v Edwards Engineering (Perth) Ltd* 1985 SLT 128.

decision lies in its approach to the issue of reasonableness, which seems absolutely sound.

CONSTRAINTS ON TERMS: THE SOFTWARE DIRECTIVE

Legislation originating in the Legal Protection of Computer Programs Directive 1991[47] confers certain rights upon users of software which may override contrary contractual terms. Thus there is a right to make a back-up copy of a computer program and a right to decompile the program when necessary to obtain the information necessary to create another, inter-operable program.[48] Another provision allows the end-user to copy or adapt the program when necessary for his lawful use, giving as a particular example the correction of errors in the program. But it is further provided that such acts are only possible if there is no contractual term to the contrary.[49] Thus here the law seems to give with one hand and take away with the other; as Colin Turpin remarks, "the result then appears to be that the supplier of a computer program is still able to restrict the use of the program as much as he wishes".[50]

CONSTRAINTS ON TERMS: NO DEROGATION FROM GRANT

In *British Leyland v Armstrong Patents*[51] the House of Lords held that the owner of the copyright in the design of the exhaust pipe of a Morris Marina could not enforce that copyright against a copyist who was producing replacement exhausts for commercial sale to owners of Morris Marinas. The basis for this was that to enforce the copyright derogated from the grant made to owners of Morris Marinas by manufacturing and selling the cars, these owners having the undoubted right to repair their vehicles as inexpensively as possible. The reasoning is extremely dubious, but the principle of "No derogation from grant" as a brake on the exercise of copyright has haunted the law ever since, in particular in relation to software.[52] However, the Privy Council has recently given a very strong indication that the principle should not be used in copyright cases, and its future in this area now looks short indeed, if not non-existent.[53]

[47] EC Council Directive 91/250.
[48] Implemented in the UK by Copyright, Designs and Patents Act 1988 ss 50A, 50B.
[49] Ibid, s 50C.
[50] C Turpin, "Some aspects of contractual licences for software", in F D Rose (ed), *Consensus in Idem: Essays in the Law of Contract in Honour of Guenter Treitel* (1996), 282–296 at 296. See ibid, 293–296 for further critical comment on the Software Directive's user rights in general.
[51] [1986] AC 577.
[52] Turpin, "Some Aspects", 289–290.
[53] *Canon Kabushiki Kaisha v Green Cartridge Co (Hong Kong) Ltd*, The Times, 1 May 1997. See further my "Copyright and the Internet", in this volume, 90–91.

CONSTRAINTS ON THE FREEDOM NOT TO CONTRACT: THE MAGILL DECISION

Having discussed the legal constraints upon the freedom to include what terms one pleases in a contract, the picture should be balanced by necessarily brief observations on the constraints which may prevent the owner of a copyright deciding not to grant licences at all. In 1995 the European Court of Justice held in the *Magill* case[54] that broadcasting organisations could not exercise the copyright which they enjoyed in their programme schedules to prevent others from publishing weekly advance listings magazines to compete with their own products, since this was "abuse of a dominant position" contrary to Article 86 of the EC Treaty. The case raised the possibility that a party could not decide to exploit a copyright by its own initiatives alone, and that the competition law of the Community in effect required the grant of licences where there was a significant consumer demand for a product. This had significant implications for the manufacturers of software. *Magill* is however concerned with a pure information product which could only be presented in one way for all practical purposes, namely as a chronological sequence. The only effective competition would be through presentation of the same basic information in the same basic way. If the function of the product can be achieved in another way without infringing copyright, then competition will exist and the refusal to licence will not be abuse of a dominant position.[55] The case is therefore likely to be most significant in relation to the copyright in the operating systems underpinning computers, where there is a very small number of dominant producers such as Microsoft, standardisation is arising partly from market pressures and partly from governmental ones, and others wish to create products which will run with these operating systems.[56]

CONCLUSIONS

The application of contract and supply law to software transactions and in particular to those transactions involving software which take place on the Internet does present a number of analytical difficulties, but not insuperable ones. Many if not most can be overcome by the drafting of appropriate and enforceable clauses. The great difficulty which is likely to remain is the one which has only been touched upon briefly here, namely that of incorporation of the well-drafted clauses into the contract between supplier and customer. But the electronic medium in which these transactions are taking place may itself provide the solution, as described at the beginning of this paper, inasmuch as part of the procedure may involve the flagging-up of the existence of

[54] Joined Cases C-241-2/91, *Raidio Telefis Eireann v Commission* [1995] I-ECR 808.
[55] See for further comment H L MacQueen, *Copyright, Competition and Industrial Design*, 2nd edn (1995), 21–23.
[56] See further Turpin, "Some aspects", 291–293.

terms and requiring the customer to indicate assent thereto before completion of the contract can be achieved. There seems little reason to doubt that procedures like this are capable of meeting the tests of incorporation. If this is right, then, while transactions on the Internet will never be free of legal difficulties, many of them can be smoothed away by the draftsman, with a check being provided by the twin policemen of unfair contracts and competition law.

8

Legal Barriers to Electronic Contracts: Formal Requirements and Digital Signatures

IAN LLOYD[1]

INTRODUCTION

It is an aspect of the general principle of freedom of contract that parties entering binding legal contracts are usually free to enter into contracts in such manner and under such terms as they may choose. Agreements may be entered into in writing, verbally, or may even be implied from the parties' actions. The fact that a contract is entered into electronically should in theory have no impact upon its legal validity, with any legal concerns restricted to the manner in which its terms might be evidenced should dispute as to the contract's existence or content later arise. In a number of jurisdictions, however, legal provisions sometimes require that a contract is constituted in writing, implicitly of a tangible rather than electronic nature, and that it be signed by the parties involved. In a 1990 report, the United Nations Commission on International Trade Law (UNCITRAL) identified four reasons which had historically prompted a requirement that contracts be concluded in writing. These were the desire to reduce disputes, to make the parties aware of the consequences of their dealings, to provide evidence upon which third parties might rely upon the agreement and to facilitate tax, accounting and regulatory purposes. There would seem no reason why these objectives could not be attained without restrictive requirements of writing, by the incorporation of satisfactory safeguards into systems for electronic contracting. As will be discussed, however, legal requirements of writing do currently exist, and may pose insuperable barriers to the growth of electronic contracting in certain areas. Since contract is the fundamental basis of most commercial enterprise, restrictions on the validity of electronic contracts present significant obstacles to the development of Internet trade and on-line business.

[1] Professor, Centre for Law, Computers and Technology, University of Strathclyde; email i.j.lloyd@strath.ac.uk.

Calls for national action to remove such barriers have been a feature of much of the UN's work in the field to date, with calls being made to member governments to remove legal barriers to electronic commerce. Initially, the calls focused specifically on EDI (Electronic Data Interchange) with the publication of a draft UNCITRAL 'Model Law on Legal Aspects of Electronic Data Interchange (EDI) and Related Means of Communication'. By the time the measure was adopted in June 1996, the title had been changed to the more generic 'Model Law on Electronic Commerce'.

This paper will examine legal barriers to electronic contracting under a number of headings. First, consideration will be given to those contracts which are required to be constituted in writing. Second, consideration will be given to the notion of what is a signature. This will require an expedition into the world of cryptography. Finally, an examination will be made of the law relating to documentary evidence with a view to determining, in particular, whether information stored in electronic format might satisfy the legal requirements for a document. Linked to this is the issue whether the making of electronic copies of paper originals will satisfy evidential requirements.

REQUIREMENTS FOR WRITING

As noted above, many legal systems require writing as a necessary component for the formal validity of certain juridical transactions. In Scotland, for example, the Requirements of Writing (Scotland) Act 1995 codifies the existing common law requirements and provides that writing would only be required for the valid constitution of three categories of legal act:

- gratuitous unilateral obligations (in other words, enforceable promises) except where these are entered into in the course of a business
- contracts relating to dealings in land
- the making of a will or establishment of a trust

The rationale behind these exceptions is broadly similar to that identified in the United Nations' report cited above. Similar requirements of writing are found in English law, although, of course, the existence of the doctrine of consideration renders otiose the notion of a gratuitous unilateral obligation.[2] Additionally, a wide range of statutory provisions provide that information is to be supplied "in writing" e.g. company accounts. In a number of such instances, specific statutory provision has been made for the acceptance of computer-generated information. In the taxation field, for example, electronic copies of invoices will be accepted for purposes connected with Value Added Tax. Generally however, statutory requirements for the supply of information

---

[2] Full details on English requirements of form in relation to writing and documents can be found in C Reed *Digital Information Law* (1996, Centre for Commercial Law Studies).

in writing will be subject to the terms of the Interpretation Act 1978 which applies throughout the UK and defines "writing" as including:

> "typing, printing, lithography, photography and other modes of representing or reproducing words in a visible form, and expressions referring to writing are construed accordingly."

A document which exists solely in digital form, for example an electronic mail message stored on the hard disk of the recipient's computer, will not be capable of coming within this definition as the electronic impulses representing its contents are not visible.

It seems clear that the 1978 definition was introduced at a time when communications between computers was limited and as with other statutory definitions of that era relating to concepts of recording and storage is ill suited to the modern age. An alternative approach more favourable to electronic contracts is found in the UN Model Law of 1996, which introduces the concept of "a data message", defined as:

> "information generated, sent, received or stored by electronic, optical or similar means including, but not limited to, electronic document interchange (EDI), electronic mail, telegram, telex or telecopy".

and goes on to provide that:

> "Where the law requires information to be in writing, that requirement is met by a data message if the information contained therein is accessible so as to be usable for subsequent reference."

This approach has been criticised in a recent report by the Legislative Working Party of the Society for Computers and Law as introducing a new requirement that communications wishing to be regarded as writing must be *retained*. Although significant evidential problems will arise if a written document should be lost, retention is not a prerequisite for the validity of a contract constituted in ordinary "hard copy" writing. Various options for reform are canvassed in the Working Party's report. For England, it was suggested that a new definition of writing should be developed which would define writing as

> "any recording of a representation of a representation of words symbols or numbers."

The definition would further state that where a representation of words, symbols or numbers is transmitted by one person to another, that transmission shall be treated as having been made in writing if the symbols are recorded by the sender or receiver.

As an alternative, the Scots law section recommended that an additional term, "electronic equivalent", should be developed which could be attached to the existing definition. This might provide:

"In relation to writing, the expression 'electronic equivalent' includes any mode of representing or reproducing words in digital form."

In terms of ultimate effect, there appears no significant distinction between the two proposals. Although it may not be anticipated that many houses will be bought and sold following an exchange of emails (and signature requirements as discussed below will also require to be satisfied) there would appear no reason of principle to require that writings should be confined to marks on paper.

REQUIREMENTS FOR SIGNATURE

The final requirement to be considered relates to the addition of a signature to a document. In many instances, documents will be signed by or on behalf of a contracting party. For the vast majority of cases, there is no specific legal requirement that there be a signature, and its prime purpose will be to evidence the fact that the document has originated from, or been approved by a particular individual. In some instances, statutory provisions may require that a document be signed as a prerequisite to its validity. In particular, requirements for signature invariably accompany requirements that contracts be constituted in writing. In this section, consideration will be given first to the question of what is a signature, and second, to the emerging concept of a digital signature. Typically, this term refers not to an electronic representation of an actual signature, but is instead an electronic device which performs the *function* of a signature, in that it involves the use of encryption techniques to provide a degree of assurance that a message was composed by a particular individual and has not subsequently been modified prior to receipt by the other party to the agreement.

The nature of a signature

What is a signature? The nature of the requirement varies according to the legal document in question and from legal system to legal system. In a number of cases, it has been provided that a variety of methods of signature may be applied. Under the terms of the United Nations Convention on the Carriage of Goods by Sea, it is provided that a signature may be made by "handwriting . . . or . . . by any other mechanical or electrical means". Comparatively few statutory definitions exist in the United Kingdom, but a substantial body of case law has sanctioned the use of mechanical aids to produce a signature. In *Goodman v. Eban*[3] the Court of Appeal (Denning LJ dissenting) held that a solicitor satisfied the requirement under the Solicitors Act

---

[3] [1954] QB 550.

1932 that bills be signed by using a rubber stamp embossed with the name of his firm. As was stated by Lord Evershed:

> "where an Act of Parliament requires that any particular document be 'signed' by a person, then, prima facie, the requirement of the Act is satisfied if the person himself places on the document an engraved representation of his signature by means of a rubber stamp. . . . the essential requirement of signing is the affixing in some way, whether by writing with a pen or pencil or by otherwise impressing upon the document, one's name or "signature" so as personally to authenticate the document."

In the case *In Re a Debtor (No 2021 of 1995)*,[4] it was held by Laddie J that a faxed copy of a signed proxy form complied with statutory requirements for signature:

> "Once it is accepted that the close physical linkage of hand, pen and paper is not necessary for the form to be signed, it is difficult to see why some forms of non-human agency for impressing the mark on the paper should be acceptable while others are not."

It is possible today for a fax to be transmitted directly from a computer without the need for a paper original. Coupled to this, a copy of a signature can be digitised and when appended to such a transmission will be printed out as a facsimile of the original signature on the recipient's machine. This will be the only paper based copy of the document and signature. Although the comment must be regarded as *obiter*, Laddie J suggested that this document should be regarded as having been "signed" by its author.

These cases indicates that the concept of a signature in UK law will be interpreted very broadly, so long as there is the attachment to paper of some physical mark which can be identified as indicating its adoption or approval. Although it would be normal for a signature to take the form of the signatory's name, a glance at many signatures will indicate that legibility is seldom a feature of these instruments and in general any mark will be acceptable so long as it can be evidenced that this is the signatory's normal method of endorsing documents. The letter 'X', for example, has traditionally been used as a means for imprinting the mark of an illiterate person.

What is a digital signature?

The International Standards Organisation define the concept of a digital signature as "data appended to, or a cryptographic transformation of a data unit that allows a recipient of the data unit to prove the source and integrity of the data unit and protect against forgery'."

---

[4] [1996] 2 All ER 345

Although the form is very different, the purpose of a digital signature is equivalent to that of the more traditional, analogue, version, namely, authentication that the document has come from the sender. The manner in which this is accomplished digitally is somewhat different however. It is possible for the digital signature to be created by the signor inscribing his or her name on an electronic tablet. This will cause the shape of the signature to be digitised and stored in this format. A copy of the original signature can then be displayed on a computer screen or can be printed onto paper. In the latter situation, there would seem to be no more legal barrier to the recognition of a digital signature than there was to the recognition of the faxed signature discussed above—although the process is obviously susceptible of misuse and forgery.

The term "digital signature" is however more commonly used to refer to the situation where the text of a data message is encrypted in such a way that a recipient can be confident that it did originate from the identified sender and that it has not been subject to any modification or amendment during the course of transmission. To this extent, the entire message becomes the digital signature. Modern developments in cryptography have rendered a digital signature far less susceptible to forgery, and indeed much of the current discussion concerning the use of encryption techniques for electronic transmissions centres round the fear that the encrypted messages may not be insecure, but rather too secure so as to be impervious to interception and deciphering by third parties. Whilst this provides obvious benefits for the privacy and security of messages, it might also allow criminals or terrorists to transmit messages concerning their nefarious plans, secure in the knowledge that, even if these were intercepted by law enforcement agencies, the contents could not be decoded. As a result, in the United States, cryptographic tools have been classed as a form of munitions, and subject to corresponding export restrictions, whilst in France, it is illegal to transmit a coded message via the public telecommunications network.

Forms of encryption

Techniques of encryption date back to at least the time of Julius Caesar. The two classical forms of encryption have involved substitution and transposition of letters. The Caesar code, for example involved shifting letters an agreed number of spaces along the alphabet. With a shift of three, for example, the letter C would become F, A become D and T, W. CAT would read FDW.

Throughout history there has been a constant battle between those seeking to use encryption to preserve secrecy and those wishing to break the codes. One of the most famous episodes in the ongoing contest involved the Allied cryptographic operations during the second world war. These led to the development of the world's first practical computing machines. Although limited by today's standards, the processing power of these computers transformed code breaking from what had been an intellectual pursuit into an exercise in number crunching. The analogy might be made with a combination lock on a safe and the contrast between the stereotypical image of a skilled safe breaker using a stethoscope to detect the correct combination and the random selection of numbers continued until the correct combination is achieved. Whilst the effort of trying several million possible combinations would be too great for humans, the task is comparatively simple for a computer.

In response to the vulnerability of traditional forms of encryption, modern systems are place reliance upon mathematical techniques. One of the first of a new generation of cryptographic techniques was implemented in the United States' Data Encryption Standard or DES. DES has been a source of some controversy since its inception in 1977, with allegations made that its effectiveness was deliberately reduced at the behest of the United States' National Security Agency. DES is an example of a single key or symmetric encryption system. A message is encoded and decoded using the same mathematical key. So long as only the sender and recipient know the key, the system is reasonably secure. A 56-bit DES key has some seventy quadrillion combinations. A massive figure for human calculators but one which provides a more manageable challenge to modern computers.

A totally new form of cryptography was identified in 1976 by two mathematicians, Diffie and Hellman. The concept of public key or asymmetric cryptography was brought to practical fruition by three further mathematicians, Rivest, Shamir and Adleman after whom the RSA system is named. Essentially, the system involves use of two keys, a public key and a private key. Messages can be encrypted using either key but possession of the other key will be required in order to decrypt them. Although the mathematics are beyond the comprehension of mere lawyers, the system is claimed to be significantly more secure than single key systems although it also operates considerably more slowly. It has been estimated that no single computer built or envisaged would be capable of decoding a message within a period of thousands of years. However, in yet another significant demonstration of the power of the Internet, it has been reported that messages have been successfully decoded using several thousand computers linked together over the Internet and operating throughout the night whilst their normal users slept.

The RSA system has proved contentious in a number of respects. Although much of the funding for the work was provided by the United States government, the system is patented with the rights belonging to a private company RSA Data Security. Further, the mathematical algorithms underlying the system have been used as the basis for a rival system, PGP (Pretty Good Privacy) created by Phil Zimmerman. Whilst observance of export laws has prevented the RSA system being used outwith the United States, the PGP system has been made freely available over the Internet, an act which has lead to harassment of Zimmerman by the FBI on suspicion of illegal export of munitions.

Encryption itself represents only one element of the problem. In the pub-lic/private key system, the owner of a key may receive an message. It may be clear that the message has been encoded using the public key. The message may indicate that the message has been sent by a particular individual. The use of cryptography may provide a guarantee that the message has not been altered subsequent to its transmission but cannot of itself provide conclusive evidence that it did originate from the alleged sender. Even where a message is encoded using a private key, this cannot of itself provide assurance that a third party has not obtained knowledge of this by illicit means. One method of overcoming this difficulty is to involve a third party, effectively to act as witness to the fact that a message truly has been sent by a particular person. This participation by what are generally referred to as "trusted third parties" is intended to provide assurance to the parties involved. One of the major areas where this application of cryptography is welcome is in the field of elec-tronic commerce. Whilst systems of EDI are well established, a feature of more generic forms of electronic commerce is that contracting parties may have had no previous dealings with each other. As will be discussed below, the "trusted third party" concept has become an important element in gov-ernmental attempts to regulate the use of cryptography.

Controls over the use of encryption have become a topic for heated dis-cussion at national and international level. In the United States, enormous controversy followed proposals to introduce a mandatory new system of encryption, the Escrowed Encryption Standard, more commonly referred to as the "Clipper Chip". The attraction of this system was that any form of digi-tised data would be encrypted in such a way as to ensure a high level of secur-ity. The less welcome aspect of the system was that its structure would enable 'keys' to be made available to government agencies so that they could readily decipher messages in the name of national security. Concerns were expressed whether the legal controls envisaged concerning release of the keys would pro-vide adequate safeguards. Although legislation implementing the Clipper pro-posals foundered due to popular opposition, and has not passed through Congress, it was announced in the autumn of 1996 that export controls on encryption software would be reduced in return for an industry commitment to the introduction of a "key recovery" system requiring that copies of all keys be held by a "Trusted Third Party". It would appear in this case that the prime motive was that the third party should be trusted by the government, rather than by the contracting parties.

In March 1997, the Council of the OECD adopted Guidelines for Cryptography Policy. In a manner similar to that adopted in the field of data protection, the Guidelines identify eight principles which should inform national legislation in this field.

1. Cryptographic methods should be trustworthy in order to generate confidence in the use of information and communications systems.

2. Users should have a right to choose any cryptographic method, subject to applicable law.
3. Cryptographic methods should be developed in response to the needs, demands and responsibilities of individuals, businesses and governments.
4. Technical standards, criteria and protocols for cryptographic methods should be developed and promulgated at the national and international level.
5. The fundamental rights of individuals to privacy, including secrecy of communications and protection of personal data, should be respected in national cryptographic policies and in the implementation and use of cryptographic methods.
6. National cryptographic policies may allow lawful access to plain text, or cryptographic keys, of encrypted data. These policies must respect the other principles contained in the guidelines to the greatest extent possible.
7. Whether established by contract or legislation, the liability of individuals and entities that offer cryptographic services or hold or access cryptographic keys should be clearly stated.
8. Governments should co-operate to co-ordinate cryptographic policies. As part of this effort, governments should remove, or avoid creating in the name of cryptography policy, unjustified obstacles to trade.

A strong relationship can be identified between these principles and a number of those applying in the data protection field. Although the Guidelines recognise the need for some state controls over the use of cryptography, it is stressed throughout that these must "respect user choice to the greatest extent."

In June 1996, the UK Government published a paper detailing its proposals "for encryption on public telecommunications networks". This recognised:

> "the need to set the right balance between commercial and personal confidentiality and the continuing ability of the law enforcement agencies to fight serious crime and terrorism"

and proposed the introduction of a system "of licensing of Trusted Third Parties (TTPs)". TTPs would provide a variety of services in the field of information security. These might include managing encryption services, and providing facilities akin to a form of recorded delivery service, certifying the fact that information was supplied by a certain person at a certain time, and was encrypted in a particular way. Additionally, the TTP would allow encrypted documents to be decoded under specific circumstances. Examples might include the situation where an employee controlling encrypted files might leave a company without leaving details of the private key used. Again, a solicitor might be required to decode documents following the death of their author. For law enforcement, the paper proposed the establishment of a system of warranted interception, with terms similar to those applied to phone tapping under the Interception of Communications Act. TTPs would be "required to release to the authorities the encryption keys of their clients under similar safeguards to those which already exist", that is, the legal safeguards currently in place in respect of phonetapping.

Following on from this document, a public consultation paper 'Licensing of Trusted Third Parties for the provision of Encryption Services' was published in March 1997. This proposed the introduction of a system of compulsory licences for organisations wishing to establish themselves in the role of TTP. In addition to the verification and data recovery roles discussed above, a number of advantages were claimed for such a licensing system. These included:

> Consumer protection against dishonest, incompetent or insolvent organisations purporting to offer such services.
>
> Enhanced interoperability of encryption services. A great variety of encryption products are available on the market creating considerable problems of interoperability. By centralising the role of key management, TTPs are considered to have a useful role to play in developing standards and thereby enhancing the accessibility and usage of encryption.

One of the major fears expressed concerning the use of TTP systems is that users might be compelled to use only forms of encryption which would be compatible with the system. The paper offers an incentive to cryptography developers in this field by suggesting that:

> Products that are designed to operate within a TTP environment will be subjected to simpler export licence procedures, thus allowing them to be exported with minimum restrictions.

This perhaps touches on one of the key issues of the subject and the source of much of the debate and controversy over cryptography policy. The Consultation Paper makes it clear that its legislative proposals are "directed solely towards the *provision of encryption services to subscribers in the UK* and *not the use of encryption.*" [emphasis in original]. Individuals would remain free to use any form of cryptography they might wish but it is clear that the commercial viability of encryption products would be enhanced were they to conform with the features of the TTP system, including access to keys for law enforcement agencies.

Legal aspects of digital signatures

As discussed above, it is clear that legal requirements requiring the use of 'writing', and signatures, cannot be satisfied by digital signatures. Given the fact that there is ready acceptance of mechanically produced signatures, which can offer little guarantee as to the identity of the person causing the signature to appear, it seems unfortunate that more effective forms of identifier should not be accepted. Whilst any form of encryption can be broken, it is not unreasonable to suggest that greater confidence can be placed in the authenticity of a digital signature than in most manual counterparts. Accepting that legislative change would be required to produce this result, the SCL Working Party recommended that it should be provided that:

> "An electronic equivalent of a writing is signed if any process has been performed on it by or under the authority of a person ('the signatory') which (a) alters it or adds to it and (b) identifies the signatory and evinces his acceptance of it."

Electronic documents: evidential issues

Until now we have been concerned with the formal requirements for legal constitution of a transaction or deed. Difficulties also arise, however, in relation to the use of electronic documents as evidence, eg, in order to prove that a crime has been committed. In the recent Scottish case of *Rollo v. HMA*,[5] evidence relating to the appellant's involvement in a drug dealing case was discovered by police stored on a electronic notepad computer seized during a search conducted, under a warrant empowering the recovery of any "document directly or indirectly relating to, or connected with a transaction" [prohibited under the Misuse of Drugs Act 1971]. Holding that the device in question was a document, Lord Milligan held that:

> "the essential essence of a document is that it is something containing recorded information of some sort. It does not matter if, to be meaningful, the information requires to be processed in some way such as translation, decoding or electronic retrieval."

A similar conclusion was reached in the English case of *Alliance and Leicester Building Society v. Ghahremani*[6] where the deletion of part of a word processed file held on a computer was held to constitute contempt of court when this was done subsequent to the making of a court order for discovery of documents.

Although these cases concerned the criminal law, there would appear no reason to doubt that information held on a computer storage device will be classed as a document for civil law purposes also.

Electronic copies of paper documents

For many organisations, such as banks, life insurance companies, and local government departments, significant costs are incurred in maintaining paper records of transactions. Savings could be made if these documents could be transferred, perhaps by use of optical character readers and digital scanners,

[5] 1996 SCCR 875.
[6] [1992] RVR 198.

into electronic form. The technique known as Document Image Processing has considerable attractions for such organisations whose activities inevitably generate considerable amounts of data. Until the entry into force in England of the Civil Evidence Act 1995, statute required in such circumstances that "original" documents be produced if needed as evidence in court proceedings. As a result, original records had to be retained against any need in future legal proceedings, even though day to day operations might be conducted on the basis of electronic copies. The 1995 Act now provides however that:

> "Where a statement contained in a document is admissible as evidence in civil proceedings, it may be proved –
> (a) by the production of that document, or
> (b) whether or not that document is still in existence, by the production of a copy of that document or of the material part of it.
> authenticated in such manner as the court may approve."

The Act came into force on 31 January 1997 following the making of the necessary Rules of Court. In Scotland, the Civil Evidence Act 1988 contains broadly similar provisions which have been in force for some time, with the requirement that the copy should be authenticated by a person responsible for its being made. The provisions of a British Standards Institute Code of Practice on 'Legal Admissibility of Information Stored on Electronic Document Management Systems' give useful guidance as to best practice in issues related to data storage.

CONCLUSION

Operating efficiently, systems of electronic contracting can provide users with significant savings in time and money. One producer has estimated that it costs $70 to process a paper purchase order as opposed to 93 cents when the order is processed electronically. Although this may constitute an extreme example, it demonstrates the commercial imperative that legal requirements should not place unnecessary barriers in the path of those wishing to take advantage of information technology in the course of their business activities.

As has been indicated in the preceding sections, in the vast majority of cases, existing legal principles and requirements allow complete flexibility to contracting parties. In a very small, though significant, range of circumstances, eg sales or purchases relating to land, electronic communications will not comply with the legal formalities. Reform is advocated on two grounds. First, given that systems of electronic communication can satisfy the considerations put forward as justifying requirements of writing and signature, there is no principled case for maintaining an exclusion. Second, the continued existence of even a small number of situations where legal barriers prevent the exploitation of information technology may create a false perception that significant legal obstacles exist. Law reform as suggested above would transmit a signal that electronic contracting is to be welcomed and may have a beneficial impact far beyond the somewhat narrow categories of transaction directly involved.

9

The Taxation of Electronic Commerce

SANDRA EDEN[1]

A common theme of the papers in this collection is how existing legal frameworks are responding (or not) to the challenges posed by technological advancements. This is not a new problem—developments in communication systems from the advent of the postal system onwards have caused headaches for contract lawyers—but the demands to be made of legal systems by the existence of the Internet have no historical precedent. The Internet not only offers methods of providing and paying for goods and services which are from the realms of science fiction but has generated a whole new range of products and applications. The novelty of Internet applications, together with the sheer scale of the commercial opportunities created, may be stretching traditional legal concepts beyond breaking point.

The purpose of this contribution is threefold. First, to examine the problems caused by Internet trading and Internet applications for the tax system, focusing particularly on the position in the UK. Second, to review the responses that there have been so far to the challenges posed. Finally, it will consider whether traditional tax concepts are apt to deal with the potential of the Internet.

There are three areas of particular concern that raise overlapping but separate issues. Of most importance is the application of indirect taxes, particularly VAT. The next issue is that of direct tax on business profits, and of how one decides whether a tax nexus has been established in a particular tax jurisdiction. Finally, the problems of classification of income from services provided over the Internet are briefly considered. Recurrent themes are the difficulties caused by the ethereal nature of Internet trading and the potential for distortion caused by the patchwork of different tax jurisdictions.

A INDIRECT TAXATION/VAT

The issues surrounding taxes on consumption in general, and VAT in particular may be obvious, but are worth stating nonetheless. Ideally one would

[1] Senior Lecturer, Department of Private Law, University of Edinburgh. Email sandra.eden@ed.ac.uk.

expect of such a system that it will be robust, i.e. not easy to evade, that it will not unduly distort economic or consumer decisions and that it will not impose an excessive administrative burden on those who are required to account to the tax authorities. Translated into practice for VAT, this requires, one, that transactions should be taxed once, and once only, two, that they should as far as possible be taxed in the country of consumption,[2] and three that there are clear rules for determining how and at what rate an individual transaction should be taxed.

Before looking at the problems that are posed by use of the Internet for VAT, it is necessary to understand a little of the workings of the tax in order to judge the potential for economic distortion caused by avoidance and evasion.[3]

VAT is currently charged by some 120 tax jurisdictions in the world, although there are still many powerful economies, for example the USA, where a sales tax is applied. Member states of the European Union are required to operate a system of VAT, and the basic framework is imposed by the Sixth VAT Directive.[4]

VAT is functionally a tax on consumption of goods and services, and is at present designed to accrue to the taxing authority in which consumption occurs. Although the person with the legal responsibility for accounting for the tax is normally the supplier of the goods and services, the tax is borne by those who buy these for private use.[5] In the paradigm case, VAT is charged at each stage of production but the tax is not factored into the cost of production as a result of the system of output tax charges and input tax credits. This is best illustrated by example. Take a company that manufactures goods. When it purchases the raw materials necessary to make the goods, the company will be charged VAT by its suppliers. When the manufacturer sells its goods, it will in turn charge VAT on the sale price of the goods, but it is only required to hand over to the tax authorities the difference between the tax it charged, the output tax, and the tax it paid on acquiring its raw materials, the input tax. In practice, a business keeps records of output and input tax over a period, and either pays over the balance to the tax authorities, or, if the input tax exceeds the tax charged, the excess is repaid to the business.

This output/input tax mechanism operated at each stage of production may seem clumsy in comparison with a single stage tax, such as the sales tax in the United States, but it has certain advantages. First, from the point of view of the tax authorities, a multi-stage tax system has a self-policing mechanism—

---

[2] See "Taxing Consumption", Organisation for Economic Cooperation and Development, 1988.

[3] Using "avoidance" here to signify legal "tax planning", for example the setting up of a business operation in a low tax jurisdiction, and "evasion" to mean some illegal activity resulting in the non-payment of tax, for example not declaring the importation of goods.

[4] Council Directive 77/388.

[5] Strictly, the tax is borne by anyone who cannot fully set off the input tax as a tax credit; this includes partially exempt and non-taxable business entities as well as consumers: see later.

each time a person charges output tax to a taxable person, there will be a corresponding claim for an input tax credit, which creates a paper trail. Second, and most importantly for the purposes of this exercise, it avoids certain economic tax distortions. Because input tax is fully credited, the rate of VAT payable by the taxable trader is irrelevant except from a cash flow point of view. It is of no special advantage to a VAT registered trader to acquire goods at a lower rate or even at zero rate of VAT.

The potential distortion created by differential VAT rates only becomes apparent when taxable goods or services arrive in the hands of someone who, for whatever reason, cannot claim the input tax as a deduction. Obviously private consumers are one example, and small enterprises not registered for VAT are another.[6] But there is one further important category of purchasers of taxable goods and services for which VAT is wholly or partially irrecoverable: those who make exempt or partially exempt supplies, for example banks and insurance companies. Where a person makes only exempt supplies, he cannot be registered for VAT. Where he makes both exempt and taxable supplies, he can only claim a portion of the input VAT he has paid. The input VAT referable to his exempt supplies is not permitted as a deduction, and so becomes an absolute cost of production to the supplier.[7]

For all the above categories of persons, there is a clear incentive to acquire goods and services at reduced or zero rates of VAT, and as the capacity to do this by way of purchases from the same tax jurisdiction is limited, the rules concerning international transactions become of critical importance.

VAT ON THE INTERNATIONAL TRADE OF GOODS

i) Goods traded within the European Union

Since 1993, intra-EC trade should technically be referred to as acquisition and dispatch, with the terms "import" and "export" reserved for trade with non-EC countries.

The system which is described below is the so-called "transitional" system. There have been proposals around since 1985 that intra-EC trade should be taxed on the "definitive" or "origin system", i.e. goods should circulate in the EC bearing the supplier's rate of VAT.[8] Recent proposals from the Commission[9] for the implementation of the definitive system, which could not

---

[6] Unless one makes taxable supplies of over a certain amount each year, currently £48,000, registration is only permitted with permission of the Customs and Excise. Permission will only be granted where business supplies are made: VAT Act 1994 Sched 1, para 9.

[7] VAT Act 1994 ss 25 and 26, SI 1995/2518. There are a number of ways of apportioning input tax , for example, by reference to the ratio of taxable to exempt supplies.

[8] Commissioner's White Paper "Completing the Internal Market" Com(85) 210 final.

[9] "A Common System of VAT- A programme for the Single Market" COM (96) 328 final.

be implemented until about 2001 at the earliest, have already run into difficul-ties,[10] and the proposed system is not further discussed here.

In brief, goods traded between taxable persons[11] in different member states cross borders free of tax and bear the tax of the country where they are acquired.[12] So a taxable person in the UK purchasing goods for business use from France will be required to account for VAT on these goods at the UK VAT rate when he completes his next VAT return.[13] The French supplier will not be required to account to the French tax authorities for any VAT as the goods are going to a taxable person abroad.

The position is in principle different where goods are purchased from a source in another member state by a non-taxable person. In such cases the gen-eral rule is that VAT is charged by the supplier, and is accounted for to the tax jurisdiction of the supplier, in the same way as the supplier's domestic sales: the tax accrues to the country of origin. So a domestic consumer living in Strasbourg in France, where the standard rate of VAT rate is 20.6% can do his shopping in Germany where the rate is 15%. The potential for cross-border shopping by non-taxable persons in order to take advantage of lower tax rates elsewhere is evident, although the associated travel costs provide a natural brake, and the experience of the United States, where sales tax varies from state to state, suggests that a rate differential of up to 5% can be tolerated. The avail-ability of mail order, and now electronic commerce, clearly reduces the effec-tiveness of this brake, because the rules of the place of supply of goods generally means that goods are treated as being supplied in the place where the supplier is based. One could, for example, have a healthy mail order business in Germany for the sale of small high cost goods, eg CDs and videos, to consumers in France. Accordingly in order to prevent the distortion caused by the potential of distance selling, a special regime now applies to intra- EC distance selling

The distance selling provisions apply only to goods traded within the EC and operate by shifting the place of supply for tax purposes to the place where the consumer belongs. A taxable person in one member state who makes sales over a particular limit in a year to customers in another member state is required to register locally and to account for VAT at the local rate. So, if the German mail order firm had sales in the UK in excess of £70,000 per annum, it would be required to register with the UK Customs and Excise, and account to them at UK rates on these sales.[14]

---

[10] The proposals require a degree of harmonisation, and the first stage, to impose a band between 15–25% for the basic rate of VAT was rejected by the European Parliament in September 1996, even though all member states have rates which are currently within this band. For criti-cism of the Commission's proposals, see Smith "A Definitive Regime for VAT" Institute for Fiscal Studies, 1997.

[11] I.e. someone registered for VAT.

[12] Where goods leave the UK for an EC destination, VAT Act 1994, s 7 deems the place of supply of goods to be the UK when the supply is to a non-taxable person, and as outside the UK when the supply is to a taxable person.

[13] VAT Act 1994, s 10.

[14] VAT Act 1994, Schedule 2.

A similar potential for distortion is caused by the existence of large non-taxable consumers, for example government departments, where the sheer scale of their purchases might make cross border shopping worthwhile and similar rules apply to reduce this potential. If the intra-community acquisitions from a particular state by a non-taxable legal person are over a certain value, that person is required to register and to account for local VAT in that state as if it was a taxable person.[15]

ii) Imports and exports: trade with non-member states

UK VAT is due in respect of the import of taxable goods into the UK, whether the goods are imported by a taxable or a non-taxable person.[16] This is the broad general rule and there are of course some exceptions, for example goods carried in travellers' personal luggage up to a certain amount, and small non-commercial transactions, but these are not significant for present purposes.

UK VAT paid on entry can generally be claimed as input tax by a taxable person, but not of course where the purchaser makes only exempt supplies, or acquires the goods for private consumption. A partially exempt supplier may only reclaim a proportion of the input tax.

No UK VAT is due in respect of goods exported from the UK.[17]

iii) VAT on international services

The above principles apply to supplies of goods. Supplies of services are taxed according to a separate set of rules which require to be more fully set out.

Although the general rule is that taxable services are taxed in the tax jurisdiction to which the supplier belongs,[18] this is again subject to important exceptions which are designed to limit distortion of competition caused by tax differentials between tax jurisdictions in relation to purchases by those who are not permitted to set off the input tax credit.

The most important exception[19] for present purposes are the special rules which apply to "relevant services", often called Schedule 5 services,[20] the range of which is extremely wide and includes:

---

[15] VAT Act 1994, Schedule 3. The present limit in the UK is £48,000 per annum.

[16] VAT Act 1994, s 1(4).

[17] VAT Act 1994, s 30(6).

[18] VAT Act 1994, s 7(10).

[19] Other important exceptions, although not central to internet commerce, include services relating to land, which are deemd to be carried out where the land is situated, and "physical services" (including cultural, artistic, sporting, scientific education and entertainment services) which are deemed to be supplied where performed: VAT (Place of Supply of Services) Order 1992 (SI 1992/3121) Arts 5 and 15.

[20] VAT Act 1994, Sched 5.

i)   the transfer of copyright, patents, licences, trademarks and similar rights,
ii)   advertising services,
iii) services of consultants and other similar services, data processing and provision of information,
iv)   banking, financial and insurance services,
v)   from 1 July 1997, telecommunications services,

Where "relevant services" are supplied by a person who belongs in a country other than the UK, whether another member state or elsewhere, and are received for business purposes by a person who belongs in the UK, the recipient is treated as having supplied the services.[21] This has the result that the *supplier* is not required to account for VAT on the services, and may give rise to what is known as the reverse charge, in terms of which the *recipient* is required to account for UK input VAT.[22] To take an example, suppose a business in the UK receives data processing services from a company situated in the U.S. The U.S. company will not charge VAT on its services, but the UK business will be required to account to Customs and Excise for VAT at 17½% on the value of the services it received, as if the business had supplied them itself. This input VAT will, as usual, generally be available as an input tax credit, and so imposes no cost to the recipient. Even if the recipient is not otherwise registered for VAT, if the services he receives push him over the registration limit, this will require his registration. Where the recipient is not registered for UK VAT, and is not required to do so as a result of the deemed supply, there will be no requirement to account for UK VAT, and, provided the services are either from a country outside the EC, or are from a EC country where the rules mirror those in the UK, there will be no VAT payable at all.

As it makes no economic difference to the fully taxable trader what rate of VAT he bears, it is evident that the reverse charge rules operate primarily to prevent partially exempt persons from gaining a tax advantage from purchasing overseas services. Fully exempt suppliers, and domestic purchasers who are not subject to the reverse charge will still gain an advantage from buying services from a low or no-VAT jurisdiction.

Where a UK supplier supplies "relevant services", these are treated as supplied where the recipient belongs in two situations:

i)   where the supply is to a person who belongs outside the EC, and
ii)   where the supply is to a person in another member state and the supply is for the purposes of that person's business.[23]

---

[21] VAT Act 1994, s 8.

[22] There are significant cash flow and administrative advantages of the reverse charge as it enables taxable persons to purchase such services from other member states and to account for the VAT in their own jurisdiction, which will normally be available immediately as an input tax credit. The alternative, that of paying VAT in the state of supplier and subsequently reclaiming it, is frequently a lengthy and frustrating process.

[23] VAT (Place of Supply of Services) Order 1992 SI 1992/3121, Art 16.

In both cases no UK VAT will be charged, although in the latter situation, one can generally anticipate that the reverse charge will be applied by the recipient's member state. The above rules mean that the UK supplier of Schedule 5 services abroad will only account for UK VAT on these where they are for non-business use by an EC recipient.

The definition of "belong" is clearly central to the operation of the reverse charge. The UK definition is that a supplier broadly belongs where he has his business establishment or some other fixed establishment, or, where he has more than one business establishment, that which is more directly concerned with the supply of the services under consideration deterimines the place of "belonging".[24] Where a recipient of supplies receives supplies in his personal capacity, then he is treated as belonging in whatever country he has his usual place of residence.

The Sixth VAT Directive does not use the term belong, instead providing that services are supplied where the supplier has his established his business or has a fixed establishment from which the service is supplied.[25] One matter is clear, the existence of a server in a jurisdiction will not on its own constitute a fixed establishment: the European Court of Justice has held that an installation can only constitute a fixed establishment where there are also staff permanently present in the jurisdiction to operate the installation.[26] Although this decision concerned gaming machines, it would apply equally to other forms of machine and would mean, for example, that a supplier of services in electronic form, say from Canada, through a server situated in the UK will not by virtue of the site of the server at least be required to account for UK VAT.

The above rules on the supply of international goods and services are summarised in the following tables on page 158.

summarised in the following tables on page 158.

POTENTIAL FOR DISTORTION

Assuming the tax systems of other countries mirror the UK rules, which they broadly will within the EC, the scope for economic distortion caused by differential rates of VAT is limited when goods and services are traded between taxable persons as such supplies will be generally be taxed at the purchaser's local VAT rate irrespective of where the supplier belongs.[27]

Turning to acquisitions by non-taxable persons, goods acquired from other member states will in principle bear the VAT of the country of the supplier rather than local VAT, except where the distance selling rules or the large scale consumer rules apply. There is some scope for economic distortion here,

---

[24] VAT Act 1994, s 9.
[25] Dir 77/388, Art 9.
[26] *Berkholz v Finanzamt Hamburg-Mitte-Altstadt* [1985] ECR 2251.
[27] The unweighted average of the standard VAT rates in member states in July 1996 was 19.3%, ranging from 25% in Denmark and Sweden, to 15% in Germany and Luxemburg: Smith "The Definitive Regime for VAT" Institute for Fiscal Studies July 1997.

1 SUPPLIES MADE BY A UK TAXABLE SUPPLIER

i Supplies of Goods

To an EC taxable person	Local VAT	
To an EC non-taxable person	UK VAT	Provided the distance selling/large consumer rules do not apply
To a person outside the EC	No VAT	

ii Supplies of Schedule 5 services

To an EC business person	Local VAT	Assuming the reverse charge provisions apply
To an EC non-business person	UK VAT	
To a person outside the EC	No VAT	

iii Supplies of other services
UK VAT

2 SUPPLIES TO A PERSON IN THE UK

i Supplies of goods

From the EC to a taxable person	UK VAT	
From the EC to a non-taxable person	Local VAT	Provided the distance selling/large consumer rules do not apply
From a non-EC supplier	UK VAT	

ii Supplies of Schedule 5 services

From the EC to a taxable person	UK VAT	Assuming the reverse charge provisions apply
From the EC to a non-taxable person	Local VAT	
From outside the EC to a taxable person in the UK	UK VAT	Assuming the reverse charge provisions apply
From outside the EC to a non-taxable person in the UK	No VAT	

iii Supplies of other services

Local VAT (if any)		Any local VAT paid can usually be reclaimed by a UK taxable person

but it is clearly limited, not least by the rule that member states are not permitted to charge less than 15% VAT on standard rated items.[28] Where there is only a couple of percentage points at stake, there is obviously less incentive to go to the trouble to shop around within the EC.

---

[28] Council Directive 77/388 (the 6th Directive) Art 12(3)(a) as amended by Directive 96/95 Art 1. This is effective until the end of 1998.

Goods acquired from a non-member state are in principle charged with UK VAT on import, whether supplied to a taxable or a non-taxable person, and the normal procedures for policing imports through customs officials and postal companies are operated. So, there is no legal VAT advantage to be gained from the purchase of goods from the Bahamas rather than Basingstoke, although there is of course a major difficulty in policing cross border trade in "goods" which can be downloaded directly from the Internet by the purchaser, with no physical medium to cross borders. This is a topic to which we shall return in the context of the discussion on the distinction between goods and services.

So, the main opportunity for legal tax arbitrage involves the acquisition of cross border *services* by non-taxable persons. Of particular attraction is the provision of services by a supplier who belongs to country where VAT is not charged, as the saving is not then a few percentage points, but the full rate of VAT. Especially where services can be supplied directly over the Internet, it may require relatively little planning on the part of the supplier to ensure that he belongs in a low tax jurisdiction.

So far, it has been assumed that tax jurisdictions adopt matching rules, but even within the EC, the Sixth VAT Directive permits scope for a certain amount of deviation. Where a supply is given different treatment as between two taxing jurisdictions, the potential for double or under taxation is obvious. For example, both jurisdictions may treat the place of supply as being within their borders, or one jurisdiction may categorise an item as a good, and the other as a service, or one may treat a supply as exempt and the other as taxable. The problems caused by the imperfect meshing of tax systems are not unique to transactions involving the Internet, but the increasing importance of such transactions, coupled with the difficulties in finding the appropriate analogies in the physical world, makes this area a productive seam for avoiders, and a trap for the unwary.

VAT IMPLICATIONS FOR THE INTERNET PLAYERS

Internet Service Providers (ISPs): Telecommunications Services

ISPs rent or buy phone line space from telecommunications companies such as BT or Mercury. They will typically be given free access to lines rented by other ISPs in return for allowing these other ISPs free access on their own space. The ISP then charges users for the facility to use this communication link. In order for the domestic user to gain access to the Internet, he must first be linked to his local ISP connection point ("Point of Presence" or "POP")[29]

[29] The POP is typically a leased room with modems and routing equipment, generally unstaffed. It is thought that its presence would be insufficient to establish a place of belonging for the purposes of VAT: see *Berkholz* supra n 26

which he will do through a modem, using the ordinary phone lines. He will be charged by the phone company, generally at local rates, for using the phone line in the same way as when the lines are used for making telephone calls. Where the user requires continuous connection, typically a large business, it is likely to have a direct connection to the POP, but still may lease the connection from the telephone company. From the POP, the user gains access to the communications channel provided by his and other ISPs, from which he can then access whatever information or other services he is seeking from anywhere in the world. All transmission costs beyond the POP are borne by the ISP, which receive payment from users for providing such access, or an "account", by subscription and/or usage fees. In addition to Internet access, other services are often provided by the ISP to the user, typically email and additional software which might for example enable the user to establish a Web site, or to engage in Web searches, or to filter access to Web sites.

For the purposes of VAT, telecommunication services were until recently excluded from the list of Schedule 5 services, and were thus charged to tax in the country to which the supplier belonged. EC providers were accordingly finding themselves at a significant competitive disadvantage in comparison to their counterparts in jurisdictions with no VAT, who could provide services at particularly attractive rates to non-taxable persons for whom VAT is an absolute cost. Accordingly, member states have been granted a temporary derogation[30] to add telecommunications services to the list of services which are treated as supplied in the country of the consumer, and all member states agreed to adjust their domestic legislation by 1 July 1997 to accommodate these changes.[31]

There has been some debate over whether ISPs provide telecommunications services or whether they provide a package which provides, amongst other things, Internet access which just happens to involve the use of telephone lines.[32] This has been a particularly sensitive issue in the US where there is a separate tax on the provision of telecommunication services. As we have seen, the number of times VAT is levied during the production process does not affect the final amount of VAT borne by the consumer, but this is not the case with stand-alone type consumption taxes. If there is a charge to telecommunications tax both on the supply from the telecommunication company to the ISP, and then again on supplies from the ISP to the user, this creates a pyramid effect which distorts the final price and makes ISPs uncompetitive in comparison to the telecommunications companies.

[30] Derogation from Article 9(1) of Council Directive 77/388, made by Council Decision 6236/97

[31] In the UK the changes have been implemented by the following regulations: VAT (Reverse Charge) (Anti-avoidance) Order 1997 SI 1997/1523, VAT (Place of Supply of Services) (Amendment) Order 1997 SI 1997/1524 and VAT (Amendment) (No 2) Regulations 1997 SI 1997/1525

[32] See e.g. "Straight Talk: Internet, Tax and Interstate Commerce" http://www.itaa.org/P7.htm; "Logging on to Cyberspace Tax Policy" http://www.caltax.org/taxwhpap.html

The argument put forward by the ISPs is that the telecommunications services bought by the ISPs are simply an ingredient of its product, and are not services which are resold to the consumer. An analogy has been made with the production of a Boeing 777, involving millions of minutes of telephone calls in the course of designing, manufacturing and selling of the plane, but with no suggestion that Boeing is providing telecommunications services.[33] One might add that the analogy is clearly not perfect, as when the passenger is sitting in the aeroplane he is not actually gaining access to telecommunication services, unlike a user of the Internet.

In the UK, it is thought that the problem has been avoided by defining telecommunications services as "services relating to the transmission, or reception of signals, writing, images and sounds or information of any nature by wire, radio, optical or other electromagnetic systems, including the transfer or assignment of the right to use capacity for such transmission emission or reception".[34] This definition does not require that the service is the *provision of* telecommunications services, but that it *relates* to the transmission and reception of signals etc. "Relate" is clearly a word capable of different interpretations, but it seems probable that the part of the service provided by an ISP which gives access to the Internet is a service "relating" to a transmission.

For the sake of completeness, one might add that the final part of the definition, that which refers to the transfer or assignment of the right to use the capacity, is apt to cover the transaction between the telecommunications company and the ISP,[35] but does not seem to cover the relationship between the ISP and the user as the ISP sells access to the Internet rather than transferring or assigning its right to use the lines.

Although the point cannot be regarded as being authoritatively settled, it is assumed here that the UK definition will cover at least the part of the service provided by the ISPs which concerns access to the Internet.

The new rules on telecom services contain a special feature which does not apply to any other Schedule 5 services, namely the "effective use and enjoyment" provisions, which might broadly be regarded as there for anti-avoidance purposes.[36] As discussed earlier, it is still generally advantageous for private consumers to purchase Schedule 5 services from non or low VAT

[33] This is taken from "Straight Talk: Internet, Tax and Interstate Commerce" supra published by the ITAA. The ITAA is the national trade organisation in the United States representing the computer software and services industry, so its views may be not be entirely neutral.

[34] New para 7A Schedule 5 to the VAT Act 1994 inserted by VAT (Reverse Charge) (Anti-avoidance) Order 1997 SI 1997/1523 See Customs and Excise Information Sheet 2/97 June 1997, available on http://www. open.gov.uk/customs/info297.htm

[35] DTI authorised telecom providers buying such services from overseas operators are not required to account for the reverse charge where they fall under the provisions of the Melbourne agreement (International Telecommunications Regulations 1988), one aspect of which is to ensure that turnover taxes are not applied to the provision of telecommunications services between telecommunication providers.

[36] VAT (Place of Supply of Services)(Amendment) Order 1997 SI 1997/1524, amending SI 1992/3121.

jurisdictions. The "effective use and enjoyment" provisions operate to shift the place of supply of telecom services to the place where the services are used, but only to in relation to supplies to and from countries outside the EC, and only where the supplies are not covered by the reverse charge already.

If a non-EC supplier provides telecom services which will be used in the UK, either for non-business purposes, or for business purposes in circumstances in which the reverse charge rules do not apply,[37] that provider will be required to register for VAT in the UK and account for tax on the services in similar fashion to the distance selling rules, although with no minimum threshold of value.[38] The effect of these rules is that a non-EC provider will be required to register in each of the member states in which it has non-business customers, unless, in order to minimise the number of tax jurisdictions with which it has to deal, it sets up a fixed establishment in one member state from which it can route all services to EC customers. If it chooses a low VAT member state, for example Germany which currently applies the lowest rate of VAT in the EC, it will be at a competitive advantage in relation to its supplies to the domestic market.

If a UK provider of telecom services supplies them to someone outside the EC which are to be used in the UK, UK VAT on these services will have to be accounted for irrespective of whether the services are used for business or private use. Where the UK provider supplies services which are not subject to the reverse charge to someone in the EC, and those services are to be used and enjoed outside the EC, then VAT is not to be charged.

The place of supply of services provided and used within member states of the EC are not shifted by these provisions.

Administratively, these provisions have the potential to create great difficulties for the ISP. Take as an example an ISP situated in the UK. It is required to charge VAT on services provided to UK customers, *unless* those services are used and enjoyed outside the UK. It is required to charge VAT on supplies to EC non-business customers, again, *unless* the services are to be used outside the EC. It is *not* required to charge VAT on services provided to *business* customers elsewhere in the EC (these will account for VAT locally under the reverse charge). It is *not* required to charge VAT on any services provided to a customer, business or domestic, outside the EC *unless* those services are used and enjoyed in the UK.

[37] This will typically be where the services are supplied to an overseas branch of a UK company.

[38] A supply of Schedule 5 services is treated as being made within the UK where it is supplied to someone in the UK for business purposes: see text related to footnote 21. Services supplied for business purposes will generally be caught by the reverse charge, but this will still not apply to supplies for business purposes to non-taxable persons, for example exempt suppliers where the value of Schedule 5 services is not high enough to bring them into the net for registration. These recipients will not pay VAT, as they are neither affected by the reverse charge, nor by the "use and enjoyment" provisions if they acquired the services for business purposes, as these provisions only apply where the services would otherwise be treated as supplied outside the EC. In practice, however, the number of businesses receiving overseas services who will remain under the registration limit is insignificant.

This places an astonishing administrative burden on the supplier. Not only must the ISP know where the customer *belongs* for tax purposes, which is not necessarily unproblematic,[39] it must also know whether the services are to be used for the purposes of a business or not, and in addition it must now know in relation to supplies made to non-EC customers whether any of those supplies are to be used and enjoyed in the UK. How is an ISP to know what use is made by a UK branch of services supplied to an international company? If a US company uses telecom services to access a data base for the purposes of the UK branch, are the services being used and enjoyed in the UK or does the actual use of the service have to originate from a computer situated in the UK? If in doubt, the ISP will be likely to charge VAT on the services and require the recipient to argue the point with the tax authorities if a refund appears to be appropriate.

The economic effect of the new rules is that it is no longer of any particular advantage for VAT purposes to locate the ISP in a non-VAT jurisdiction. One point to note however is that the use and enjoyment provisions are not presently applied to other international services which, when provided for non-business purposes to non-taxable persons, are still taxed where the supplier belongs.[40] Accordingly, where the non-EC ISP provides services over and above access to the Internet, such services will generally escape VAT in the hands of a non-taxable recipient. There may therefore be some advantage in charging for such services separately rather than at present subsuming the whole cost within one fee.

Content Providers

At one level, the Internet offers suppliers an unrivalled advertising medium. A Web page describing the range of goods on offer is infinitely more sophisticated than a paper catalogue and has the capacity to carry information on thousands of products including up to date prices and stock availability. However, the commercial uses of the Internet extend far beyond a sophisticated mail order catalogue: new services are available, and old ones can be delivered at a speed and cost hitherto unimaginable. New goods and services are developing all the time, and again, old ones such as books, CDs and video, or banking services, can be delivered electronically

---

[39] See p. 157.

[40] Member States are permitted to apply the use and enjoyment provisions to any of the Schedule 5 services (Article 9(3) of the Sixth VAT Directive), but so far the UK has chosen not to apply them to anything other than telecommunications services (and, outside the Schedule 5 provisions, hire of means of transport), which they were required to do by the terms of the derogation. Depending on how the use and enjoyment provisions work with telecommunications services, thought might be given to extending their scope.

i) Access to information and other services

Content providers typically offer fee-based access to information by subscription and/or charge for incremental use. In the past, such services have tended to be used by businesses, for example Lexis/Nexis, or credit reporting agencies, but with the expansion of the domestic market as a result of the growth of home computers, the range of services on offer are changing. Already some newspapers and magazines offer on-line access as an alternative to the purchase of a hard copy. In the United States, some companies provide access to electronic games and music videos, and there is at least one Internet casino in the Caribbean.

Generally the services provided by such content providers will be covered by the Schedule 5 rules, with the result that taxable purchasers will account for UK VAT under the reverse charge, and non taxable purchasers will bear the local rate of EC VAT where the services are from a member state and no VAT where the services are provided by a non-EC supplier. There will be a clear incentive for domestic users and unregistered or partially exempt businesses to acquire such services from overseas.

In passing, one might note that whilst the printed word is commonly subject to reduced rates of VAT,[41] the service of providing access to information is standard rated and the question might arise as to whether the downloading of a newspaper for example should be treated as a supply of a newspaper or the provision of information. This is simply one example of the problem of categorisation, discussed further in the next section.

ii) Internet Sales

a) Physical goods   Interactive web sites, where a purchaser can access information about a product, place an order electronically and pay by credit card, are already well established. The method of placing an order does not change the nature of the transaction so there is no particular relevance for VAT of goods ordered over the Internet.[42] As with mail order, goods from an EC supplier will either bear the supplier's or the recipient's rate of VAT, depending on the application of the distance selling rules, and whether the recipient is acquiring the goods for business or domestic purposes. Goods from a non-EC supplier will be subjected to UK VAT on import.[43]

So, the advent of the computer age does not create any new tax problems in relation to the international trade of physical goods, or at least as long as

---

[41] Books, magazines and newspapers are zero rated in the UK: VAT Act 1994, Schedule 8. Group 3.

[42] *Emphasis Ltd v HM Customs and Excise* LON/95/2355A. which concerned an order by e-mail to a take-away food shop. This was rather engagingly described by the providers as an "e-meal" facility.

[43] See earlier discussion at pp 157–8.

the tax which is due is actually accounted for. Evasion is still an issue of course, but only to the extent that the increased use of computers has created a market for small expensive software, which may be more easily able to slip unnoticed across borders than, say, a bed.

Although the main focus here is the problems caused by VAT, it is of interest at this point to compare the position in the United States, where a major tax distortion exists in favour of distance selling, including orders placed via the Internet. In *Quill Corporation v North Dakota*[44] the Supreme Court held that it was unconstitutional to allow a state to tax sales to its residents by an out-of-state supplier unless the seller had a significant sales operation in the state. To expect distance sellers to account for local sales tax in each state would be to place an unreasonable burden on the supplier, and without having connections with a state such as business premises, showrooms or employees, there was no taxable nexus between the supplier and the state. This places distance selling operators in the US in a position which will be envied by their European counterparts who are faced with the requirement to account for local VAT.

b) Computer software   The differences in the VAT treatment of goods and services noted earlier makes accurate identification of the supply particularly important. A domestic purchaser can acquire *services* from outside the EC without paying VAT, but VAT is due on imports of *goods*. The place of supply can depend on whether the supply is of a good or a service and if there is no clear definition which applies across tax jurisdictions, there is the potential for double or under taxation. Suppliers have to know when they should charge VAT on the supply and purchasers when they have to apply the reverse charge.

Again, it is worth noting that a similar debate has proceeded in the United States, as the sales/use tax which operates in 45 states in the US generally only applies to sales and use of tangible corporeal property, so whilst the sale of software on a physical medium is generally taxed, many states exempt the electronic transmission of such software.

In the olden days, a purchaser could be moderately sure whether he was buying a good or a service. With the development of computer software, the concept of a product has changed and life is less certain. Computer software can be purchased in a myriad of ways: it can be bought off the shelf or downloaded or already installed when the hardware is purchased. It may be standard or customised, in a final state or subject to further development. It is not bought outright by the consumer but conditional use is granted, which may be perpetual or limited, restricted to a certain number of users or not. Payment may be one-off or by instalments, and may be of a fixed price or subject to use or profitability, and payment may entitle the user to varying degrees of continuing support.

---

[44] 504 US 298.

Clearly, the disk or CD on which the software is supplied is a good. Equally clearly, the provision of ongoing support is a service. The rest is difficult to classify. It is evidently not like buying a bed. Analogies only work so far: the purchase of software from a computer shop is similar to the purchase of a book or a CD as, in all cases, the purchaser owns the physical matter but does not acquire the unrestricted right to use the material contained thereon. However, the purchaser of the book and the CD can at least lend them to friends.

There is as yet no case law in the UK on the distinction between goods and services in the context of taxation of supplies of software, and although this distinction has been considered in other contexts, for example contract law,[45] the relevance of these cases will be limited in the light of the specific definition provided by statute and the Sixth VAT Directive.

For the purposes of VAT, the UK definition of the distinction between goods and services is not especially helpful:

> "Any transfer of the whole property in goods is a supply of goods, but . . . the transfer
>
> a) of any undivided share of the property, or
> b) of the possession of goods,
>
> is a supply of services".[46]

This has been amplified in the context of imported software in the UK by Customs and Excise.[47] Software already installed in hardware at the point of sale and included in the price is treated as a sale of goods. Other supplies of software are divided into "normalised" (off the shelf) and "specific" (customised) products. Normalised products are regarded as made up of goods (the carrier medium) and services (the information), although if there is no separate identification of these, the whole supply can be treated as one of goods. If they are separately identified, there is no VAT paid on the services element on import from outside the EC, although a taxable person will be required to account for VAT under the reverse charge. Specific products are specially designed or adapted programmes, or updates or enhancements to specific programmes, or to normalised programmes purchased under a contract to supply updates or enhancements. The supply of specific products is treated as a supply of services.

The references to the carrier medium sprinkled though the Customs and Excise notice makes it evident that it does not specifically apply to downloaded products, although the notice does state that information provided by "satellite, telephone, telex, facsimile etc." is a provision of services, and this may be apt to cover downloaded programmes. The definition of goods and

---

[45] See MacQueen p. 124.
[46] VAT Act 1994, s 5 and Schedule 4.
[47] CE Notice 702/4/94 "Importing Computer Software".

services in the VAT Act 1994 tends to suggest that downloaded software is a supply of services, but there are other jurisdictions, for example Germany[48] and Spain, where downloaded software is treated as "goods".

Apart from the fact that there is no clear dividing line between "normalised" and "specific" software, it is clear that there are still some unresolved difficulties with the supply of software.

A practical problem faced by content providers is that of knowing where their customers are located. Services provided for non-business purposes to individuals in the same or other member states should be charged to VAT whilst services provided elsewhere should be supplied VAT free. Where a product is physically delivered, the destination is known, but in the case of a supply made electronically, there may be nothing other than an Internet address. This will contain a country code (except for addresses in the United States), but this does not have to be the country where the purchaser "belongs", or "uses and enjoys" the services supplied. Even the billing address will not generally be known by the supplier as payment will normally be by credit card. Suppliers will obviously be able to ask their customers where they "belong", but they have no means at present of checking that this information is accurate.

Further problems arises when it comes to the appropriate categorisation of the supply. Is it reasonable to treat software contained on a physical medium as a sale of goods, when the value of the goods is minimal? Although the legal nature of the acquisition is not one of sale but of use, the reality is closer to sale where the purchase is off the peg, and would point towards treating it as an acquisition of goods. Is it then reasonable to treat "physical" and downloaded software differently? If all software should be afforded the same treatment, should this be as a good or as a service? There is no clear answer as to what this treatment should be. To treat it as a service will create the potential for economic distortion, as non-taxable consumers will prefer to purchase software from suppliers outside the EC. To treat all software as goods may deal with one problem of legal distortion, but may create another difficult dividing line: that between the provision of software and other services. In any event, to treat all software as goods does not remove the potential for evasion in relation to downloaded software which is virtually impossible to police.

SOLUTIONS?

From the above discussion, it is evident that the difficulties posed by the Internet for VAT arise as a result of several factors: the imperfect mesh between tax jurisdictions, the problems of using analogy to squeeze new concepts into old bottles, the ease with which service providers can be moved around and the lack of tangible presence.

---

[48] For an account of the tax problems of internet trading in Germany see Brodersen "International Tax Issues in Cyperspace: Taxation of Cross-border Electronic Commerce" INTERTAX (1997) Vol 25 p. 133.

There is of course no easy answer. Work has and indeed continues to be done on the lack of consistency between different tax jurisdictions. Already a certain amount of progress within the EC has been made, further work is continuing in the Taxation Policy Group to explore the issues at EC level with Member States.[49] But, it is not in relation to transactions within the EC that the greatest distortions arise but those with the rest of the world. The history of tax harmonisation within the EC, where progress has been at best patchy, and at worst glacial, is testimony to how difficult and how closely related to sensitive issues of sovereignty such a project is. And this is in the context of a group of states who have undertaken to work together. It is as unrealistic to contemplate a fully harmonised world tax system as it is to anticipate universal agreement on the world's most palatable food. Tax systems are economically and culturally specific, and generally have grown in a piecemeal, almost organic way, in response to the needs and values of the society which they serve.[50] The existence of different tax systems, and in particular of tax havens, is something with which the world has learned to live. As international tax arbitrage is inevitable, all a jurisdiction can do is to make what internal adjustments it can in order to minimise its effect, and the moves made by the EC in response to the problems for the providers of telecommunication services within the EC form an example of such a response.

Much of the above discussion centred on the distinction between goods and services, and the competitive advantage given to non-EC suppliers of services to domestic purchasers. Perhaps the concept of belonging is outdated in the context of the provision of electronic services. If the tax charge depends on the place of belonging of the supplier, and if it is easy for a supplier to locate in a low tax jurisdiction, is not the solution to shift focus to the place of consumption, and, as with telecommunication services, to charge tax according to the jurisdiction of the consumer rather than the supplier? Not only is this less likely to encourage tax distorted behaviour (unlike suppliers, consumers are unlikely to change their place of residence to another tax jurisdiction simply because certain services are cheaper), but it is consistent with the notion of VAT as a tax on the consumer. Whether this can be done without imposing a significant extra administrative burden on overseas suppliers is not clear, and the UK tax authorities will be watching closely to see how the use and enjoyment provisions imposed in relation to telecommunications services work out in practice.

There are relatively few telecommunications companies and ISPs in comparison with the unimaginable number of content providers,[51] and the services

---

[49] Commission Document "A European Initiative in Electronic Commerce" Com(97) 157 final.

[50] If this seems to overstate the case, consider the relative rates of tax on petrol in the car-loving US in comparison with Europe and, within Europe, the rates of excise duty on alcohol in the fastidious north in contrast to the convivial south.

[51] In 1996 it was estimated that there were 250,000 commercial sites: Department of the Treasury, Office of Tax Policy "Selected Tax Policy Implications of Global Electronic Commerce" November 1996, ftp://ftp.fedworld.gov/pub/tel/internet.wp. This figure will already be out of date.

provided by an ISP tend to be concentrated within one state. This will not be the case in relation to distributors of software for example. The practical difficulties of registering and policing the use and enjoyment provisions in relation to potentially millions of providers, who may have difficulties identifying the location of their customers, may well prove to be overwhelming, in which case other solutions may have to be found.

If it is decided that the difficulties of policing transactions and the consequential potential for evasion are insurmountable, or that the administrative burdens imposed on suppliers are becoming untenable, some consideration of entirely new tax methods might be appropriate. The idea of a "bit" tax has been around for some time, but concrete proposals have not yet been put forward.[52] The general idea of a bit tax is that there is a minute tax on every megabit of data passed over the Internet by the establishment of tax "toll booths", so the challenges of taxing transactions are bypassed by a tax on use. Superficially attractive, difficulties with the bit tax become quickly apparent when one ponders questions of jurisdiction, allocation, and perhaps above all, enforcement and collection. There is a view that such a tax would be entirely impossible to operate given the anarchic and amorphous nature of the Internet.

A further difficulty with replacing VAT with the bit tax in relation to certain transactions is that a line is being drawn from a tax point of view between transactions which are essentially identical. It is evident that the Internet will be a powerful tool in international commerce and should not be discouraged by a heavier tax burden. It is equally clear that one does not want to permit the tax take to be diminished by under-taxing Internet transactions. It would be extremely difficult to design a bit tax which in respect of an individual transaction would even approximate with the sales tax or VAT which it is replacing.

In any event, the bit tax seems to be off the current agenda. The United States seems to have ruled it out in their recent policy document on electronic commerce:[53]

> "Therefore, the United States will advocate in the World Trade Organisation (WTO) and other appropriate international fora that the Internet be declared a tariff-free environment whenever it is used to deliver products or services.
>
> This principle should be established quickly before nations impose tariffs and before vested interests form to protect those tariffs.
>
> In addition, the United States believes that no new taxes should be imposed on Internet commerce. The taxation of commerce conducted over the Internet should be consistent with the established principles of international taxation, should avoid inconsistent national tax jurisdictions and double taxation, and should be simple to administer and easy to understand."

[52] See Soete "The "BIT TAX ": the case for further research" (April 1997) for further discussion http://www.lovotax.nl/tax/onderwerp5/15.html.

[53] "The Framework for Global Electronic Commerce" July 1997 published by the Inter-agency working group under Vice President Gore, available on the Whitehouse web page: www.whitehouse.gov/WH/New/Commerce/.

In addition, it is not at present finding favour with the EC, and has been publicly dismissed as a possibility by the EC Commissioner for the Internal Market, Mario Monti.[54]

An alternative answer might be, as suggested in the first part of the above quote from the US policy document, to relieve software and computer services from VAT or sales tax altogether. An argument used by the industry is that their supplies do not involve the use of infrastructure or the resources of a jurisdiction in the same way as the production of tangible goods, so they should not bear the same tax burden as other suppliers. The weakness with this argument is that it not only presupposes that it is appropriate to collect tax according to the benefit gained by the taxpayer rather than on other measures such as ability to pay, or place of consumption, but also ignores the fact that consumer taxes are supposed to accrue to the state of consumption rather than the state which has contributed most in the way of infrastructure, the state of production.

A more pragmatic argument for the removal of VAT on software and other computer services is that it will remove one of the incentives for suppliers of such services who are aiming at the European domestic market to establish themselves in jurisdictions where no VAT is imposed, for example the United States. The VAT foregone may conceivably be recouped by an increased tax take on corporate profits arising in the UK if, by taking VAT out of the equation, suppliers establish themselves in the UK. The extent to which this will be successful depends in large part on how confident suppliers are of tax havens which charge little or no direct tax. If VAT is taken out of the equation there is no overwhelming direct tax incentive to set up in the United States, but there is in a tax haven such as the Bahamas, which deliberately offers corporate tax incentives to encourage the establishment of companies. Whether businesses will be put off tax havens by other drawbacks, such as reduced legal protection or the existence of a less skilled workforce, will remain to be seen.

It is all very well for the US to suggest abandoning any attempt to tax Internet commerce, as there is in general no tax on services, and as mentioned earlier, out of state supplies of goods escape local sales taxes. It is at the moment very difficult to estimate what the potential loss of revenue would be should the EC decide that neither the provision of services over the Internet nor the downloading of computer software should be subject to tax. There would be limited tax losses in respect of supplies to the business market as transactions between taxable persons generate no revenue, so the losses will largely concern supplies to the domestic consumer, which may not be enormous at present, but are only likely to increase. Careful calculations on the likely loss of revenue would require to be undertaken to establish whether this is a step which can be afforded.

[54] Speech by Monti on 8 July 1997 to the European Ministerial Conference "Global Information Networks" http://europa.en.int/rapid/cgi/rapcgi.ks. See also Commission document "A European Initiative in Electronic Commerce", op. cit. note 48.

B DIRECT TAXATION

Before a state can levy a tax on profits, a connection, or "tax nexus", must be established between itself and those profits. The rules which establish nexus are varied, but are generally in some way associated with physical or legal presence in a state. For example, the UK taxes the profits of companies which are resident in the UK, and also seeks to tax profits of non-resident companies trading in the UK through a branch or agency. Residence is established in the UK either by incorporation in the UK,[55] or by having a place of central management or control in the UK.[56] Other jurisdictions adopt other criteria, such as place of registered office, place of effective management, place of residence of controlling shareholders, domicile of controlling directors, place where the shareholders' meetings are held and so on. Two things should be immediately apparent. First, a company can easily be regarded as resident in more than one jurisdiction. Second, its overseas profits can be subject to tax by two jurisdictions: the country of *source* (ie the country in which the profits are actually made), and the country of the company's *residence*.

The potential for double taxation is not new and for many years countries have negotiated with each other to establish a network of double taxation treaties. One thing which such a treaty will do is to provide a tie breaker rule to establish one country of residence, and then allocate profits between competing tax jurisdictions. Most treaties operate on the basis that the profits of an enterprise will be taxed in the state in which that enterprise is resident, only ceding the right to tax to the country of source where there is sufficient presence in the country of source to amount to a "permanent establishment".[57] In either case, the profits are taxed in the country where the business is, rather than where its consumers are.

The issues which the Internet raises for corporate taxation fall into two main categories, although both concern jurisdictional issues caused by the slippery nature of electronic presence. The first question is to what extent a computer presence in a tax jurisdiction will be regarded as establishing a tax nexus. This is already a pressing issue as it concerns traditional business organisations, albeit using the global communication network to market and perhaps distribute their goods. The second question concerns how one taxes an enterprise which lacks very much at all in the way of any physical presence. This is likely to become an increasingly important issue as the design, production, marketing and delivery of new goods and services take place electronically, with no offices, factories or warehouses to link the business to a specific physical location.

---

[55] Finance Act 1988, s 66(1).
[56] *De Beers Consolidated Mines Ltd v Howe* [1906]AC 455.
[57] Article 7 in each of the OECD, the UN and the US model conventions is to this effect.

Can a computer constitute taxable presence?

A business which uses the net to help sell its products can do so in a variety of ways. It may simply take advantage of a Web page to advertise its wares, providing no interactive facility. However, it may provide an application form, which the user completes, giving credit card or e-cash details, which is transmitted to a distribution centre for checking and delivery. Finally, where the order is for electronic goods or services, the order may be processed by the server which then "delivers" them automatically without any outside involvement at all. If a Web page has any physical location at all, it must be on a server. However, a business will frequently not own its own server, but will share one with other users through an ISP. There will often be more than one server in operation, to avoid traffic jams or to provide local reduced-rate access. The point is, whether a transaction is conducted from one server rather than another, and where a particular server is located, is often a matter of chance.

Does the existence of a server performing any of the activities described above add up to a permanent establishment?

a) Treaty Provisions

Typically, a double tax treaty will provide that a permanent establishment is a fixed place of business through which the business of an enterprise is wholly or partly carried on. The term in the model treaties is expressly stated to include a place of management, a branch, an office a factory and a workshop,[58] all of which require some physical presence. So, would a computer in a room on its own suffice? Finding the appropriate analogy in the physical world is not easy. On one view, the server which can deliver the goods is rather like a catalogue store, which does constitute a fixed place of business. Even a shared server might be regarded as similar to space rented in a shopping centre. However, if there is no individual making decisions or taking action where the server is situated, the analogy begins to break down.

The Commentary to the OECD model treaty states "a permanent establishment may nevertheless exist if the business of the enterprise is carried on mainly through automatic equipment", going on to give particular examples of "gaming and vending machines and the like", but gives the impression that the machines must be operated and maintained by the business or a dependent agent.[59] The European Court of Justice has decided in the context of VAT that the mere presence of gaming machines in a territory without permanent personnel was not sufficient to constitute a "fixed establishment".[60]

---

[58] Article 5 of the model conventions.
[59] Commentary to Article 5(4) of the OECD Convention, paragraph 10.
[60] *Berkholz* supra note 26.

It seems unlikely in light of the above that simply to advertise on a server could render that server a permanent establishment. It may even come within one of the specific exceptions to a permanent establishment provided by the model treaties, namely "the use of facilities" and "the maintenance of a stock of goods or merchandise" which in both cases are "solely for the purposes of storage, display or delivery".[61] If the server is capable itself of delivering the product, does this come within the exception? Not presumably if it receives orders and runs credit checks as then it is not solely for the purposes of storage, display or delivery. In any event, are electronic products "goods" for the purposes of the exception?

Where the server does process the order, there is the possibility it may come within the "dependent agent" rule. A permanent establishment may be created through the use of an agent if such agent is "acting on behalf of an enterprise and has, and habitually exercises, in a Contracting State an authority to conclude contracts on behalf of the enterprise".[62] The Commentary adds that the agents may be individuals or companies, but is silent on the significance of a computer acting on an enterprise's behalf, and the rule in the UK at least appears to be that an agent must be a juristic or natural person, and that a machine is just an extension of the legal person for whom it acts.[63]

b) UK domestic provisions

If issues of this kind arise between the UK and a country with which the UK has no double tax agreement, then the matter is resolved by domestic law.[64] The existence of a server in the UK will not on its own constitute the place of central management and control, but could it amount to trading there through a branch or agency? The case law, which does not concern the new technologies, has identified the place where the contract is made as being an important factor,[65] and, as has been pointed out elsewhere, this is not unproblematic in the context of contracts made over the Internet.[66] However the place of the contract is not decisive, and more recent cases have sought to identify "the place from which the profits in substance arise".[67] Without clearer judicial guidance, it must remain dubious to what extent computer presence in the UK can amount to taxable presence.

---

[61] OECD Model Convention, Article 5 para 4(a) and (b).

[62] Ibid. Article 5, para 5.

[63] *Thornton v Shoe Lane Parking* [1971]2 Q.B.163.The case concerned an automated parking ticket machine.

[64] The UK has one of the most extensive networks of DTAs—over 100 compared with the US's 48.

[65] E.g. *Grainger and Son v Gough* [1896] AC 325, in which a French wine merchant with sales agents in Britain was held not to be trading in the UK as the orders were sent to him in France for acceptance, thus the contracts were made in France.

[66] See MacQueen and Davies at pp. 121 and 97 respectively.

[67] Atkin L.J. in *F.L. Smidth & Co. v Greenwood* 8 TC 193 at 203–4, cited with approval in *Firestone Tyre and Rubber Co. Ltd. v Llewellin* (1957) 37 TC 111 at pp. 142–3.

If the presence of a server *can* constitute a taxable presence, the next issue is the allocation of taxable profits between the state of residence, and the state or states of taxable presence. In the UK, trading income from the branch, or royalty income from property held by the branch, is taxable in the UK in the absence of a double taxation treaty.[68] Under treaty, it is usually the profits "attributable" to or the royalties in respect of property "effectively connected" with the permanent establishment which are taxable in the country of permanent establishment.[69] Even where a business operates through one server this is problematic, but where there are two, in different jurisdictions, or which are changed from time to time by the ISP, the difficulties multiply.

Two conclusions can be drawn from the above discussion. First, the issue as to whether a server can create a tax nexus is profoundly uncertain. Second, the problems created if it can are so messy as to be virtually insoluble. Given that it is largely a matter of expediency where a server is located, it is suggested that a server should be afforded no more status than a mere warehouse, even where it is able to process and deliver orders. This does not mean that the profits will remain untaxed as there will still usually be a state which is able to establish a tax nexus through other means. This however leads on the second matter of particular concern for corporate taxation, where much more intractable problems are caused by the mobility of electronic businesses and the potential lack of physical presence.

Source or residence taxation of cyberspace companies

It was mentioned earlier that the traditional method of taxing profits is to look to where the business is physically carried out. In the electronic world into which we are entering, there may be no physical presence: directors may hold board meetings and take decisions by video link or other electronic means, the workforce can be linked together by email, deliveries or services can be provided on-line, and its finances could be dealt with by an electronic bank. And satellites have not even been mentioned. The concept of permanent establishment, bound up as it is with the idea of physical presence, simply cannot cope.

The US Treasury's preliminary response has been to suggest a move away from concepts such as permanent establishment, of which an enterprise may have many, back to the principle of taxation by the country of residence:

"The growth of new communications technologies and electronic commerce will likely require that principles of residence-based taxation assume even greater importance. In the world of cyberspace, it is often difficult, if not impossible, to apply traditional source concepts to link an item of income with a specific geographical location. Therefore, source based taxation could lose its rationale and be rendered

[68] ICTA 1988 s 11.
[69] Article 7.

obsolete by electronic commerce. By contrast, almost all taxpayers are resident somewhere. An individual is almost always a citizen or resident of a given country and, at least under US law, all corporations must be established under the laws of a given jurisdiction. However, a review of current residency definitions and taxation rules may be appropriate."[70]

The experience of the use of double taxation agreements is that it is generally possible to establish one place of residence for companies, even if this is finally done by reference to its place of incorporation or registration, but the benefit of certainty attained by the use of this criterion has to be set against the resistance which will be generated among states which will lose revenue as a result of such a move. It may not be entirely coincidental that this proposal has emerged from the United States, which currently enjoys a virtual monopoly on software producers, but if new businesses engaged in the production of electronic products start to locate themselves in "flag of convenience" countries, one might imagine that the attraction of residence based taxation might diminish even to the US. Perhaps the answer then is to return to the concept of permanent establishment, but to refine it, for example, by defining it as the country where the majority of residence criteria apply. Alternatively, the unitary taxation method of allocating profits between tax jurisdictions, depending on factors such as sales, premises and workforce, although recently having taken a nose-dive in popularity might provide another solution.

C TRADING INCOME OR ROYALTY INCOME?

The final matter to be dealt with is the correct classification of payments for the receipt of software, or the use in general of Internet services. Earlier discussion in the context of VAT assumed that the payments were either for goods or services. There is another possibility: that the user is paying royalties for the use of an intangible.

There are a number of departure points from a tax point of view between trading income and royalty income:

i) royalty income is often subject to withholding tax when paid overseas: in the UK for example, tax at basic rate must be deducted from periodical payments of copyright or design royalties where the usual place of abode of the owner of the copyright or design is outside the UK[71] unless the payment is to be paid gross under treaty;[72]

---

[70] US Department of the Treasury, Office of Tax Policy "Selected Tax Policy Implications of Global Electronic Commerce" November 1996"para 7.1.5 op cit. supra n. 51.

[71] ICTA 1988 s 536, s 537B. This does not cover copyright in a cinematograph film or video recording, but if these are downloaded, it is not clear the exemption would apply.

[72] Article 12 of the OECD model concerns income from royalties, and provides for taxation in the state of residence of the owner, thus limiting the right of the source country to apply

ii) certain countries do not allow royalties paid to be deducted for the purposes of the payer's tax unless the recipient also resides in the same state or is taxable in that state;

iii) royalty income will not be subject to VAT, import taxes or customs duties;

iv) royalty income may be treated differently from trading income for the purposes of setting off deductions and expenses.

The term royalty is defined in the OECD model treaty as a payment "of any kind received as a consideration for the use of or the right to use, any copyright of any literary, artistic or scientific work, including cinematograph films, any patent, trade mark, design or model, plan, secret formula or process, or for information concerning industrial, commercial or scientific experience." In the UK, computer programmes are regarded as literary works.[73]

Solutions to the classification problem have been suggested by the OECD[74] and appear in the revised commentary on the relevant article on royalty income in the OECD model which explicitly deals with the problems associated with sales of computer software.[75] Broadly the Commentary attempts to characterise income from the sale of computer software according to its substance rather than its form, and generally treats it as giving rise to business profits where the software is used for the purchaser's personal or business use, and treating it as royalty income only where the purchaser is to exploit the software for commercial purposes.

The Commentary identifies three situations: the partial transfer of rights, the alienation of rights and payments under mixed contracts and make recommendations in relation to each.

The normal transaction relating to software is for a partial transfer of rights to take place, as the acquirer receives certain rights of use or exploitation, whilst the owner retains ownership. In cases of a partial transfer of rights, the payment will be treated as business income of the recipient where the payment is for the personal or business use of the purchaser. It is of no relevance that the purchaser's use of the software is limited or that the copyright remains with the seller. Only in unusual situations will payments for partial transfer of rights be treated as royalty income, for example where the original author places part of his rights at the disposal of a third party to enable the latter to develop or exploit it.

---

withholding tax. The corresponding article in the US model simply provides for the state of residence to have the primary right rather than the exclusive right.

[73] Copyright, Designs and Patents Act 1988 S 3(1)(b).

[74] OECD "The Tax Treatment of Software, Issues in International Taxation No 4" (1992)

[75] Revised Commentary on Article 12 paragraphs 12–17 (post 1992 version). Article 12 concerns income from royalties, and provides for taxation in the country of residence of the owner. The corresponding article in the US model simply provides for the state of residence to have the primary right rather than the exclusive right.

Where rights are fully alienated as a result of payment, this is clearly not a payment of a royalty, which is a payment for the use not the transfer of rights. Where the alienation is extensive although not partial, it is still unlikely that the income will be royalty income, even if it is paid in instalments or related to a contingency, and in such cases the disposal will normally be regarded as disposal of capital.

An example of a mixed contract is a contract of purchase of hardware with built-in software and concessions for the right to use the software combined with the provision of services. In such cases the Commentaries recommend that the starting point is to break down the contract into its various parts and to apportion the payments into, for example, payment for the hardware, payment for the use, and payment for the continuing services, and to tax them appropriately. In light of the view on the partial transfer of rights discussed above, even the part relating to use will not normally be classified as a royalty.

Whilst the OECD has been applauded for its work on payments for computer software,[76] in practice a number of countries have placed reservations on the article. For example, Spain reserves the right to tax payments for the use of software as royalty income even where the use is not exploitation. Canada and the US have also placed less extensive although still important reservations on the article. For example the US reserves the right to treat payments for software as royalty income where the payments are related to profitability.[77]

The United States is similarly in the process of addressing this issue and has proposed regulations which attempt to classify income from the sale of computer programmes.[78] The term "copyrighted article" is used to apply to the restricted rights of use a purchaser of computer software receives, in contrast to the normal copyright rights such as the right to reproduce the work, make derivative works, or distribute copies of the work. The acquisition of a "copyrighted article" is to be treated as a purchase of goods even where it is characterised by the parties as the grant of a licence, and even where it is downloaded rather than supplied on a physical medium. The sale of substantially all the rights in the software is to be treated as a sale of goods, and where the sale is for the exploitation rather than the use of the software, the income is to be treated as royalty income.

The issue of classification into royalty or other income is the one which, with international co-operation, is probably most easily capable of resolution.

[75] Sprague and Chesler "Comments of the Commentary to Article 12 (Royalties) of the 1992 OECD Model Convention" Intertax (1993) 310

[76] See Klaus Vogel on Double Taxation Conventions (2nd ed. with supplement) for a full list of reservations.

[77] United States Department of the Treasury *Proposed Regulations on the Classification of Certain Transactions Involving Computer Programs* Reg.-251520-96

[78] "Managing the value network" Ernst and Young, May 1997.

Both the OECD and the United States Treasury appear to be thinking along the same lines, although there are still points of divergence which will need to be worked out. There is an underlying issue of tax jurisdiction which might make universal acceptance of their proposals more problematic than might be anticipated. The point is that most software companies operate out of the United States. Where their products are provided through permanent establishments situated in other countries, this creates a tax nexus sufficient for that other country to share in the tax take on the profits. Where the product is supplied electronically, there is unlikely to be a tax nexus in the state of the user, and withholding tax on royalty income is the only way in which the state of the user is able to take a slice, although before the United States are accused too quickly of tax imperialism, one should add that under most treaties, withholding taxes are reduced or removed.

CONCLUSION

As computers become more sophisticated and more secure the volume of transactions conducted over the Internet is bound to increase. A recent report by Ernst and Young[79] predicted that the proportion of financial services companies using the Internet is set to rise to 60% by 1999 as compared with 13% now. The Chartered Institute of Taxation has warned of the potential loss of billions of pounds of revenue as a result of cyberspace trading,[80] and if they are right, these billions would have to be made up from other sources, shifting the delicate balance of various tax revenue sources in the UK and elsewhere and threatening the integrity of tax systems. The existence of readily available encryption software up to military standard, and the unregulated and amorphous nature of the Web make it near inevitable that tax evasion on individual transactions is going to take place, and without adopting an entirely different approach such as a bit tax, there will undoubtedly be loss of revenue.

Accepting this, there is massive room for improvement in tax systems worldwide and it may be that the best starting point lies in international co-operation in seeking consistent definitions. The lack of interface between tax systems makes avoidance easier, but, perhaps even worse, often makes it impossible for those who want to comply to do so. Tax co-ordination across state borders is critical to establishing systems which will go even close to dealing properly and fairly with Internet commerce and one of the easiest ways for states to cooperate is in developing workable classifications which can be operated by the users of the tax system. The OECD's work on the classification of income from sales of software is an example of what can be achieved. Fitting Internet transactions into traditional classifications created

---

[80] *Financial Times*, 9 June 1997. The CIoT is the professional organisation of the tax profession in the UK.

for a tangible environment has not worked well, and even within the EC there are inconsistencies of interpretation. Further work on this area is urgently needed.

The US policy document quoted above identifies the following aims for a tax system: that it does not distort or hinder commerce; that it is simple, transparent and places a minimum burden on those who are required to account for it; and that it can accommodate tax systems world-wide.[81] Even if these aims are too lofty, on the above evidence the taxation of Internet commerce has some way to go.

---

[81] "The Framework for Global Electronic Commerce" July 1997 op cit. supra n 53.

PART 4
Liability for Content on the Internet

10

Defamation and the Internet

LILIAN EDWARDS[1]

In recent years, defamation or libel on the Internet has become one of the hot topics of Internet law. Many gallons of both real and virtual ink have been spilled in computer and legal journals, as well as on-line electronic fora, as the impact of "terrestrial" defamation law on both suppliers and consumers of Internet services has been debated.[2] This article will not attempt a comprehensive treatment of the area[3] but will focus on two crucial points.

(i) why users of the Internet are more likely than ordinary citizens to be found publishing comments which are actionable as defamatory, and

(ii) what problems (or, looking at it from the other side of the fence, opportunities) arise if those who are the victims of defamatory comments on the net attempt to seek compensation by taking legal action.

Two preliminary points are worth emphasising at the start. First, any lawyer looking at the problem of Internet libel is immediately struck by the fact that it is has an inherently transnational nature. Because of the international connectivity of the Internet, its speedy transmission of huge amounts of data simultaneously to multiple destinations, and general lack of respect for national borders, it is extremely easy for an individual to make a defamatory comment via a computer situated in (say) Scotland attached to the Internet, which can then be read by thousands if not millions of people similarly equipped in multiple other national jurisdictions—where (as discussed below) the law of, and defences to, defamation may be very different than those found in the Scottish legal system. In pre-Internet days, such transnational

---

[1] Lecturer in Private Law, University of Edinburgh; email L.Edwards@ed.ac.uk.

[2] See for only a small selection, T A Cutrera "Computer Networks: Libel and the First Amendment" (1992) 11 Computer Law Journal 557; E J Naughton "Is Cyberspace a Public Forum? Computer Bulletin Boards, Free Speech and State Action" (1992) 81 Georgetown Law Journal 409; T Arnold-Moore "Legal Pitfalls in Cyberspace: Defamation on Computer Networks" (1994) 5 Journal of Law and Information Science 165 ; N Braithwaite "The Internet and bulletin board defamations" (1995) 145 New Law Journal 1216; F Auburn "Usenet News and the Law" (1995) 1 Web LJ; H Pearson "Liability of Bulletin Board Operators" [1995] 2 CTLR 54; S Dooley "Specific Risks on the Internet: Defamation" (1995) Computers and Law, Oct/Nov, 10; D Howarth *Textbook on Tort* (Butterworth, 1995) pp 563-565; C Waelde and L Edwards "Defamation and the Internet: A Case Study of Anomalies and Difficulties in the Information Age" (1996) 2 Int Rev of Law, Computers and Technology 263.

[3] For such a survey, see Waelde and Edwards, op cit n 1.

publication would have, for economic reasons, been almost exclusively the preserve of a large traditional publisher, such as a newspaper, TV station or book publishing house, who would be likely to have both the resources and the foresight to take legal advice, and to have a system of prior checking in place, to avoid incurring exactly such legal liability. Very few of the individuals now setting up home page Web sites, contributing to newsgroups, sending email or taking part in Internet Relay Chat (IRC) will have such defensive strategies or knowledge of what speech might be legally actionable. Where defamatory statements cross national boundaries, inevitably problems of international private law are invoked, with difficult questions raised such as what country (or countries) will have jurisdiction to hear any action for damages raised, what country's law should govern the action (the choice of law question) and if a decree is obtained, how can it be enforced if the defender lives outwith the jurisdiction of the court (as will frequently be the case)? Those libelled on the Internet may find then that their case is not the simplest to pursue. By way of comfort, however, Internet libel defenders may also be dismayed to find that they can be sued in the courts of multiple countries to which they have little or no connection, and where the law applied is foreign to them in the extreme. Hardened libel lawyers will say there is nothing very new here, which is, formally, true—but the problems of traditional publishing and defamation are so multiplied when applied to a forum as large, as accessible, as cheap and as transnational as the Internet, that it is not hard to see why there is a perception that the law of libel has been transformed by its application to the new electronic highway.

Secondly, Internet users cannot be regarded as a homogenous group. In particular, it is important to separate out the potential liability of those who give individuals and corporations *access* to read, and write to, the Internet : not just the so-called Internet Service Providers (ISPs) such as CompuServe, Demon, Pipex, America On-Line et al, who typically provide access to the Internet on monthly subscription or at an hourly rate, but also non-commercial hosts such as universities, who give Internet access for free to many students and staff, and corporate hosts, who have an Internet link (whether dedicated, or via an ISP) and allow their employees, and perhaps their clients, access to the Internet via their facilities. The particular problems of Internet Service Providers (and equivalent hosts) in this area are considered below.

SITES OF DEFAMATION ON THE INTERNET

In considering why the Internet is a defamation prone zone, there are at least four distinct sites where defamation may occur on the Internet that can usefully be separated out, as to some extent they raise distinct problems.

(i) One to one email messages

As anyone who has used email will know, it is remarkably quick and easy to use. Comments can be typed in haste and sent at the press of a button. Compared to conventional written correspondence, where there is typically time to draft the statement, print or type it out, re-read, re-draft, and then *think* before signing, putting the message in an envelope, attaching a stamp and putting in the post, transmission of email is virtually instantaneous and usually, once sent, is irrevocable. As a result, email correspondence is often in substance more like spoken conversation than written interaction for habitual users—hasty, ungrammatical and rash—and tends to lead parties to say things they would not only not normally commit to writing, let alone widely published writing, but would in fact often also not say in face to face interaction with the other party. Psychologically, electronic interaction combines a sort of deceptive distance—one is after all sitting safe behind a terminal in one's own office when writing—with a kind of equally deceptive intimacy. Studies and anecdotal evidence show that there is a lack of body language, eye contact or spoken cues, as there would be in conversation or on the phone, to prevent the making of inappropriate statements.[4] All this means that those sending email are dangerously prone to making remarks that turn out to be legally actionable.

To add insult to injury, it is very easy to repeat or forward the defamatory comments of *others* via email, and in the libel law of many countries, a re-publisher is just as liable as the original publisher (barring the possibility of innocent dissemination defences, discussed below).[5] For example, party A receives an email concerning the foul practices of a competitor and forwards it with a few keystrokes to parties C and D who later send it on to E and F.[6] Only later is it discovered that the message is not true; subsequently the competitor discovers the re-publication and sues party A rather than or as well as the original author who may be (say) without funds. In this way, actionable email statements can be re-published far and wide with the speed of transmission of any other computer virus.

Sending an email containing defamatory statements about person B from person A to person B will in some legal systems not be regarded as "publication" for the purposes of libel law, since there is no communication to the public but only to the libelled recipient. This is true, for example, of English law,[7]

---

[4] See Cutrera, op cit n. 1, at 559-560.

[5] In Scots law, for example, any repetition of a defamatory statement is actionable (see *Hayford v Forrester-Paton* 1927 SC 740.)

[6] These were very much the facts of the recent Western Provident case, discussed below at p. 187.

[7] *Pullman v Hill* [1891] 1 QB 524. It is possible however that emails might be regarded as inherently insecure and so as akin to postcards, which may be read by anyone in transit, in which case communication to a third party is not essential for publication even in English law (*Sadgrove v Hole* [1901] 1 KB 1 and see B Napier "Logging on To Libel Laws (1995) 92 Law Society Gazette 21.)

but not apparently, of Scots law.[8] However, as is true with Internet publication generally, emails can be, and often are, sent across national boundaries eg from Scotland to England, or to France or the US. As already mentioned, this may mean that the law governing any potential action may not be that of the defender's residence or domicile. Thus the risk will not go away just because the email sender (or their ISP) are resident in England.

(ii) Mailing lists

The format of an electronic mailing list is that various parties subscribe by email to the list, which is administered by some central host. The subject of discussion of the list may be anything from Internet law to real ale to homosexual fantasies. Usually the list is set up so that, by default, any email message sent by any one subscriber to the list, is "bounced" or "exploded out" to every other subscriber (many of whom will, as the parlance goes, "lurk" and never be known to exist to the person commenting). Mailing lists combine all the general problems of email discussed above, with some extra difficulties of their own. It is very easy for the slightly careless or inexperienced user of such a list to think they are replying *only* to the maker of a particular comment— but *actually* send their reply to every member of the list. The embarrassment factor can be considerable, particularly where the members of the list form a small professional community within which the professional reputation of the person defamed can be severely damaged. It is not a coincidence that one of the very few cases across the globe on Internet libel not settled out of court, *Rindos v Hardwick*,[9] revolved around comments made on a mailing list for academic anthropologists in which comments were made implying that Rindos, the Australian plaintiff, had been denied tenure because he was not a properly ethical researcher and was academically incompetent.

(iii) Newsgroups, the USENET and discussion fora

Newsgroups are discussion fora which are made up of comments from their subscribers, sorted by subject matter. All it takes to subscribe and post comments to a newsgroup is rudimentary software, obtainable for free as shareware, and an Internet connection. Collectively, the newsgroups available to Internet users are sometimes known as the "Usenet".[10] There are something like 14,000 Usenet newsgroups subscribed to en masse by millions of subscribers, located in every country where there is Internet access. As a result, any comment posted to a Usenet newsgroup is virtually guaranteed to be published, and read, within days if not hours, in many hundreds of national

---

[8] See K McK Norrie *Defamation and Related Actions in Scots Law* (Butterworths, 1995), p 28.
[9] Unreported, Supreme Court of Western Australia, 31 March 1994. See comment in Auburn, op cit n 1.
[10] See further Terrett, p. 22.

jurisdictions. As can be imagined, the volume of material published in these fora is enormous—one estimate is that around 4 million articles are available at any particular time.

Newsgroups are even more problematic from the defamation point of view than the rest of the Internet because of what may be described as traditional "Internet culture". Until very recently—roughly, the early Nineties—the Internet was largely the domain of technophiles, students, academics and workers in the computer industry, principally in the US. These users largely accessed the Internet for free and used it for non-commercial purposes. There was a strong collective sentiment towards anarchy, libertarianism and free speech rights—and a strong corresponding dislike of corporate, governmental or legal authority or control. In this culture, full, frank and unfettered discussion known as "flaming", which was often indistinguishable from rudeness and abuse, was not only tolerated but by and large encouraged. The usual remedy for being flamed was not to post a writ for libel, but extra-legal self help—in other words, flame back. It was and is not uncommon for newsgroups to degenerate into "flame wars"—torrents of abusive comments which destroy all sensible discussion in the group. This was all very well, perhaps, when most Internet users shared a similar cultural background. But in recent years the Internet has ceased to be the domain of "netizens" and become extensively used by individuals and families, including children, who pay for Internet access and expect it to respect the same standards of decency and courtesy as other media. Even more importantly, corporate use has expanded enormously, as firms who see the Internet as a domain for commercial expansion establish their own connections and Web sites. For these users, flaming and abuse are not acceptable, nor are self-help remedies, and preservation of corporate reputation is paramount. Corporate culture now seems to have firmly encountered the Internet as in July 1997, the first corporate email libel case known to be settled in the UK received extensive publicity. This case was brought by Western Provident Association who sued Norwich Union Healthcare for spreading allegedly untrue rumours on its internal email system about Western's financial stability.[11] A settlement was reached under which Western Provident paid out the not insubstantial sum of £450,000.[12]

(iv) The World Wide Web

The Web is now so large, and increasing in size so fast that it is impossible even to pin down estimates of its size. In September 1996, there were 30

---

[11] *Scotsman*, 18 July 1997.

[12] The asserted clash between "traditional" Internet culture and "new" corporate Internet culture can be seen in many other areas under discussion in this volume. In the field of trademarks and domain names, for example (see further Waelde, p. 45) there have been running clashes between Internet "pirates" who have "poached" the domain names normally associated with corporate brand names such as MacDonalds and Harrods, and the corporations in question, who have turned to conventional legal remedies for trademark infringement to rectify what they perceive as interference with their business interests.

million Web pages, located on 275,000 servers, indexed by the Alta Vista search engine. At around the same date, it was estimated that the Web doubled in size every 45 days.[13] Like newsgroups, Web sites can be accessed and read in multiple jurisdictions, and they therefore share many of the problems of transnational publication discussed above. But perhaps the major unique problem with the Web is how far it allows any individual to mimic traditional publishing at very low cost. "Home pages" can be set up which do a good job of looking like electronic journals or glossy magazines and which can be extremely attractive, with good design and graphic content. However many of the parties setting up Web sites—often fans of popular music or TV programmes, students, pressure groups, or amateur associations—are not already hard copy or traditional publishers, have no knowledge of the law of defamation or libel, and may well find themselves publishing defamatory statements without fully appreciating their potential liability.[14] There has already been one at least one case in the UK where proceedings have been initiated against a Web publisher for libel. In February 1996, the Poetry Society was sued for publishing a Web page in which a vanity publishing company was accused of "preying on poets who could not otherwise get their poems published". The matter appears to have been subsequently settled out of court. Interestingly, although the Poetry Society's web site at the time was itself physically hosted by the BBC server, there seems to have been no attempt made to involve the BBC as co-defenders, possibly because the aim was removal of the offending statement rather than financial compensation.

PROBLEMS AND OPPORTUNITIES FOR INTERNET LIBEL PURSUERS AND DEFENDERS

Jurisdiction, choice of law and enforcement

As mentioned above, one of the major features of Internet libel or defamation is that it will often have been transmitted across national boundaries. In such cases, it will be necessary for a plaintiff or pursuer to work out where he or she may, and perhaps may most advantageously, raise any action. Once jurisdiction is established, there is then the question of establishing choice of law. There are self-evidently crucial differences between national laws of defamation which may favour either the pursuer or defender. For example, if we take a random scenario :

[13] *Scotland on Sunday*, 26 May 1996. For further information on the Web, see Terrett, p. 19.
[14] Equally they may well unknowingly breach the law of copyright and trademark. See, for example, the rock group Oasis's warning of their intention to crack down on unauthorised use of copyrighted material relating to the band by amateur "fan" Web sites (*Financial Times*, June 5 1997).

> *An individual resident and domiciled in Scotland posts a defamatory comment about a person also resident and domiciled in Scotland, but having a national reputation throughout the UK, to a Usenet newsgroup. The group is read by subscribers in many countries, including England. The defamed party wishes to sue.*

The obvious court in which to sue is the Court of Session in Scotland. But under the Civil Jurisdiction and Judgements Act 1982, Schedule 8 (which applies in cases between two Scottish domiciliaries) there can be jurisdiction *either* in the court of the defender's domicile—Scotland—*or* in the place where the delict is committed. Where is a delict such as defamation committed? There are two obvious interpretations—firstly, the place where the remark was originally made (the "source" of the delict); and secondly the place where the remark is "published " ie, where it is made public and has an impact on the reputation of the person defamed (the "target" of the delict). Case-law from the European Court of Justice interpreting the Brussels Convention—notably the recent referral to the ECJ from the House of Lords in the case of *Shevill v Presse Alliance S.A.*[15]—seems clearly to establish that either interpretation is a valid alternative for the purposes of fixing jurisdiction. Thus in our scenario, notwithstanding the fact that both the pursuer and defender are Scots, there is jurisdiction in both Scotland and England. Where there is both publication, and a reputation to be affected in England, the pursuer may well wish to think about suing in England, where the damages award will almost certainly be higher than in Scotland. This is legitimate forum shopping, but one important caveat must be made; another matter clarified in *Shevill* is that if the action is raised in England on this kind of basis, damages can only be sought in respect of damage caused to the reputation in that jurisdiction. To sue for damage caused by the defamatory statement in *every* jurisdiction where it was published—which could be every country where the newsgroup was read in the case of a global celebrity with a matching reputation—the action must be raised in the courts of the domicile of the defender (in this example, Scotland). It should also be noted that *forum non conveniens* is still a possible plea in actions involving intra-UK jurisdiction only,[16] although not actions between parties from different states party to the Brussels Convention.[17]

The logical next question in this scenario is what law will govern the action. Actions for defamation are still subject to the common law requirement of "double actionability", ie, the requirement that there must be a successful cause of action under both the *lex loci delicti* (the law of the place of the delict) and the *lex fori* (the law of the forum) before the action can

---

[15] (Case C-68/93) [1995] 2 WLR 499, and see comment by Forsyth at [1995] CLJ 515. Note that *Shevill* is an authoritative interpretation of the place of the delict for the purpose of fixing jurisdiction only, not of choice of law.

[16] See *Cumming v Scottish Daily Record and Sunday Mail and others* [1995] EMLR 538.

[17] Art 21 of the Brussels Convention provides that the first court seised of any action must hear it, barring a small exception in Art 22 on related actions.

succeed.[18] In the example chosen, both the *lex fori* and the *lex loci delicti* are English law—so double actionability is not a problem. (This is on the assumption—as seems likely but is not wholly clear—that for the purposes of choice of law, the place of the delict is also the place where damage is caused to the reputation of the victim, ie, the "target" jurisdiction.)[19] But the rule of double actionability *can* have invidious effects for the pursuer or plaintiff where two legal systems are involved, and the law differs between them. Let us vary our scenario a little:

> *The person defamed is a public figure, eg, a media celebrity, originally an American national, but who has established his principal home in Scotland. Both pursuer and defender are resident and domiciled in Scotland. The defamatory comment, as before, is published in a Usenet newsgroup readable in many countries including Scotland, England and the United States. The principal harm done to the pursuer's reputation is in the United States.*

Will the action by the celebrity succeed if raised in Scotland? There is jurisdiction to sue in the place of the defender's domicile—Scotland—for the whole damage caused to the pursuer's reputation in all countries. To successfully sue for damages in respect of the damage to the reputation in the US, there must however be a successful cause of action under both Scots and US law.[20] In the US, it is a defence to an action for libel that the pursuer or plaintiff is a "public figure."[21] In such cases according to US law, the burden is put on the *pursuer* to show by clear and convincing evidence that the defender made the comments with actual malice. In Scots law, by contrast, such malice is presumed. It is quite possible then that although the action would *succeed* under Scots law, the pursuer may fail as a result of the double delict rule—an example of US law controlling the result of an action between two Scots domiciliaries. The only possible line of attack for the pursuer in this example lies in the approach taken in the cases of *Boys v Chaplin*[22] and *Red Sea Insurance Co Ltd v Bouyges S.A & Others*[23] in which the House of Lords and the Court of Appeal, respectively, chose to approve the possibility that in appropriate circumstances the double actionability rule might be displaced in favour of a "proper law" approach. In a case of the kind above, there might conceivably be a conclusion that the "centre of gravity" of the action was in Scotland and that Scots law should be the proper law.

---

[18] This restrictive requirement has recently been abolished in both Scottish and English law for most transnational delict or tort actions under the Private Law (Miscellaneous Provisions) Act 1995—but was specifically retained for actions for libel and defamation.

[19] See *Bata v Bata* [1948] WN 366 (CA). Scots law seems to have reached a similar conclusion in *Longworth v Hope and Cook* (1865) 3 M 1049 and *Evans v Stein* (1904) 7 F 65. An unresolved problem however is the fact that in this scenario there are at least two jurisdictions where there is publication and loss to reputation, while for the purposes of choice of law (unlike jurisdiction) there can only be one "place of the delict".

[20] The example is simplified. In reality the relevant law would be of a particular US state.

[21] See *New York Times Co v Sullivan* 376 US 254 11 L Ed 2d 686 84 S.Ct. 710 (1964).

[22] [1971] AC 356.

[23] [1994] 3 All ER 749.

Finally it is important to remember that winning the action is only half the battle. Where the defender in an Internet libel case lives abroad, the judgement will still need to be recognised and enforced by the courts of the defender's residence (unless he happens to leave major assets in the pursuer's country of residence). Many countries may choose not to so recognise, either because they have no clear mechanisms in place for recognition of foreign decrees, or because the legal basis of the judgement runs against principles of their own legal system, eg, an over-riding constitutional preference for freedom of expression. Such problems have already arisen in respect of judgements for libel obtained in the English courts where enforcement was then sought against a U.S. defender.[24]

Liability of Internet Service Providers

The key role of ISPs such as CompuServe, Demon at al is to provide access to the Internet for their subscribers. This access includes allowing subscribers both to read and write to Usenet newsgroups; and to surf the Web. ISPs also sometimes host "local" discussion fora—newsgroups accessible only by their own paid up subscribers and not therefore part of the general Usenet—and almost invariably agree to act as physical hosts to Web pages set up by their subscribers (generally to a maximum storage of a few megabytes). In all these cases, the ISP runs the risk of being regarded as the publisher of libellous remarks, originated by another person, but published by them in one of these forums. As noted above, it is clear in principle that in both Scotland and England,[25] any repetition or re-publication of a defamatory statement is in itself actionable. Action is possible against all intervening persons who are responsible for repeating, publishing or otherwise circulating the defamation. The person defamed may thus choose whether to sue the original defamer, or the repeat publisher, or both—and in many cases, will be best advised to sue the party with the deepest pockets, usually the ISP, rather than the original author. But as a practical issue, far too much material passes through Usenet newsgroups alone at any one time for an ISP to physically scrutinise it all in advance of publication, and it is generally impossible to exclude any particular message in a newsgroup, only the whole newsgroup. ISPs thus have almost no control over much of the material they are "publishing". Software does exist to search for and block access to material of an offensive or pornographic nature on the Internet,[26] but it is of little use in relation to defamation, where there are no specific words or images which can be predicted as attracting legal risk. As we have seen, someone's reputation may be savaged

[24] See *Matusevitch v Telnikoff* 877 F Supp ; Civil Action no.94-1151 RMU (see comment at 23 Media L.Rep. 1367).
[25] See *Truth New Zealand v Holloway* [1960] 1 WLR 997.
[26] See further Akdeniz, p 236.

as easily in an amateur poetry forum as a newsgroup on bestiality or sexual fantasies. This adds up to a liability time-bomb for ISPs, which could seriously affect their ability to operate commercially, unless defences of some kind are made available to them.

In both the US, the UK, and elsewhere, ISPs have tried to claim that they should be exempted from liability on the basis of concepts of innocent dissemination—essentially claiming that have no effective control over the material they re-distribute, and thus should not be held legally liable in respect of it as publishers. To some extent this argument rest on whether ISPs are seen as more akin to conventional hard copy publishers, or TV and radio broadcasters—who have control over what they publish, and a corresponding duty to check that the material they publish is *not* defamatory—or whether they should be seen as more like "common carriers" such as the phone company—who are seen as "mere passive conduits" for information, with no effective control over it, and who are thus usually not held liable for whatever material they carry. Somewhere between the two a third analogy can be drawn, to news-stands or bookstores—persons who are responsible for distributing large quantities of potentially defamatory material and have some chance to examine it, but who cannot reasonably be expected to check it all in detail if they are to stay in business.[27]

Two widely discussed US cases[28] have failed to settle in detail the issue of whether ISPs should have the benefit of an innocent dissemination defence. In *Cubby v CompuServe*,[29] CompuServe were sued in respect of a message appearing in a local forum hosted by them, called "Rumorville USA". CompuServe had employed a third party specifically to edit and control the content of this forum. The third party posted the information on the Internet once it was edited, with no intervening opportunity for CompuServe to review the material prior to publication. CompuServe argued that they were merely a distributor of the information, not a publisher, and should therefore not be held liable. The New York District Court agreed, holding that CompuServe was here acting in a way akin to a news-stand, book store or public library, and that to hold it to a higher standard of liability than these distributors, would place undue restrictions on the free flow of electronic information.

But in *Stratton Oakmont Inc v Prodigy Services*,[30] the decision went the opposite way. On similar facts, Prodigy was sued in respect of comments posted to a local discussion forum it hosted. Again , Prodigy had employed persons known as "board leaders" to monitor and edit the content of the forum and had empowered these board leaders to remove material, although

---

[27] While this three category analysis is commonly accepted in US law and has by extension penetrated global Internet law, it should be noted that it has been rejected in English law, albeit in the context of hard copy magazine publishing: see *Goldsmith v Sperrings* [1977] 1 WLR 478.

[28] See the articles cited at n.1., plus a useful summary of the issues in I Lloyd "Liability for the Contents of On-line services" (1995) 3 IJLIT 273. See also now *Zeran v AOL*, discussed at p. 195.

[29] 766 F Supp 135 (SD NY 1991)

[30] 1995 NY Misc. 23 Media L. Rep. 1794.

only after it was posted. The crucial difference from the CompuServe case (such as there was) was that Prodigy had explicitly marketed itself as "a family oriented computer network", which as part of its "value added" services, would control and prevent the publication of inappropriate messages. This seems to have been enough to lead the court to regard Prodigy as the publisher of the libels in question, rather than as a mere distributor, and accordingly they were held liable.

The most unfortunate aspect of the *Prodigy* and *CompuServe* decisions is that the ratio that can most easily be extracted from the two contrasting results is that to avoid liability, an ISP should do as little as possible to monitor and edit the content of the messages or other material it carries. This, it can be argued, will make it seem more like a news-stand, and less like a publisher. Such a "head in the sand" approach is an extremely unhelpful message for improvement of Internet services, where as any user will know, one of the key problems for real commercial use is the huge volume of unedited, disorganised, misleading and often offensive text that has to be worked through to reach any useful information. What the Internet needs is more editorial control by ISPs, not less.

More unfortunately still, these "head in sand" aspects of the *Prodigy* decision may have been adopted for the UK in the new legislation on defamation which came into force throughout the UK in September 1996, and had as one of its explicit aims the clarification of the defence of innocent dissemination for Internet providers in both England and Scotland.[31]

Section 1(1) of the Defamation Act 1996 provides that:

"In defamation proceedings a person has a defence if he shows that—(a) he was not the author, editor or publisher of the statement complained of,
  (b) he took reasonable care in relation to its publication, and
  (c) he did not know, and had no reason to believe, that what he did caused or contributed to the publication of a defamatory statement."

Although this section is an improvement over the vagueness of the pre-existing common law, its phrasing still leaves much to be desired from the viewpoint of ISP liability. The defence of proving "reasonable care" provided by s 1(1)(b) is only available to persons who are not "publishers" according to s 1(1)(a). A "publisher" is defined in s 1(2) as a commercial publisher, ie, a person whose business is issuing material to the public. This would certainly seem to exclude non-commercial hosts such as universities, but to embrace commercial ISPs. Furthermore, if an ISP monitors or edits content, as both Prodigy and CompuServe did, it is also likely to be regarded as an "editor" as this is defined as including any person "having editorial or equivalent responsibility for the content of the statement or the decision to publish it." However s 1(3) goes on to state that

---

[31] See Chapter 2 of the Lord Chancellor's Consultation Document on the draft Defamation Bill, *Reforming Defamation law and Procedure,* July 1995.

"A person shall *not* be considered the author, editor or publisher of a statement if he is *only* involved . . .

(c) in . . . operating or providing any equipment, system or service by means of which the statement is retrieved, copied, distributed or made available in electronic form; . . . [or]

(e) as the operator of or provider of access to a communications system by means of which the statement is transmitted, or made available, by a person over whom he has no effective control." [parts omitted and emphasis added]

It is clear that section 1(3)(e) was intended by Parliament to be the umbrella under which ISPs could shelter themselves from liability.[32] But this subsection is problematic in that it seems to require, in a style rather reminiscent of the *Prodigy* decision, that to get the benefit of the s 1(1) defence, the ISP must *only* provide Internet access, and not do anything else—not, for example, exercise editorial control or spot-check content—for if they do, it would seem they will be exercising "effective control" over the maker of the defamatory statement. Yet it seems unlikely that an ISP which neither monitors nor edits can succeed in proving, as s 1(1)(b) requires, that it took "reasonable care" to prevent the publication of the defamatory statement. There is thus an inherent catch 22.

One possible escape for ISPs might lie in claiming that a person who edits content is only exercising effective control over the defamatory *statement*, not the person who makes the statement. Another approach might be to seek exemption from publisher/editor status under s 1(2)(c) rather than 1(2)(e), which although less apparently descriptive of an ISP does not contain any "hands off" requirement.

If either of these arguments is accepted, what must an ISP do to be seen to exercise reasonable care? Section 1(5) provides that a court should have regard to the nature or circumstances of the publication, and in particular to the "extent of the responsibility of the defender for the content of the statement." In relation to a Usenet newsgroup, for example, where very large amounts of material arrive by the hour from all over the globe, and the system operator has almost no control except to censor the entire newsgroup, this would, one hopes, be very little responsibility at all. It is noteworthy that both the CompuServe and Prodigy cases involved local rather than Usenet discussion fora, where the ISPs had at least a reasonable chance of keeping an eye on the material complained of.

Finally if all attempt at claiming a s1(1) defence fails, an ISP may wish to avail itself under ss 2 and 3 of an offer to make amends. If such an offer is accepted, further proceedings against the offending party are barred. ISPs are in a particularly good position to offer "a suitable correction" of the statement complained of and to publish it, as required by s 2(4)(b), far and wide,

---

[32] See *Hansard*, HL Vol 571, col 605. The wording of this section was changed from its original form following criticism of the Draft Bill in, inter alia, Charlesworth "Legal issues of electronic publishing on the World Wide Web" (1995) 26 Law Librarian 524.

since they can at almost no cost distribute the apology to the whole of the Internet.

Although ss 2 and 3 may be of practical use, it seems there are no panaceas to be found in s 1 of the 1996 Act. Even if the interpretation of s 1(1) does run favourably to ISPs, the Act will, of course, only operate to relieve an ISP of liability where the litigation in question is governed by the law of England or Scotland. If Demon, for example, is sued in France by a French resident for a statement posted in a Demon local newsgroup, then the defence in s 1(1) will only be relevant if UK law is the governing law of the cause, which is more than likely not to be the case. However it is not, of course, just the 1996 Act which lacks extraterritorial reach, but the whole of UK defamation law. In the end the simplest solution for ISPs afraid of being sued in the UK may be to physically locate their business overseas, in a jurisdiction with less exorbitant libel damages than England, and where foreign decrees for damages are not easily enforced.

SOLUTIONS?

Before considering what solutions there are to the problems identified above in relation to Internet libel, it is worth asking if there is really a need for anything more than legal inertia. In the last five or six years of frenetic Internet expansion, after all, there have been only a handful of Internet libel cases receiving international attention. It is submitted however that these cases are merely the tip of the iceberg. Because of the uncertainty of the law on innocent dissemination, and the scale of potential risk, it is likely that far more Internet libel cases have been settled out of court or by apology, than have ever even made it to the stage of serving a writ.[33] This artificial hiatus will not however last forever, especially as commercial enterprise on the Web becomes more prevalent. In the US, an artificial brake may have been applied to Internet libel cases by the introduction of the Communications Decency Act 1996 (CDA), which provided criminal sanctions for Internet operators who published offensive material on the net, but also granted (in section 230(c)) immunities from liability to ISPs who were only publishing information provided by another person. In *Zeran v America Online Inc.,*[34] the Eastern Virginia

---

[33] At least three other Internet libel cases have been reported in the UK other than those discussed elsewhere in this article. All appear to have been settled out of court. The first such case was that of Dr Philip Hallam-Baker in 1994, who was sued for placing an allegedly libellous notice on the Usenet concerning Dr Lawrence Godfrey (*The Lawyer*, 25 January 1994). Asda paid a police constable "substantial" damages when he discovered untrue statements alleging fraud against him had been placed on Asda's internal email system (*Daily Telegraph*, 20 April 1995). Finally, David Braben, a computer games designer, sued his former partner, Ian Bell over statements made by Bell in an interview published on the Internet (*Times*, 7 December 1995).

[34] US District Court of Eastern Virginia, 21 March 1997, Civil Action 96-952-A, available at http://www.bna.com/e-law/cases/zeran.html.

District Court found that this provision of the CDA pre-empted the right of the court to hear an action for libel and failure to remove a offending statement brought against America Online. Imposition of common law liability on AOL would have frustrated the objective of section 230(c), which was to encourage ISPs to put in place monitoring and blocking controls so as to restrict circulation on the Internet of offensive material. Accordingly the action was struck out. Even although the CDA has now in large part been struck down[35] as in breach of the constitutional right of freedom of speech, the immunity granted in section 230 still stands, and for the moment, seems to have staunched the American flow of cases.[36]

In the UK, however, there are signs that Internet libel is not only becoming more prominent, but that the risk of suit is being spread even wider than the original author and the ISP or host site. In July 1997, we have seen not only the Western Provident case already discussed, but also the Jimmy Hill case. This concerned a Web site known as the "Tartan Army" which posted information about the Scotland football team, and was sponsored by the brewers Scottish Courage.[37] The site contained a forum where fans could directly post their views about "the beautiful game". Unfortunately one of the main topics of discussion was Jimmy Hill, the sports broadcaster, and various obscene, rude and defamatory comments and jokes were posted about him in a variety of languages. The most interesting point about the case, perhaps is that Mr Hill chose not to sue the Web site owners themselves, nor their ISP, but instead Scottish Courage, the sponsor.[38] This is a worrying precedent for other sponsors and advertisers on the Web, who have next to no control over what is displayed in proximity to their name, and might seriously impede commercial exploitation of the Web.

So what steps can be taken to reduce the risks to ISPs and other parties of being sued for Internet libel? As discussed above, national legislation such as the Defamation Act 1996 is of little use when attempting to regulate, and provide defences in respect of, transnational Internet libel. Self help solutions are possible, such as the imposition by contract of an indemnity against possible legal liability arising out of the acts of any person who subscribes to an ISP. Such "shrink wrap clauses in cyberspace"[39] are however of limited utility: first, they will be subject (whatever the proper law of the contract is) to mandatory consumer protection rules such as the UK Unfair Contract Terms Act 1977 and the EC Directive on Unfair Terms in Consumer Contracts; secondly, they are likely to make informed consumers simply turn to another ISP in what is an increasingly competitive market for Internet

---

[35] Supreme Court decision in *Reno v ACLU*, (1997) 2 BNA EPLR 664, available at http://www.aclu.org/court/renovacludec.html. See further, Akdeniz at p. 232.

[36] See also *Doe v America Online Inc.*, FlaCirCt, Palm Beach Cty, No. CL 97-631 AE, 6/13/97.

[37] See http://www.ontonet.be/~ont082/tartan.html.

[38] Pending resolution of the dispute, Scottish Courage have withdrawn their sponsorship.

[39] The term is taken from M Lemley "Shrink wraps in cyberspace" (1995) 35 Jurimetrics Journal 311.

services;[40] thirdly, and most importantly they will not provide relief where an ISP is sued in respect of a defamatory statement made by a non-subscriber but published by the ISP.

Most legal (as opposed to cyber-activist) commentators accept that in this field, as in others such as breach of copyright, trademark infringement, obscenity and pornography on the net, single nation legislative strategies are pointless and that a better way forward is by multilateral agreement leading to an international convention.[41] Certainly an international agreement on defences of innocent dissemination would be of use both to ISPs and to individuals, as would an agreement to harmonise or clarify the rules of international private law in relation to transnational torts. The crucial question, however, is whether there is sufficient political imperative to push such an international agreement into being. Not only do such agreements require abandonment of national sovereignty on matters of acute local interest such as definitions of obscenity, but there is increasing agreement in the computer industry and among politicians and businessmen that over-regulation of the Internet at this early stage of its commercial development may be harmful. Furthermore external regulation runs counter to the deep-rooted anti-regulatory culture of "traditional" Internet users and may prove to be unenforceable.[42]

An alternative approach is international co-operation on voluntary or self-regulatory approaches to control of offensive material. Following the downfall of the CDA, it appears that the US government is leaning towards a regime of industry and private sector self-regulation in relation to harmful content, rather than state regulation which runs the risk of being embarrassingly felled as in breach of constitutional rights and freedoms.[43] A similar development can be perceived in Europe, in the Green Paper recently released by the European Commission on illegal and harmful content on the Internet.[44] As the European Commission recognises therein, defamatory material on the Internet is just one small part of a wider problem, which is how to control

[40] The power of consumer protest in relation to ISP standard form contracts can be seen from the incident in October 1996 when CompuServe was forced to drop an amendment to its standard agreement which gave the company the right to alter as it pleased any software uploaded to CompuServe (*Guardian*, October 24 1996).

[41] See for example Rubens, Fraser and Smith "US and international law aspects of the Internet: fitting square pegs into round holes" (1995) 3 IJLIT 117; Cairns "Opportunities, Risks and Some Intellectual Property Constraints Surrounding the Provision and Use of On-Line Services" (1995) 4 IJLIT 19.

[42] See M Gould "Rules in the Virtual Society" (1996) 10 Int Rev of Law, Computers and Technology 199, who cites the difficulties encountered by Canada in enforcing its pre-trial prejudice rules against the collective will of the Internet community in the Homolka child murder case (see further Bonnington, p. 202).

[43] See "Clinton backs curbs on porn sites to protect children", *Scotsman*, 23 July 1997; also reports at (1997) 2 BNA EPLR 700 and 741.

[44] *Illegal and Harmful Content on the Internet*, Communication to the European Parliament, the Council, the Economic and Social Committee and the Committee of the Regions, October 1996. Available at http://www2.echo.lu/legal/en/internet/content/communic.html.

the spread of material on the Internet whose content is either harmful or actively illegal—for example, material (pictures as well as text) which is criminally obscene, blasphemous, liable to incite racial hatred, illegally copied or altered in breach of intellectual property rights, etc. The solution tentatively espoused in principle by the EC to this deluge of unwanted material is self-regulation by Internet content providers in the form *inter alia* of voluntary subjection to a ratings scheme. One such scheme is PICS (Platform for Internet Content Selection) which was launched in May 1996 by the WWW Consortium and provides a scheme of so-called "neutral labelling" rather like that used to describe films in TV magazines. The idea is that rather than imposing censure or censorship on Internet service providers from without, consumers may *themselves* recognise and screen out content that offends them. A Web site, for example, may label itself using PICS "tags", as containing adult content, bad language and nudity. This will of course instantly up its hit rate! But it will also allow parents to tag it as "not to be accessed at any cost" by their children. Although such ratings schemes may conceivably be a partial answer to the problem of pornography on the Internet, it has to be said they can do little to reduce the risk of—and liability for—on-line defamation—which almost by definition may occur where you least expect it. However there does seem to be a common appreciation discernible in the recent pronouncements of the Clinton administration and the EU that making ISPs liable for harmful content outwith their control is unfruitful. The Bonn Declaration of 8 July 1997 puts it this way: ". . . third party content hosting services should not be expected to exercise prior control on content which they have no reason to believe is illegal".[45] Given the political will behind this sentiment, it would not be surprising if before long we may see an international solution at least to the problem of ISP liability for Internet libel, if not a cessation of the phenomenon itself. That awaits a sea-change in either human nature or Internet culture, neither of which seem alterable by legislative will alone.

---

[44] Declaration of Ministers of EU Countries at the conference "Global Information Networks: Realising the Potential", July 6-8 1997 (see report at (1997) 2 BNA ELPR 744.)

11

News Without Frontiers: Pre-Trial Prejudice and the Internet

ALISTAIR BONNINGTON[1]

The legal profession is often accused of being rather staid. However, even in this enclave, few can be unaware of the astonishing progress made over the past few years in communications technology. Information can now be transmitted worldwide by cable, satellite and telecommunications systems so quickly that to all intents and purposes it is instantaneous. Broadcasters, who may be situated at any location in the world to cover news stories as they break, possess what are known in the trade as 'fast response vehicles'. These are specially designed mini television studios capable of sending television pictures via satellite from the remotest part of the countryside all over the globe within minutes of being set up. The Internet is another medium where there is almost instantaneous communication and which is used regularly for the dissemination of information.

The result is that information can be communicated with ease across international borders. But this cross border communication brings with it a number of problems, one of which is the danger of pre-trial prejudice. One of the functions of the media is to report on news stories as they break. Sometimes these stories will involve horrific crimes. In covering these stories, personal opinions, whether of the journalists involved, or of others present at the scene will be broadcast, as will pictures, relevant historical events, in depth interviews from experts and so on. It may be that the events are of such a nature, the authorities may wish to bring criminal proceedings against one or more of those involved. But to what extent might the information that has already been broadcast as news around the world prejudice the chance of the accused having a fair trial particularly where it is a trial by jury? Will there not be a danger that those who are to be jurors will have already made up their minds of the guilt (or innocence) of the accused, basing their prejudices on what they have read and heard in the media and on the Internet? The question then becomes, do we have the law to regulate the sort of communication that may result in pre-trial prejudice and hence contempt of court?[2]

---

[1] Solicitor to the BBC in Scotland. Email: alistair.bonnington@bbc.co.uk.
[2] In the UK the Contempt of Court Act 1981 deals with pre-trial prejudice/publicity. For an

This article brings together a number of themes that emerge in this discussion. The first is to illustrate that problems with pre-trial prejudice are most serious where a jurisdiction operates a system of jury trials. Although witnesses may be similarly influenced by pre-trial publicity, the problems are most acute in relation to jurors. The second is to highlight the problems posed by cross border communication. It is relatively easy to control information through sanctions imposed on the media located within a single jurisdiction. However, news, and the reporting and communication of that news whether by way of traditional broadcasting or over the Internet results in world wide dissemination. Within this global community single jurisdiction attempts at control are almost impossible. The third theme is the tension in these various jurisdictions between freedom of speech and prejudicial pre-trial publicity; reporting of news events as they occur and commenting on those events is just one form of freedom of speech, but exercising that freedom may result in prejudice to an accused; the difficulty arises where the one philosophy meets head on with the other.

The dangers of pre-trial prejudice are particularly severe in the context of communication of news stories. News, by its nature, is communicated virtually immediately and regularly without much opportunity for full legal checks. When a tragic incident takes place such as that experienced in 1996 in Scotland in Dunblane, there is immediate worldwide media interest. Within two hours of the Dunblane shootings, information was being transmitted via the internet, radio and television throughout the world. Newspapers, because of the need to produce hard copies were much slower in the distribution of information on the tragedy. The story was first published in a number of evening editions. By broadcasting standards, that is equivalent to a work of ancient history.

The problem of prejudicial pre-trial publicity did not, in fact, arise in the Dunblane case as Robert Hamilton had killed himself after murdering the children and their teacher. He therefore never stood trial. However, for about three and a half hours after the initial news of the incident, the police would not comment on whether Hamilton was dead or not. Had he not been dead, he would have had to stand trial. By that time, stories, speculation, rumours and so on had been broadcast all over the world. The shock felt by many was palpable. Could Hamilton have ever had a fair trial thereafter, should the need have arisen? Would too many people not already have made up their mind as to his guilt (or innocence)? This terrible incident illustrates very clearly the sort of legal difficulty posed by worldwide instantaneous electronic communication.

Prejudicial pre-trial publicity is of particular concern in those jurisdictions which have trial by jury as it is the jury who may be most influenced by what they have heard or seen. Witnesses in a trial may also be affected by specula-

analysis in this area see Walker 'Fundamental Rights, Fair Trials and the New Audio-Visual Sector' [1996] 59 MLR, 4, 517.

tion, rumour and media hype. For this reason, the Lord Advocate issued a warning to newspapers and broadcasters at the time of the appointment of Lord Cullen to look into the Dunblane shootings. There was no question of Lord Cullen being influenced by media hype, but it was felt that there was a real possibility of witnesses being affected. In Scotland, the Courts impose some of the strictest rules in the world on prejudicial pre-trial publicity. The Scottish judges believe that from the time a person is arrested, there should be nothing broadcast or printed in a newspaper which might prejudice the minds of witnesses or jurors against them. To create a risk of prejudice is enough to break the law[3]. It is no defence to show that in reality there was no prejudice—for example, because the accused plead guilty. Any broadcaster or newspaper editor who offends against this may find himself in severe trouble. Substantial fines have been imposed by the Scottish Courts on errant editors and, on some occasions, imprisonment has been considered[4].

If media interest in the incident is domestic or local then, at least to an extent, their activities can be controlled and sanctions imposed and enforced accordingly. Scottish courts can control what happens in Scotland. And that can hold true for limited cross-border control. For instance, English news organisations who are used to the more liberal approach taken to prejudicial pre-trial publicity in that jurisdiction, are at times subject to the Scottish Courts in respect of publishing activities. Publication is the offence[5]. If a newspaper is printed in England but distributed in Scotland, that amounts to publication in Scotland and therefore attracts liability. The Daily Mail has found this to its cost on a number of occasions when it has published prejudicial material about Scottish cases. In 1978 it took a particular interest in a bisexual butler, Archibald Hall, who murdered his employers the MP Walter Scott Elliott and Mrs Elliott. He also murdered a prostitute named Mary Coggle and a couple of his gay lovers. A murdering bi-sexual occasionally transvestite butler was too much to resist for the Daily Mail and they published an extraordinarily detailed account of what they, in their wisdom, believed to be the crimes he had committed. The were found to be in contempt of the Scottish High Court as a result[6].

At around the same time, an English broadcaster found itself suffering severe financial penalties in the Scottish Courts over contempt of court. London Weekend Television investigated and reported on the question of what is now called Persistent Vegetative State—or PVS. PVS at that time was 'hot news', and the subject was being debated around the world due to the

---

[3] Contempt of Court Act 1981 s 2(2).
[4] *HMA* v *George Outram & Co. Ltd* 1980 SLT 13 where a fine of £20,000 was imposed on the publishers of the Glasgow Herald newspaper. Imprisonment of the editor was considered.
    See also *HMA* v *Newsgroup Newspapers and Express Newspapers* (the Vindico Sindic case) where fines of £20,000 and £30,000 were imposed against The Sun and The Express newspapers respectively.
[5] Contempt of Court Act 1981 section 2.
[6] *Hall* v *Associated Newspapers* 1978 SLT 241.

petition to the American Courts by the parents of Karen Quinlin. Karen had been rendered unconscious in a road accident and, having been advised by their doctors that she would never recover, Mr & Mrs Quinlin wished to switch off the life support machine. They went to court to seek authority for that purpose. London Weekend Television looked at the dilemma facing Karen's parents and her doctors and the surrounding legal issues. They linked into their programme mention of a trial which was due to take place at the Sheriff Court in Edinburgh the next day. The accused in that case was a nursing sister called Atkins. She was accused of attempting to murder a 13 year old patient who was suffering from severe brain damage in the intensive care unit of the hospital. Putting it in simple terms, Nurse Atkins was accused of attempting to "mercy kill" the young girl. Although it was made clear in the television programme that Nurse Atkins denied the charge and would be proceeding to trial, the Scottish High Court found London Weekend Television to be in contempt. The Company was fined £50,000; the Editor of the programme £5,000; the Managing Director of LWT £5,000 and the Programme Producer £1,000[7].

In the past, it has been possible to contain, if not eliminate these problems of pre-trial prejudice because of the nature of distribution of news—by way of hard copies, or else television broadcasts which were pre-recorded and thus allowed time to make full legal checks of the contents. However, this is no longer the case, and not only is news broadcast live by these fast response vehicles, but the speed of response is further magnified many times over by the rapid expansion of the Internet. Further, digital (as opposed to analogue) broadcasting, the next major technological advancement about to be launched, will increase to an extraordinary extent the amount of news information which can be transmitted world wide. The BBC has already announced a 24 hour news channel.

How are domestic courts to police transborder news communication in the modern world? Can they hope to exercise any form of control? If a broadcaster is set up in Paris to broadcast in the English language to Member States of the European Union, and they broadcast information which is in contempt of court in Scotland, which prejudices an accused having a fair trial, is a Scottish Criminal Court to send the Sheriff's Officer marching up the Champs Elysee with an Order to serve on the editor of the television company? If news is distributed on the Internet, there are no borders, and indeed no concept of borders, either physical or psychological.

A recent experience between Canada and America illustrates the difficulties which may arise with crossborder communication. There was a most terrible case in St Catherines, Ontario, Canada involving a man called Barnardo and a woman call Homolka[8]. They were accused of horrific crimes against children involving abduction, sexual abuse and then murder. The crimes were

---

[7] *Atkins* v *London Weekend Television* 1978 SLT 76.
[8] *R* v *Barnado* [1995] Ont. C. J. Lexis 339

very similar to those of the Moors Murderers in the 1960's in England. In Canada, the law on prejudicial pre-trial publicity seems to be similar to that in Scotland. The Canadian judges were anxious to prevent prejudice to Barnardo's trial after his wife Homolka plead guilty to reduced charges on the basis that she would turn Crown evidence and speak against Barnardo. Although the domestic media complied with a court order issued preventing pre-trial publicity, journalists from other jurisdictions were not so bound by the order. Huge amounts of traffic on the details of the trial entered Canada over the Internet by way of mailing lists and Usenet newsgroups, much of which originated from the US. In the US, it has been found almost impossible to regulate pre-trial publicity because of the First Amendment to the US Constitution which allows freedom of speech. Freedom of speech and contempt of court by way of pre-trial publicity do not sit happily together, and there are numerous examples of the superiority of the requirement of freedom of speech. One of the most recent examples in the context of pre-trial publicity being that in what has been dubbed the 'O.J. Simpson circus', where the accused was tried and found guilty on many television shows before the first juror was sworn. In the Homolka case it may, ultimately, have been possible for the Canadian authorities to determine where the information entering the jurisdiction emanated from, but undoubtedly, the sheer volume of communication made it impractical to either trace, prosecute or enforce contempt of court orders against the perpetrators. This case not only illustrates the difficulties in policing cross border news travelling on the Internet, but also is indicative of the inevitable clash between the philosophies of freedom of speech and pre-trial publicity; pre-trial publicity being but one form of freedom of speech. US newspapers and citizens were entirely entitled under US Law to print whatever and discuss they wanted about Mr Barnardo and Miss Homolka.

Hard copy is somewhat easier to police than the Internet. There was one incident during the Canadian proceedings where a man was arrested for bringing American newspapers into the area where the trial was to take place. This rather blunt instrument, in theory, might be one way of enforcing domestic law against foreign offenders. But towards the end of the 20th Century can one realistically expect that there will be acceptance of the enforcement of criminal penalties against the media who are obeying their domestic law but offending against the law of a receiving country? It seems highly unlikely that such criminal penalties would go unchallenged before the European Court of Human Rights. The UK Government has now signalled its intention to incorporate the European Convention on Human Rights into the domestic law of this country. Article 10 of that Convention gives the right to freedom of speech; in the event of incorporation into domestic law, it is likely that these same tensions that have arisen in the US, between freedom of speech and pre-trial 'censorship' will surface and be litigated in our domestic courts.

Closer to home, there has been controversy about international pre-trial publicity over the bombing of Pan Am Flight 109 which came down near

Lockerbie in Scotland just before Christmas some years ago. On the third anniversary of the bombing, warrants were issued for the arrest of two Libyan citizens, both by a US court and by the Sheriff at Dumfries in Scotland. The legal team acting for these men comprising of a number of lawyers from various countries raised the question of prejudicial pre-trial publicity as one of the reasons as to why their clients should not stand trial. The peculiarity about Lockerbie was that after the warrants granted by the Sheriff at Dumfries had been extant for one year, the strict liability rule on publishing material which would constitute pre-trial prejudice imposed under the Contempt of Court Act 1981 ceased to apply[9]. Accordingly, the media were under a more relaxed regime than for a domestic case where normally the granting of the warrant and the arrest are virtually contemporaneous. This appears to be the only case to date where the terms of the schedule to the Contempt of Court Act 1981 which lays down this provision about a warrant which is unexecuted for a year or more resulting in the more relaxed rule on pre-trial publicity has been relevant.

Despite the relaxation of the normal rules, it is difficult to believe that it would be impossible to find a jury of fifteen people to try these men in Scotland should that eventuality ever arise. In contempt matters the courts, both in Scotland and England, have recognised that the lapse of time between the reporting of the incident and the date of trial, means that potential jurors will almost certainly have forgotten what they have heard in relation to the incident, whether they read it in the newspapers, saw it on the television, heard it on the radio, or now, became aware of it through the internet. And that applies no matter how prejudicial the item may have been.[10]

It should be remembered that the law of contempt, as developed in the UK, arises out of the presumption that a criminal trial will take place before a jury of lay persons. That presumption would, of course, be untrue in many countries in Europe where the accused is tried before a judge alone. Sadly, there has to date been little research into the effect of pre-trial publicity on jurors. The Lord Chancellor's Department has been lobbied on many occasions by academics[11] and the media to relax the terms of the Contempt of Court Act 1981 to allow research to take place into this interesting issue. It may be that analysis would indicate that there is little, if any, real prejudice caused by pre-trial publicity.

Following on from the Lockerbie bombing and the difficulties with the prosecution of the two Libyan suspects, the International Bar Association, amongst others, has suggested the setting up of an international criminal court for the trial of "international crimes". If such a court were set up, there would be perfect opportunity to deal with this vexed question on what advanced

---

[9] Contempt of Court Act 1981 Schedule 1 paragraph 11.

[10] *Sturman* v *HMA* 1980 JC 51. *Attorney General* v *ITN and Others* [1995] 2 All ER 370.

[11] Most recently by Professor Ross Harper at a conference on Legal Aid in Edinburgh on 28th June 1997.

publicity would be allowed. However it is likely, such trial court would comprise only professional judges in which case the question of pre-trial publicity would not be a major issue.

CONCLUSION

So what would be the way forward in this difficult area? A comparative study of the law of pre-trial publicity within the European Union, or indeed world wide would be of assistance. It cannot escape the notice of even the most traditional Scots lawyer that the approach in this country is extremely restrictive when compared with the practice elsewhere. That, in part, may be explained by the fact that serious criminal cases in Scotland and tried by jury. But even then, the Scottish judges proceed on the assumption that jurors will be adversely affected by what they read, see and hear about a case prior to the commencement of evidence. There is absolutely no scientific basis for that approach. Since the Contempt of Court Act 1981, any research has become illegal. As mentioned above, interest has been shown in carrying out investigation in this area with the result that the Lord Chancellor's Department has recently indicated its willingness to consider the possibility of relaxing the 1981 Act for the purpose of proper research into the workings of the jury system. This is to be welcomed and it is to be hoped that any such research will include research into the effect of pre-trial publicity.

It could transpire that the Scottish courts' fears are misplaced and that the public who make up the members of the jury can still try the accused "according to the evidence" despite some degree of pre-trial publicity. The experience of such cases as "the Glasgow Rape Case"[12] indicates that it is still possible for the jury who are dealing with a case which has received widespread pre-trial publicity to bring in a discerning verdict.

If that proves to be the outcome of research, it may be possible for Scots law and systems like it to move gradually towards a more relaxed approach to this issue whether by way of relaxation of the rules relating to pre-trial publicity, or relaxation of the requirement that trials should be heard by jury; they could instead be heard by judge alone. This would also sit more happily with the incorporation of the European Convention into domestic law with the attendant move towards a recognition of the right of freedom of speech.

If it was found that adverse pre-trial publicity was a major problem, then the solution, as with so many other areas connected with the Internet may be to proceed by way of a Convention on Prejudicial Pre-trial Publicity. with all the attendant difficulties of harmonisation of laws. However, it has to be said that it is difficult to see any uniformity of approach in the European Union to this question, let alone on a global basis.

---

[12] *X v Sweeney* 1982 S.C.C.R. 504; 1982 JC 70; 1983 SLT 48.

In this morass one thing is clear. Lawyers must move quickly. Advances in modes of communication are astonishingly quick; lawyers must respond accordingly or they will find that there is no room for any element of choice in the solutions to the problems of pre-trial publicity and prejudice which will be imposed by necessity in this fast moving world of global communication.

12

Computer Crime

PAUL CULLEN QC[1]

Computers affect us all. They have an impact on both private and commercial life and their influence is constantly expanding. What is just as obvious, however, is that computers can provide a powerful tool for the criminally minded. This chapter is intended to address first, how far Scots criminal law is equipped to tackle offences involving computers, and secondly, some practical issues which criminal lawyers may encounter when faced with computer-related crime and evidence generated by computers. In particular, the recovery of computer evidence and its use in court will be considered. Although the principal ambit of what follows is Scots law, many rules will also apply throughout the UK. Some comparative points will also be drawn from other jurisdictions for, as will be discussed, much of the problem with computer crime is that it is of a trans-jurisdictional nature.

It may be helpful at the outset to recognise that there is a distinction to be drawn between crimes in which the use of a computer plays an incidental part, and on the other hand, crimes which can by definition be carried out only by means of or in relation to a computer. I would suggest that there are essentially three situations in which criminal lawyers may encounter computers and computer-generated evidence. First, what I shall call "computer crime proper". Computer hacking and contraventions of the Data Protection Act 1984 are examples of offences where the use of a computer is fundamental to the commission of the offence. Secondly, there are what may be called "ordinary" crimes, whether common law or statutory, which have been committed with the aid of a computer. This category would encompass most instances of computer fraud, offences of obscenity—including the dissemination of child pornography—and stalking. The third category involves offences which are not committed using a computer, but for which evidence from a computer is available. It is easy to envisage a fraud, such as car clocking, committed without any computer assistance. But the records required to prove the crime may come from a computer.

[1] Formerly Solicitor General for Scotland. Research assistance was provided by Shona Barrie of the Crown Office Policy unit and Murray Earle, PhD student at the University of Edinburgh.

"COMPUTER CRIME PROPER"

The obvious starting points for a discussion of how Scots law deals with computer crime are the consultative memorandum and subsequent report of the Scottish Law Commission published in 1986 and 1987 respectively, both entitled "Computer Crime".[2] They examined whether Scots criminal law was able to cope with the increasing use of computers and whether legislative change was needed. The Commission sought to identify the potential for criminal misuse of computers and examined the adequacy of existing criminal offences. A similar exercise was conducted by the Law Commission in England.[3] Both Commissions recommended that offences should be created to deal with computer hacking. In light of the Commissions' examination of the issues the Computer Misuse Act 1990 was passed which applies throughout the UK. This was a Private Member's Bill, introduced with Government support. The Act created various new offences in the area of what I have called computer crime proper.

The objective of the 1990 Act was to deter computer "hacking".[4] In popular culture, the term "hacker" conjures up the illicit but not necessarily the illegal. The term "hacker" was popularised in William Gibson's influential cyberpunk novel *Neuromancer* (1982) as a generic term for all occupants of "cyberspace", but has come to be applied mainly to those who seek access to data maintained on computer systems to which the hacker has no legal password or access code. In terms of the criminal law, two obvious forms of hacking activity can be identified. The first involves gaining access to information on another person's computer where that information is available to the public, but only on payment of fees. The hacker seeks to retrieve the information yet avoid paying the fee.[5] The second form involves unauthorised access to data on a computer where the information is not to be revealed to the public at all. The public perception of hacking tends to be as a crime akin to joy-riding, a prank which causes little damage to society or third parties. Yet in both forms identified, hacking may involve some or all of theft or alteration of information, breach of privacy, the planting of viruses or the causing of damage by other means to programs or data captured in the computer memory, with the possibility of considerable financial loss arising as a consequence.[6]

---

[2] SLC CM No 68, 1986 and SLC No 106, 1987.

[3] See LC WP No 110, 1988, and LC No 186, 1989.

[4] See further I Lloyd, *Information Technology Law*, Chapters 14-19. See also *Stair Memorial Encyclopaedia* , Volume 7 , para. 387. An interesting popular examination of the phenomenon of hacking can be found in B Sterling *The Hacker Crackdown* (Penguin, 1994).

[5] See for example *R v Gold* 1988 AC 1063, discussed infra.

[6] Charlesworth notes in "Legislating Against Computer Misuse: The Trials and Tribulations of the UK Computer Misuse Act 1990" (1993) 4 JLIS 80 at 88 that in the *Bedworth* case, for example, (see below, p. 4), hacking by a computer science student, while mainly done for "kicks", had allegedly caused some £10,000 of loss to a cancer charity and £25,000 loss to the Financial Times.

The Computer Misuse Act 1990, s 1 creates a summary offence of unauthorised access to programs or data held in any computer. Although obviously aimed at "hackers" as described above, section 1 may be applicable in circumstances other than these paradigm situations. "Unauthorised access" may be obtained by "insiders" attempting to gain an illicit advantage using a system to which they have legitimate access, as well as by total "outsiders" hacking from one computer to another. It was clearly established in the first case to be prosecuted under the 1990 Act, *Attorney-General's Reference (No 1 of 1991)*[7] that there does not need to be an attempt to gain access to computer B using computer A for a s 1 offence to be committed. In this case a former sales assistant took advantage of his knowledge of a shop's computer system to purchase equipment there at a reduced price. The Court of Appeal held the offence could apply to "insider hackers" who made unauthorised use of a single computer system as much as to "outsider hackers". However it is less clearly established that "unauthorised access" can occur where a person has permission to access a system on a general basis, but then does so for illicit and unforeseen purposes. In the unreported case of *Bignell*,[8] two police officers with access to the Police National Computer (PNC) searched that computer for information, not for the purposes of their employment, but to discover facts about the estranged wife of one of the accused. Although convicted at first instance under s 1, on appeal, the court found that as the policemen had general authority to access the computer, they could not be guilty of the offence. It is submitted that this is an unnecessarily restrictive approach to "unauthorised access". If adopted, it is particularly unfortunate as a recent House of Lords ruling, *R v Brown*,[9] has also confirmed that activities of this sort do not constitute the offence of improper use of personal data under the Data Protection Act 1984. In that case, another policeman again looked up the PNC to access information for personal gain in connection with his debt collection agency. It was held that mere viewing of data was not "use" of it for the purposes of the 1984 Act.

Any unauthorised access by those who are merely careless, inattentive or imperfectly informed about the limits of their authority is exempt from prosecution under section 1. Section 1 also covers the case where the hacker gains access to a computer without any clear idea what he is likely to find there, or what other systems will be opened to him.

Section 2 of the Act creates an interesting offence, sometimes known as the "ulterior intent" offence, which may be prosecuted summarily or on indictment. It involves the commission of a Section 1 offence with intent to commit or facilitate the commission of a more serious criminal offence, defined as including all common law and statutory offences for which an accused over

---

[7] [1992] 3 WLR 432.
[8] Unreported, *Computing*, October 3, 1996, p3, discussed in P Spink "Misuse of Police Computers"(1997) 4 Jur Rev 219.
[9] [1996] 1 All ER 545.

the age of 21 may be sentenced to 5 years imprisonment. The use of the word "facilitate" covers the case where person A is acting to enable an accomplice B to commit the further offence.

Section 3 is the final major offence-creating section and creates an offence of causing an unauthorised modification of computer material. This is intended to catch the quintessential teenage hacker who interferes with data in computer systems and plants viruses or logic bombs.

In Scotland, there have been no reported prosecutions under any section of the Computer Misuse Act 1990, although there has been at least one unreported (and unsuccessful) prosecution under s 1.[10] In England, one prosecution in relation to section 3, *R v Bedworth* (1991, unreported) at the time "raised considerable doubts about the effectiveness of the Act to curtail adequately the activities of computer hackers."[11] Bedworth, along with two co-defendants was charged under s 3 with conspiracy to gain unauthorised access to various computer systems, modification of those systems, and dishonest use of British Telecom services. The two co-defendants pleaded guilty but Bedworth, a 19 year old student at Edinburgh University, went to trial and was acquitted on the ground that he was "addicted to hacking" and was thus unable to form the necessary criminal intent. This rather novel defence would, however, almost certainly have been rejected had the case been tried by judge and not by a jury. Furthermore, if the prosecution had been brought under s1 rather than s 3, the Crown would not have been required to prove that the defendants had the "requisite intent and the requisite knowledge" for the crime as required by s 3(1)(b). Although convictions under s 3 remain difficult to secure due to the problems of obtaining sufficient evidence, a number of unreported but successful prosecutions have taken place in England subsequent to *Bedworth*, including that of *Pile*, a writer of dangerous computer viruses which had caused more than half a million pounds' worth of damage. Pile was sentenced to 18 months imprisonment at Exeter Crown Court in November 1995.[12]

Sections 4 and 5 give an international dimension to the Act by extending the jurisdiction of the Scottish, English and Northern Irish courts. Prosecutions for unauthorised access (the s 1 offence) and unauthorised modification (the s 3 offence) can be brought so long as there is at least one significant link with the home country. The home country is defined as one of the three parts of the United Kingdom, either Scotland, Northern Ireland or England and Wales. The significant link is defined as being either that the accused person was in the home country when he committed the offence, or

---

[10] *R v Woolhead*, unreported, Stirling Sheriff Court, March 8, 1995, cited in Spink, op cit supra n 8.
[11] Charlesworth, op cit, n 7.
[12] See for a useful summary of recent prosecutions, Y Akdeniz "Section 3 of the Computer Misuse Act 1990: an Antidote for Computer Viruses." (1996) 3 Web JCLI.

any computer to which the accused secured, or intended to secure, access, or which was modified by him, was situated in the home country.

The extended jurisdiction also applies to the s 2 offence, unauthorised access with intent to facilitate the commission of a further offence. Such an offence is not, however, dependant on the existence of a significant link with the home country. It is sufficient that the accused intended to carry out the further offence in the home country or abroad and that there would be jurisdiction under the ordinary rules to try that offence. These somewhat unusual provisions confer jurisdiction on the Scottish courts over an accused who carries out acts in country A to obtain unauthorised access to a computer in country B, with intent to commit a further offence in Scotland. Moreover, there is also a mirror provision, which allows a Scottish court (for example) to try a person who hacks into a computer in Scotland with intent to use the information obtained to commit a further offence abroad.

COMPUTER AIDED CRIME

I turn now to the range of ordinary crimes involving existing offences, carried out with the aid of a computer. It is important that the mere fact that a computer has been used to carry out a crime should not mesmerise us. We should concentrate instead on the traditional definitions of the ingredients of the crime in question, and analyse the supposed criminal conduct in the usual way. Computer-related fraud, for example, has been defined by the United Kingdom's Audit Commission as 'any fraudulent behaviour connected with computerisation by which someone intends to gain financial advantage.' But most computer frauds involve the use of a computer simply because of the automated nature of banking and commerce. The crook who composes a false invoice using computer software is not, however, really a "computer fraudster". Early problems in English computer fraud prosecutions centring around whether it was possible in law to deceive a machine, and jurisdictional difficulties,[13] have been, to a large extent, circumvented by the enactment of s 2 of the 1990 Act discussed above. In *R v Gold*,[14] computer hackers dishonestly obtained a password assigned to a British Telecom engineer so they could make free use of Prestel services. This case was unsuccessfully prosecuted prior to the 1990 Act under an English statute dealing with forgery, on the basis that the hackers had "forged" the password they had dishonestly obtained. Both the Court of Appeal and subsequently the House of Lords found the statute was inapplicable to the circumstances in this case, a result which highlighted the need for specific legislative intervention in the shape of the 1990 Act. In Scots law, however, it has been suggested that the case could have been prosecuted under the common law offence of obtaining services by

---

[13] See *R v Thomson* [1984] 1 WLR 962 and *R v Gold* [1988] AC 1063.
[14] *Supra.*

means of a false pretence, thereby avoiding the difficulty the English courts faced in *R v Gold*.[15]

OBSCENITY AND PORNOGRAPHY[16]

A similar approach can be taken in relation to offences dealing with obscenity and computers as to computer fraud. A computer, or the Internet, may well be used to circulate pornography, but again this does not amount, in my view, to true computer crime. Particular problems do however arise in relation to the detection of crimes of obscenity aided by computers, especially in relation to the use of computer evidence and the bringing of the offence within the scope of criminal statutes drafted well before computers were widely used. In *R v Fellows and Arnold*,[17] the Court of Appeal in England had to interpret such legislation in a case involving the use of a computer by two paedophiles.[18] The accused were charged with contraventions of the Obscene Publications Act 1959 and the Protection of Children Act 1978. The first accused maintained on his computer hard disk a large collection of child pornography to which other paedophiles could gain access, either to view it or copy it, in return for contributing their own paedophile material to the collection. At that stage a password would be issued to them. The second accused was such a customer. who down-loaded child pornography from the first accused's disk, and contributed material from his own collection to the computer of the first accused.

The Court of Appeal had to consider a number of problematic definitions in the legislation. The principal difficulty was that the statutory language used by the original draftsmen, which may have been adequate at the time the legislation was passed, was argued to be inadequate to describe the electronic transmission of data. Two matters were resolved satisfactorily by the court. First, was the visual image stored in a computer's memory a "copy of a photograph" as demanded by the legislation? The court held that a visual image stored on a computer disk, a visual image which is scanned from that disk for transmission to another computer, and a visual image which is stored on another computer as a result of a transmission can all constitute "a copy of a photograph" for the purposes of the 1978 Act.

Secondly, was having such images on computer disk tantamount to having them with a view to their being distributed or shown to others? Here the defence argued that the rôle played by the first accused did not involve a

---

[15] By Lloyd in Reed ed *Computer Law* (1996, 3rd edn, Blackstones) at p 250.

[16] For further comment on these issues from the perspective of English, EC and US law, see Akdeniz, p. 223.

[17] [1997] 2 All ER 548.

[18] For a fuller discussion of the *Fellows and Arnold* cases, see note by C Cobley, (1997) 2 *Communications Law* 30.

sufficient degree of active participation for a finding of guilt. The court rejected that argument and held that where a person has copies of indecent photographs on a computer disk, he has them with a view to their being shown by himself, even if all he does is to allow another person to access the material for himself, by downloading a copy of it to that other person's computer. The court adopted the analogy of a picture being left exposed in a library and the key to the door of the library being available. The court's view was that giving the key to someone, whom you knew was likely to use it to enter the library in order to look at the picture, would amount to showing the picture to the recipient of the key. At the end of the day, the convictions were upheld.

Some of the problems of definition discussed in *Fellows* have since been explicitly addressed by the Criminal Justice and Public Order Act 1994, which was not in force at the time the offences in *Fellows* were committed. This statute amended both the English legislation, under the Protection of Children Act 1978 and the Criminal Justice Act 1988, and the equivalent Scottish provision in Section 52A of the Civic Government (Scotland) Act 1982. These Acts make it an offence to possess or publish indecent photographs of children. The 1994 Act extended the definition of a photograph to include what is now described as a "pseudo-photograph". According to s. 7(7) of the 1978 Act as now amended, "pseudo-photograph means an image, whether made by computer graphics or otherwise howsoever, which appears to be a photograph." This definition is clearly intended to extend to any data stored on a computer disk which is capable of conversion into an image. The 1994 Act also extends the definition of "publication" of obscene matter under the 1959 Act to cover computer transmission of computer images and text, including pseudo-photographs.

It is possible that the more flexible nature of Scots criminal law, with its greater reliance on common law offences than is found in England or most comparable legal systems, may aid it in securing prosecution of novel offences committed with the aid of computers, which have a tendency to fit less than neatly into the confines of date-stamped legislation. In 1996, there was an unreported sheriff and jury prosecution in Stornoway in the case of *HMA v Chambers*. The accused was charged with a variety of offences including shameless and indecent conduct, a common law offence, as well as contraventions of the Sexual Offences (Scotland) Act 1976. The accused was an amateur photographer and held photography sessions with the two complainers, girls aged 12 and 13. In the course of these sessions the accused invited the girls to expose their breasts, an invitation they did not accept. However, the accused used a hidden video camera to record the girls dressing and undressing throughout. At the time of his arrest the accused was found to be in possession of a large collection of computer disks and equipment. One item recovered was a document in the nature of a sexual curriculum vitae for the 12 year old. This document was headed up with a photograph of the 12 year old showing one breast exposed. It then went on to purport to describe the child's sexual experience and sexual interests.

The accused admitted that he had used a computer programme to devise a questionnaire. The replies to the questions would then determine the route to be taken through the questionnaire. If a child gave an answer which the accused did not find promising, entire sections of the questionnaire would be omitted. This made tracking through the programme a very complex task for the police. The accused used these answers as the basis for the sexual curriculum vitae. The accused also admitted using a computer scanner and printer to doctor an otherwise innocent photograph.

He was indicted on and pled guilty to a charge in the following terms:

that you did,
"Conduct yourself in a shameless and indecent manner, and did by means of various items of computer equipment, cameras, a modem, a scanner, a printer and other devices and equipment produce and print, and on [a date] did have in your possession [at an address] a three page document of a sexual and indecent nature purporting to relate to [the 12 year old complainer] upon which an image or likeness of [the complainer] was reproduced which had been altered by you so that the image purported to depict her with one breast fully exposed".

It is worthy of note that the Crown was without too much difficulty able to frame an appropriate common law charge to meet the facts of this offence, thereby avoiding any possible problems of interpretation of statutory language as in *Fellows*. In Scotland there is no legal objection to prosecuting a crime at common law even though it might or might not be possible to bring it within the scope of a statutory crime.[19] No plea was taken to the competency or relevancy of this charge.

It is also of interest that throughout this investigation there was a real fear that the accused had an accomplice, or the technical ability remotely to destroy files and disks which the police wished to search. The accused spent a period on remand because it was of paramount importance that he did not have access to a telephone until the completion of the police enquiries.

Child pornography

No discussion of crimes of obscenity committed with the aid of a computer would be complete without mention of the Internet. Although the Internet has made some criminal activity far easier eg the distribution of pornography it has not (as yet) created fundamentally new types of criminal behaviour. The Internet does not exist in a legal vacuum; what amounts to an offence off-line, will also amount to an offence on-line. One of the developments most apparent to Internet users has been the enormous growth in undiscriminating distribution of electronic mail messages offering access to pornographic images

[19] See Criminal Procedure (Sc) Act 1995, s 312(t).

at a price, often via Web sites demanding credit card payments before viewing is allowed. It is alarming that there is now a speedy and cheap means of sending a message offering illegal pornographic material to thousands of potential customers (as well as to thousands of unwilling recipients some of whom are likely to be shocked or distressed). An electronic message, alleged to have originated in New York, was recently posted to thousands of British Internet users, offering to sell or to trade in child pornography or indeed to manipulate paedophile images from ordinary photographs.

Technological developments have enabled huge amounts of pornographic material to be reproduced more quickly and more cheaply than before in the new media such as hard disks, floppy disks and CD-ROMs. The images that can be captured are not restricted to "stills" photographs, but include animations of moving images comparable in quality with video recordings. The end user can view them on a VDU, they can be transmitted between computers, or they can be printed on computer printers. Discouragement of reproduction of such material is a difficult matter for the enforcement agencies. Whereas in the past the forfeiture of hard copy pornographic material was a fairly punitive sanction, its effect is now diluted because of the ease of copying digitised material.

In addition, those harbouring child pornography in digitised form are often able to hide it quite effectively. Detection is therefore substantially more difficult. Material can be encrypted with a code to deter prying police officers. It is usually possible to decode and access the material, but this can be a lengthy and expensive process. The immediate response of the computer is also a problem; the flick of a button can result in the contents of a disk being destroyed. An accused can configure a computer programme to respond to a "keystroke", deleting all the material sought.

Attempts to control the nature of the material available on the Internet have given rise to great difficulties in practice. The number of sites on the Net is enormous and many are transient in nature. Those which contain pornographic material are, however, usually well sign-posted. In the UK, the Department of Trade and Industry has taken steps to seek control of unsuitable materials on the Internet.[20] Their studies have revealed that whilst a very small percentage of the Internet's total information resource contains what can be deemed to be "unsuitable material", this small percentage is disproportionately accessed and downloaded. The traditional barriers which may deter people from obtaining pornography, such as the fact that it would be stored on the top shelf in a shop, the embarrassment factor, or the price of the material, are not inhibiting factors with the freedom of access provided by the Internet. In addition, there is the element of anonymity.

---

[20] With the report *Legal Issues and the Internet* commissioned from the Central Computer and Telecommunications Agency (CCTA) by the Department of Trade and Industry and published in June 1996 by HMSO.

The result of the DTI's study was a recommendation that there be a combined approach to dealing with such unsuitable material. First, users of the Internet could be made aware of the availability of tools which can filter out such material.[21] Also, UK-based content providers could be encouraged to set up a scheme labelling material available on Internet sites by its contents. Finally, it recommended regulating the Internet Service Providers to try to achieve a uniform and responsible response to illegal material.

As discussed in other papers in this volume, notably those by Edwards and Akdeniz, there is a growing belief that self regulation of the Internet is more effective as an answer to problems such as the spread of computer pornography rather than external regulation by governments. In the event, consultation with the Internet Service Providers Association (ISPA) led not to new legislation or licensing controls but to the launch in September 1996 of the Internet Watch Foundation.[22] This initiative had full Government support and was backed by the Metropolitan Police and leading Internet trade associations. It focuses on the blocking of illegal material, in particular child pornography. It is a self-regulatory initiative, which is monitored by the Internet Service Providers (ISPs). In essence the Internet Watch Foundation is an initiative along the lines of the former Conservative Government's Benefit Fraud Hotline, with Net users invited to "blow the whistle" on the posters and providers of pornography on the Net. Information provided will then be passed onto the police for appropriate investigation, if it has been posted within the UK. If the ISP in question is based outwith the UK, details will be passed on by the police to their counterparts in the appropriate jurisdiction. To date, the feedback from the Internet Watch Foundation following the opening of its telephone hot line has been positive. It has resulted in a small amount of child pornography being traced and removed by Internet Service Providers, all of which had originated from outside the UK.

ISPs have a dual interest in accepting and promoting the work of the Internet Watch Foundation. First, the alternative may well be draconian legislation by the government. Secondly, ISPs who knowingly allow their services to be used for illegal purposes will also, it is thought, be liable to prosecution. It is quite possible that the offences of possession of indecent photographs or pseudo-photographs now to be found in s 160 of the Criminal Justice Act 1988 and section 52A of the Civic Government (Scotland) Act 1982 (and the corresponding English offences), discussed above, might be applied to ISPs who

---

[21] Self regulation of Internet content is available to the individual user in the form of products like *Net Nanny* (http://www.netnanny.com/), *Cyber Patrol* (http://www.cyberpatrol.com/), *Surfwatch* (http://www/surfwatch.com/) and *CYBERsitter* (http://wwwsolidoak.com/). These programmes allow the individual user to rate or grade the incoming material and either filter out certain material, or allow in only certain specific sites. See further discussion in Edwards, p 191 and Akdeniz, p. 236.

[22] See <http://www.internetwatch.org.uk>. The Foundation has more than 50 members and all service providers are invited to become members. One of the Foundation's tasks, at the instigation of the Home Office, is to produce an Industry Code of Practice for self regulation.

knowingly act as hosts for such material, or act as "channel" for such images to individual users. There are, however, two possible defences. First, the accused may plead that they had not seen the image and had no knowledge or suspicion that the image was indecent. Secondly, the defence may plead that that they had a legitimate reason for possessing or distributing the image.[23] It would appear that no prosecutions have yet been brought against an ISP in the UK.

There have, however, been many instances where individual Net users have been prosecuted in relation to child pornography on the Internet. In January 1996, a computer consultant was reportedly the first person to be jailed in Britain for receiving child pornography via the Internet.[24] More recently, a statistician at Newcastle University admitted using the University's computers to access pornographic pictures through the Internet. He was fined £1,000. He downloaded the images onto floppy disks before feeding them into his lap-top computer. The court was advised that he was permitted access once a week to the University computers for his research. However in September 1996, the University's systems programmer noticed some unusual files had been trans-ferred from the Internet, all of which could be traced back to the computer used by the accused. The files were found to contain child pornography.

Stalking

Stalking in its non electronic form has become a matter of much public con-cern in recent months. What of electronic stalking? The offence of stalking in its ordinary form most frequently involves an accused who persistently watches, follows or in some other way harasses the victim with unsolicited and obsessive attention. Computers can add another dimension and offer great potential for the obsessed stalker. The facility offered by electronic mail can mean that the victim is bombarded with material either at home or at the work place. And of course should the stalker choose, he can remain anony-mous, thereby causing even greater alarm for the victim.

The Telecommunications Act 1984, which applies throughout the UK, makes it an offence in s 43 to use a public telecommunications system[25] to send grossly offensive, threatening or obscene material. This would seem to cover data sent via the Internet and computer modems, which use telephone lines. Such behaviour would also constitute conduct likely to cause offence or alarm to others thereby amounting to the Scottish common law crime of

---

[23] Criminal Justice Act 1988, s 160(2)(a) and (b) (England) and Civic Government (Sc) Act 1982, s 52A(2)(a) and (b) (England). It has been suggested this might apply to exclude any possi-ble liability where pictures of abuse of children were kept as medical or psychological records, or as part of academic research.

[24] *Scotsman*, 5 January 1996 "Man jailed for child porn on the Internet".

[25] Extensively defined in s 4 of the 1984 Act.

breach of the peace. Although conduct such as sending invasive or threatening emails might be seen as lacking a public element, and therefore not causing a breach of the peace, analogies can be drawn with Scots cases on the sending of "poison pen" letters on a one-to-one basis which were held to constitute an offence of this nature. Threats made via email might also be charged under the common law of assault. Here we have another example of how Scots common law is flexible enough to tackle computer aided crime.

It is also possible that electronic stalking might be curtailed using the recently enacted Protection Against Harassment Act 1997. Section 4 of the Act, applicable to England only, stipulates that "a course of conduct" which causes a fear of violence may be prosecuted as an offence under the Act if the perpetrator knows or ought to know that his conduct could have that effect. A "course of conduct" is defined in s 7 as involving conduct on at least two occasions. "Conduct" is only defined inclusively as including speech, and therefore can no doubt include elements such as harassment by multiple emails. It is probable that s 4 was not extended to apply to Scotland because of the aforementioned breadth of the common law relating to breach of peace and assault. In Scotland, however, a civil non-harassment order may be obtained if there has been a course of conduct amounting to harassment ie two occasions of such conduct.[26] Breach of such a non-harassment order is a criminal offence.[27] We are still some way, however, from the position in some American states where statutes have been drafted which overtly entertain the possibility of electronic communication as a method of stalking.[28]

Recovery and use of computer evidence in prosecutions

Once an offence has been detected the process of gathering evidence must begin. Whether evidence is sought to prove the charge, or in defence of the charge, the importance of obtaining expert assistance to recover evidence associated with computers cannot be over emphasised. As mentioned earlier, the material to which access is sought may be encrypted with a code or be password-protected. Other sophisticated security measures can be employed with the result that a clumsy attempt to gain access can trigger the automatic deletion of all the material. It is also possible for data to be erased remotely, by an associate working on distant equipment, who is alerted to the unwanted intrusion. The investigator must therefore proceed cautiously.

---

[26] See s 8. In England an injunction against harassment may be obtained under s 3, breach of which gives warrant for the arrest of the defendant.

[27] Section 9.

[28] For example, Alaska's Criminal Law Statute, Chapter 41, Offences Against the Person, makes "stalking" a criminal offence and expressly includes 'sending mail or electronic communications to that person' as one of the envisaged methods of stalking. Similarly, the Penal Code of Connecticut describes stalking in the second degree as including communication with a person by computer network.

There are complex decoding programs which investigators can run, but the police will often simply collate information about an accused's hobbies, nicknames, or even the name of his pet dog—people use all sorts of personal information to create passwords. Gaining access to password-protected files is a major practical problem. An alleged paedophile ring was prosecuted in London in March 1996. The police strongly suspected that their computers contained indecent images of children, but they were unable to gain access to the files to establish this. Ultimately, the police were able to seek only forfeiture of the computer hardware.

Another important aspect of the recovery of evidence is the careful dismantling of computers, correctly labelled and logged, as they may have to be reconstituted again in a courtroom. It is essential that the original evidence should not be altered in any way and that its integrity be maintained. It may be important to replicate the precise sequence and structure of the information recorded on the disk. For instance, in a fraud case the *absence* of one particular item of data may yield an incriminatory inference. It is also important to retain the chain of evidence so that any print-out can be retraced to its originating computer file.

That naturally leads us to consider how to use computer related evidence in court at trial. There are two aspects to this.

First, the practical problem of presenting computer evidence. Thought may have to be given to the means by which information contained on disk, for example, can be presented to a judge or jury. Back-up copies must be taken of the exact contents of disks for the purposes of displaying evidence in court, as mentioned earlier. In addition CCTV monitors may be required in the courtroom to permit demonstrations of the searches of disks as the exact contents of the disk are displayed.

Secondly, the use of computer evidence in the legal sense. The starting point is that in theory the "best evidence" rule will still hold true with computer-related evidence. The "best evidence" rule requires that a party to an action must produce the best available version of the evidence which he seeks to lead. However this is not such a problem as it once was, as legal rules requiring that originals of documents rather than computer-generated copies be presented in court are generally being diminished by legislation in both England and Scotland.[29] For criminal law, ss 279 of, and Schedule 8 to, the Criminal Procedure (Scotland) Act 1995 make special provisions for the admission in criminal proceedings of certified documentary evidence, particularly business documents.[30] These provisions also validate the use of certified copies of documents. In some instances this may contain hearsay material, as the person who entered the information, or the person who retrieved the information, may not be available. But this can usually now be accepted as the best

[29] See Lloyd, p. 148.
[30] Similar provisions exist for English law in the Police and Criminal Evidence Act 1984, s 69 and ss 23 and 24 of the Criminal Justice Act 1988.

evidence at a trial. For the purposes of these provisions a document has been specifically stated to include a computer disk.

It is also interesting to note that the Criminal Court of Appeal in Scotland recently had occasion to consider the definition of a "document" in *Rollo v HMA*.[31] The accused appealed against his conviction under the Misuse of Drugs Act 1971 for the supply of drugs. A crucial piece of evidence for the Crown was the contents of the electronic notepad of the accused. The appeal was on the ground that the contents of the notepad were inadmissible because it was not a document in terms of s 23(b) of the Act, the section under which the police were granted their search warrant. It was held that the essence of a document is that it is something containing recorded information of some sort, and that it does not matter that the information requires to be processed in some way such as translation, decoding or electronic retrieval, or that it was protected in some way against unwanted access. The appeal was refused.

CONCLUSION

It has been my intention in this article to show that criminal lawyers need not be unduly alarmed at the prospect of cases involving computers and computer evidence. Our starting point should be the definition of the crime. Is it a computer crime proper, or is it a crime committed with the aid of a computer? Paring the offence in question down to its basic definition can assist in putting it in context. Thereafter, aware of the part that the computer evidence plays, we simply revert to the rules of evidence, either in their basic form, or as specifically provided for by statute.

I also hoped to demonstrate the capability of Scots law in particular to meet the challenge of computer crime. Three examples discussed above have highlighted the capability of Scots common law to be flexible enough to deal with the novel scenarios of computer crime. The first is the example of computer fraud by illicit obtaining of passwords, which vexed the English judiciary in *R v Gold* but which Scots law might deal with under the offence of obtaining services by means of false pretences. The second is the offence of shamelessly indecent conduct tried at the Sheriff Court in Stornoway which might have presented a patently offensive set of facts which nonetheless could have been difficult to prosecute within existing legislation. The third is the example of stalking, which Scots law was competent to deal with under the offences of breach of the peace and assault without the need for specific new enactments. New legislation such as the Computer Misuse Act 1990 and the Criminal Justice and Public Order Act 1994 does, of course, have a rôle in dealing with genuinely novel offences and closing loopholes. Civil libertarians will also argue that it is best for emerging new areas of criminal behaviour to be

---

[31] 1996 SCCR 874.

governed by publicly available and clearly laid out statutes rather than the uncertainties of the common law. On the other hand, as the *Fellows* and *Gold* cases show, it is not always easy or possible for legislation to be drafted in a sufficiently flexible form to adapt to the pace of technological change. (It can easily be imagined for example that before long we will find offensive conduct occurring in virtual reality that will be hard to categorise under current concepts of criminal obscenity, publication and possession.) As the passage of time has shown, there has been little need so far in Scotland to legislate against crimes involving computers. Whilst there is no room for complacency, I would suggest the framework is in place to see computer related crimes properly dealt with by the courts.

13

Governance of Pornography and Child Pornography on the Global Internet: A Multi-Layered Approach

YAMAN AKDENIZ*

INTRODUCTION

How pornography should be regulated is one of the most controversial topics to have arisen in relation to the Internet in recent years. The widespread availability of pornography on the Internet has stirred up a "moral panic"[1] shared by the government, law enforcement bodies such as the police, prosecutors and judges along with the media in general.[2]

There have been many attempts to limit the availability of pornographic content on the Internet by governments and law enforcement bodies all around the world. While the US Government introduced the Communications Decency Act 1996 ("CDA"), the UK police attempted to censor Usenet discussion groups allegedly carrying child pornography in the summer of 1996. Both attempts were criticised and the US Supreme Court struck down the CDA in June 1997.

There is no settled definition of pornography, either in the United Kingdom itself, or in the multi-national environment of the Internet, where cultural, moral and legal variations all around the world make it difficult to define "pornographic content" in a way acceptable to all. What is considered simply sexually explicit but not obscene in England may well be obscene in many other countries; conversely what is considered lawful but not pornographic in Sweden may well be obscene under the current UK legislation.

This chapter will discuss two different issues: the regulation of potentially harmful content such as pornography on the Internet; and regulation of

---

* LL.B., MA , Ph.D. Student at the Centre for Criminal Justice Studies, Law Faculty, University of Leeds. E-mail: lawya@leeds.ac.uk. For further information, see <http://www.leeds.ac.uk/law/pgs/yaman/yaman.htm>. Portions of this article appeared in an earlier form in Y Akdeniz, "The Regulation of Pornography and Child Pornography on the Internet," (1997) 1 *Journal of Information, Law and Technology.*

[1] See S Cohen, *Folk Devils and Moral Panics: Creation of Mods and Rockers* (Blackwell, 1987).

[2] It all started with a controversial Time Magazine article in the summer of 1995. See P Elmer-Dewitt "On a screen near you: Cyberporn", *Time*, 1995, July 3, 34-41.

invariably illegal content such as child pornography. These issues are different in nature and should not be confused. It is the submission of this chapter that any regulatory action intended to protect a certain group of people, such as children, should not take the form of an unconditional prohibition of using the Internet to distribute certain content where that is freely available to adults in other media.

Before explaining the possibilities of how to govern the availability of "pornographic content" on the global Internet, this chapter will briefly discuss how and in what form these materials are available on the Internet.

The availability of pornographic content on the Internet

Pornography on the Internet is available in different formats. These range from pictures and short animated movies, to sound files and stories. Most of this kind of pornographic content is available through World Wide Web ("WWW") pages; but sometimes they are also distributed through an older communication process, Usenet newsgroups. The Internet also makes it possible to discuss sex, see live sex acts, and arrange sexual activities[3] from computer screens. There are also sex related discussions on the Internet Relay Chat ("IRC") channels where users in small groups or in private channels exchange messages and files. But as with the Web and the Usenet, only a small fraction of the IRC channels are dedicated to sex. There are more than 14,000 Usenet discussion groups all around the world but only around 200 groups are sex related, some of these relating to socially valuable and legitimate discussions, concerning, eg, homosexuality or sexual abuse.

THE GOVERNANCE OF THE INTERNET

If illegal and harmful content on the Internet needs to be regulated then the question is: how should this be achieved? Despite the popular perception, the Internet is not a "lawless place."[4] Rather the Internet "poses a fundamental challenge for effective leadership and governance."[5] Walker states that:

> "In the current stage of modern, or post-modern society, one can expect a trend towards "governance' rather than the "government', in which the role of the nation

---

[3] But see section 2 of the Sexual Offences (Conspiracy and Incitement) Act 1996 which makes it an offence to incite another person to commit certain sexual acts against children abroad. The scope of incitement for the purposes of section 2 extends to the use of Internet and any incitement will be deemed to take place in the UK if the message is received in the UK.

[4] See J R Reidenberg, "Governing Networks and Cyberspace Rule-Making" (1996) *Emory Law Journal* 45.

[5] *Ibid.*

state is not exclusive but may need further sustenance by the activation of more varied levels of power at second hand.'[6]

According to Reidenberg, laws, regulations, and standards will affect the development of the Internet and this is also true for self-regulatory solutions introduced for the availability of pornographic content on the Internet. Reidenberg states that:

> "Rules and rule-making do exist. However, the identities of the rule makers and the instruments used to establish rules will not conform to classic patterns of regulation."[7]

The Internet is a complex, anarchic, and multi-national environment where old concepts of regulation, reliant as they are upon tangibility in time and space, may not be easily applicable or enforceable. This is why the wider concept of governance may be more suitable. According to Walker, "social regulation within modern society has developed within physical bounds of time and space, but the development of cyberspace distanciates its inhabitants from local controls and the physical confines of nationality, sovereignty and governmentality leading to new possibilities in relationships and interaction."[8] The idea of "governance without government" may be the best approach for the development of the Internet. But "if such mechanisms of international governance and re-regulation are to be initiated then the role of nation states is pivotal."[9]

There appears to be no single solution to the regulation of illegal and harmful content on the Internet because, for example, the exact definition of offences such as child pornography varies from one country to another and also what is considered harmful will depend upon cultural differences. A recent European Commission Communication Paper stated that "each country may reach its own conclusion in defining the borderline between what is permissible and not permissible."[10] The multi-layered governance system should be a mixture of national and international legislation, and self-imposed regulation by the ISPs and on-line users. This should include codes of conduct by the ISPs, software filters to be used by parents, advice to parents and school teachers, hotlines and special organisations to report illegal content on the Internet.

---

[6] See Walker Clive "Cyber-Contempt: Fair Trials and the Internet" (1997) Yearbook of Media and Entertainment Law.

[7] See J R Reidenberg, "Governing Networks and Cyberspace Rule-Making" (1996) *Emory Law Journal* 45.

[8] Walker Clive, "Cyber-Contempt: Fair Trials and the Internet" *Yearbook of Media and Entertainment Law*.

[9] P Hirst and G Thompson, "Globalization and the Future of the Nation State," (1995) 24 *Economy and Societ* 408 at 430.

[10] European Commission Communication to the European Parliament, The Council, The Economic and Social Committee and the Committee of the Regions: Illegal and Harmful Content on the Internet, Com (96) 487, Brussels, 16 October 1996. An on-line copy is available at <http://www2.echo.lu/legal/en/internet/content/content.html>

Governance theorists are beginning to recognise that "objects of governance are only known through attempts to govern them"[11] and "governance is not a choice between centralisation and decentralisation. It is about regulating relationships in complex systems,"[12] and the global Internet does provide a great challenge for governance. The following headings will try to address the issues arising from the multi-layered approach to the governance of "pornographic content" on the Internet.

OVERVIEW OF UK PORNOGRAPHY LAWS

This section concentrates mainly on those aspects of UK law relating to obscenity which have particular reference to the Internet. UK obscenity legislation has recently been amended by the Criminal Justice and Public Order Act 1994 ("CJPOA 1994") to deal with the specific problem of Internet pornography.[13] The following will show, however, that there are difficulties with the application of existing national laws to a medium such as the global Internet which does not have any borders.

Obscene Publications Act 1959 and 1964

These two statutes constitute the major legislation to combat pornographic material of any kind in the UK. Section 1(1) of the 1959 Act provides that "an article shall be deemed to be obscene if its effect or the effect of any one of its items is, if taken as a whole, such as to tend to deprave and corrupt persons who are likely, having regard to all relevant circumstances, to read, see or hear the matter contained or embodied in it."[14]

Under Section 2(1) of the Obscene Publications Act ("OPA"), it is an offence to publish an obscene article or to have an obscene article for publication for gain. Section 1(3) of the 1959 Act makes it clear that the "articles" contemplated were such items as computer disks; however most of the pornography on the Internet is now transferred electronically from one computer to another using telephone lines and modems rather than via any tangible medium such as discs. This left a possible lacuna in section 1(3), OPA 1959, but this has now been plugged by CJPOA 1994, which amended the meaning of "publication" in that section, so that electronic transmission of

---

[11] A Hunt & G Wickham *Foucault and Law: Towards a Sociology of Law as Governance* (1994, Pluto Press)at p 78.

[12] RAW Rhodes, "The Hollowing Out of the State: The Changing Nature of the Public Services in Britain", (1994) *Political Quarterly* 138 at p 151.

[13] See House of Commons, Home Affairs Committee: First report on Computer Pornography, (HMSO,1994).

[14] This legal definition of obscene is narrower than the ordinary meaning of obscene which is filthy, lewd or disgusting. See *R v Anderson and others* [1971] 3 All ER 1152.

pornographic material is now clearly covered by the 1994 Act. When A sends B pornographic pictures attached to an e-mail, this electronic transmission will be a publication covered by the Act.[15]

Section 1(2) of OPA 1964 makes it an offence to have an obscene article in ownership, possession or control with a view to publishing it for gain. Following the amendments made by CJPOA 1994, this would even apply when A simply makes the data available to be transferred or downloaded electronically, by providing a password to B, so that B can access the materials and copy them.[16]

CHILD PORNOGRAPHY

The main concern of legislators and parents in relation to Internet content is child pornography, rather than other forms of pornographic content. This has been the case ever since paedophiles started to use the Internet for circulating pornographic materials related to children.[17] Paedophiles may be seen as a minority sexual group, with its own form of expression explicitly involving fantasies and imaginings about sex with children. But while it is often argued that pornography should not be proscribed on the basis of freedom of speech arguments, there is a general consensus that the line should be drawn with child pornography. In most cases, child pornography is a permanent record of the sexual abuse of an actual child (except in the case of pseudo-photographs, which are discussed below). An understanding of the special way in which child pornography is child abuse, is crucial to an understanding of the whole problem of child pornography.

UK child pornography laws

Protection of Children Act 1978

The 1978 Act was passed in response to the growing problem of child pornography. Its main purpose was to close some potential gaps in the measures

---

[15] See further Y Akdeniz, "Computer Pornography: A Comparative Study of the US and UK Obscenity Laws and Child Pornography Laws in Relation to the Internet", [1996] 10 *International Review of Law, Computers & Technology* 235.

[16] See *R v Arnolds; R v Fellows*, (1996) *The Times*, 27 September. See also section 43 of the Telecommunications Act 1984 which makes it an offence to send "by means of a public telecommunications system, a message or other matter that is grossly offensive or of an indecent, obscene or menacing character" and is an imprisonable offence with a maximum term of six months. In addition to dealing with indecent, obscene or offensive telephone calls, the Act also covers the transmission of obscene materials through the telephone systems by electronic means.

[17] The Meese Commission Report, in 1986, provides evidence that paedophile offenders and child pornographers had begun to use personal computers and computer networks for communication and distribution of materials. See Attorney General's Commission on Pornography: Final Report, 2 vols. Washington, D.C.: U.S. Government Printing Office, July 1986 [The Meese Commission] at page 629.

available to police and prosecutors.[18] The definition of "photograph" given in section 7(4) of the 1978 Act was extended to include photographs in electronic data format following the amendments made by section 84 (4) of the Criminal Justice and Public Order Act 1994 (CJPOA 1994).

The CJPOA 1994 introduced the concept of "pseudo-photographs" of children. Pseudo-photographs are technically photographs, but they are created by computer software manipulating one or more pre-existing pictures. For example, a child's face can be superimposed on an adult body, or to another child's body, with the characteristics of the body altered to create pornographic computer generated images without the involvement of a real child. It is now an offence "for a person to take, or permit to be taken or to make, any indecent photographs or pseudo-photographs of a child; (or) to distribute or show such indecent photographs or pseudo-photographs" under section 1 of the 1978 Act.

The UK police believe that the creators or possessors of pseudo-photographs will end up abusing children, so the purpose of the new legislation may be seen as to criminalise acts preparatory to abuse,[19] and also to close possible future loopholes in the prosecution of such cases, as it may be very difficult to separate a pseudo-photograph from a real photograph.[20]

Although pseudo-photographs can be created without the involvement of real children, there is a justifiable fear that harm to children is associated with all child pornography. The Williams Committee stated:

"Few people would be prepared to take the risk where children are concerned and just as the law recognises that children should be protected against sexual behaviour which they are too young to properly consent to, it is almost universally agreed that this should apply to participation in pornography."[21]

On the other hand, there are arguments that pseudo-photographs are not harmful. The children involved in child pornography may suffer physical or

[18] Gibbons Thomas "Computer Generated Pornography", *International Yearbook of Law Computers and Technology*, 1995, vol. 9, pp. 83–95, page 87.

[19] In March 1996 the author had an interview with Detective Inspector David Davis, head of West Midlands police commercial vice unit which deals with child pornography. He clearly stated that the UK police believe that if somebody creates or posses indecent pseudo-photographs of children, he is a potential child abuser and will abuse children in the future. See also Explosive Substances Act 1883 as an example for preparatory acts being criminalised.

[20] See the Canadian case of *R v. Pecchiarich* [1995] 22 O.R. (3d) 748-766, in which Pecchiarich, 19, was convicted and sentenced to two year probation, and 150 hours of community service for distributing "pseudo-photographs" of children over the Internet under section 163 (1) of the Canadian Criminal Code. Although Pecchiarich created these materials and they prove his paedophilic tendencies and fantasies, he did not commit any offence towards children. Compare the case of Jake Baker, who had fantasies about torturing, raping and murdering a female student at the University of Michigan. He also sent his story to alt.sex.stories giving the name of a classmate. His case was dismissed by a US District Count Judge ruling that he was protected by the First Amendment. Baker's case was tackled as a speech issue and although he had sick fantasies they did not involve immediate danger or any criminal activity. See *U.S. v. Baker*, 890 F. Supp. 1375 (1995).

[21] Williams Committee Report (1979) Obscenity and Film Censorship, Cmnd 7772, (London: HMSO), page 90, para 6.68.

mental injury, but with pseudo-photographs, the situation is quite different. These photographs are created only by the use of computers. There is no involvement of children in production and there is no direct harm to children in their use. However there is substantial evidence that photographs of children engaged in sexual activity are used as tools for the further molestation of other children,[22] and photographs or pseudo-photographs will be used interchangeably for this purpose.[23]

Section 160 of the Criminal Justice Act 1988

Under section 160 of the 1988 Act as amended by section 84(4) of the CJPOA 1994, it is an offence for a person to have an indecent photograph or pseudo-photograph of a child in his possession. This offence is now a serious arrestable offence with a maximum imprisonment term not exceeding six months. It has been successfully used in its new form in recent cases involving possession of child pornography.

Operation Starburst

In July 1995, the British police were involved in Operation Starburst, an international investigation of a paedophile ring who used the Internet to distribute graphic pictures of child pornography. Nine British men were arrested as a result of the operation which involved other arrests in Europe, America, South Africa and the Far East. The operation identified 37 men world wide.[24]

Possession offences

As a result of Operation Starburst, many cases of simple possession offences were brought to court. *Christopher Sharp* was fined £9000 and was the first person to be prosecuted in a case involving pornography and the Internet in the UK. Sharp admitted two charges of possessing indecent photographs of children under the age of 16 contrary to section 160 of the Criminal Justice Act 1988. In early 1996, *Martin Crumpton*, a former computer consultant, was sentenced to three months' imprisonment in a Birmingham magistrates' court. He also admitted possession of indecent pictures of children and was the first

---

[22] Attorney General's Commission [The Meese Commission] Final Report on Pornography, 2 vols. (Washington, D.C.: U.S. Government Printing Office) July 1986, page 411.

[23] See also the recent US legislation, Child Pornography Prevention Act 1996 which sets mandatory prison sentences of 15 years for production of child pornography, five years for possession of child pornography, and life imprisonment for repeat offenders convicted of sexual abuse of a minor. The 1996 Act also covers the computer generated images of children as in Canada and the UK.

[24] See further Akdeniz Yaman, "The Regulation of Pornography and Child Pornography on the Internet," 1997 (1) *The Journal of Information, Law and Technology*.

person to be jailed in the UK in an offence concerning pornography and the Internet.[25]

Distribution offences

Fellows and Arnold: The Birmingham University Case

Fellows and Arnold were charged with a total of 18 charges, under the Protection of Children Act 1978, Obscene Publications Act 1959, and the CJPOA 1994, which widened the definition of "publication" to include computer transmission. West Midlands Police Commercial Vice Squad was contacted by US Customs saying they had identified a site in the UK. Vice Squad officers then swooped on the Department of Metallurgy at Birmingham University and discovered thousands of pictures stored in the computer system of youngsters engaged in obscene acts. The material could be accessed through the Internet across the world. Fellows had built up an extensive library of explicit pornography called "The Archive," featuring children as young as three, on a computer at Birmingham University where he worked.

The judge ruled that the computerised images could be legally regarded as photographs, setting a legal precedent that a pornographic computer image was, in law, the same as a photograph. After the ruling of the trial judge, Fellows admitted four charges of possessing indecent photographs of children with a view to distributing them, and one of possessing obscene photographs of adults for publication. Arnold also admitted distributing indecent photographs of children. Fellows was jailed for three years, and Arnold for six months for providing Fellows with up to 30 pornographic pictures of children.

Owen J. stated:

> "The pictures could fuel the fantasies of those with perverted attitudes towards the young and they might incite sexual abuse on innocent children."

This decision, and Crumpton's imprisonment in 1996, both show the current judicial attitude towards traffickers of child pornography and paedophiles in general.

On appeal, Evans L.J., upheld the ruling of the trial judge that images stored on computer disc constitute photographs.[26] His Lordship reviewed the terms of the Protection of Children Act and decided that although the com-

---

[25] More recently, *Dr John Payne*, 48, a GP in Warminster, Wiltshire, admitted a string of computer child pornography charges in November 1996 and was sentenced to 120 hours' community service in December 1996, by the Trowbridge Magistrates. He had four images of children in indecent poses stored on his home computer. See Cyber-Rights & Cyber-Liberties (UK) for further information on all UK child pornography cases involving the Internet at <http://www.leeds.ac.uk/law/pgs/yaman/yaman.htm>.

[26] See *R v. Fellows, R v. Arnold,* CA, *The Times* October 3, 1996.

puter disk was not a photograph, it was "a copy of an indecent photo-graph."[27]

The US Telecommunications Act 1996, including the provisions of the CDA 1996, attempted to restrict access by minors to "patently offensive depictions of sexual or excretory activities", a provision clearly intended to cover the pornographic images and materials which are widely available on-line over the Internet. In particular the CDA specified that it covered content available via an "interactive computer service". This obviously included materials available on the Internet. In the US, speech which is not considered "obscene" but is indecent enjoys First Amendment protection, though it can still be regulated where there is a sufficient governmental interest. The fact that the CDA was intended to prohibit "indecent speech" would have had an unprecedented effect on the Internet. Information regarding protection from AIDS, birth control or prison rape, is sexually explicit and may be considered "indecent" or "patently offensive" in some communities, and this kind of speech would have been affected by the provisions of the CDA, particularly as it had no definition of the word "indecent".

Legal challenges to the CDA

The American Civil Liberties Union (ACLU) and other civil liberties groups filed a lawsuit challenging the CDA as an unconstitutional restraint on free speech on the Internet. In *ACLU v. Janet Reno*, ACLU claimed that the CDA was ill defined and did not sufficiently delineate what speech or other actions would be subject to prosecution. ACLU and the other plaintiffs argued that:

> "Not only does this ban unconstitutionally restrict the First Amendment rights of minors and those who communicate with them about important issues, but, because of the nature of the online medium, it essentially bans 'indecent' or 'patently offensive' speech entirely, thus impermissibly reducing the adult population to 'only what is fit for children'."

---

[27] See also the case of Father Adrian McLeish, a Roman Catholic priest at St Joseph's church in Gilesgate, Durham, who held the largest known collection of child pornography yet gathered electronically. He had amassed a vast store of obscene pictures and drawings in his presbytery and exchanged thousands of explicit e-mail messages with other paedophiles. McLeish was sentenced to six years imprisonment by Newcastle upon Tyne Crown Court in November 1996. His activities were exposed a year ago during "Operation Starburst." See Cyber-Rights & Cyber-Liberties (UK) supra for further information and for other cases involving child pornography and the Internet.

ACLU did not challenge the statute to the extent that it already proscribed obscenity or child pornography, merely opposing the extension of liability for speech introduced by the CDA.[28]

Following an initial temporary restraint order obtained by the ACLU, in June 1996 the Federal District Court of Philadelphia held that ACLU had established a reasonable probability of eventual success in the litigation by demonstrating that sections 223(a)(1)(B) and 223(a)(2) of the CDA were unconstitutional on their face to the extent that they covered "indecency." Accordingly, a preliminary injunction was granted. Dalzell J stated:

> "As the most participatory form of mass speech yet developed, the Internet deserves the highest protection from government intrusion. Just as the strength of the Internet is chaos, so the strength of our liberty depends upon the chaos and cacophony of the unfettered speech the First Amendment protects."[29]

The final appeal in the *ACLU* case, to the Supreme Court, resulted in a historic ruling on June 26, 1997 in which by a 7–2 vote, the online censorship provisions of the CDA were struck down. The Supreme Court affirmed the Philadelphia Court's ruling that the CDA was unconstitutional, declaring that "[t]he CDA's "indecent transmission" and "patently offensive display" provisions abridge the freedom of speech protected by the First Amendment".[30] They went on to add:

> "As a matter of constitutional tradition, in the absence of evidence to the contrary, we presume that governmental regulation of the content of speech is more likely to interfere with the free exchange of ideas than to encourage it. The interest in encouraging freedom of expression in a democratic society outweighs any theoretical but unproven benefit of censorship."

One of the principal issues addressed in the judgement was whether Internet content was more akin to content in print media or in broadcast media such as television. Because of its mass appeal and easy access by children, a higher level of scrutiny in broadcasting than in print media is justified. If part of a broadcasting program on radio or on television is patently offensive, vulgar or shocking than it may be considered indecent and banned at certain times of the day. The Supreme Court explained that the factors that are present in broadcasting are not present in cyberspace. "Neither before nor after the enactment of the CDA have the vast democratic fora of the Internet been subject to the type of government supervision and regulation that has attended the broadcast industry." The Internet was not as invasive a medium as radio or television, since communications over the Internet did not invade an individual's home, or appear on one's computer screen unbidden. Users seldom

---

[28] See 18 U.S.C. 1464-65 and 2251-52. See also *New York v. Ferber*, 458 U.S. 747 (1982), and *Miller v. California*, 413 U.S. 15 (1973), and *U.S. v. Thomas* 74 F.3d 701 (1996).

[29] *ACLU, et al.v. Janet Reno*, 929 F Supp 824 (1996).

[30] See the Supreme Court decision No 96-511, at <http://www.aclu.org/court/renovacludec.html>.

encountered offensive content by accident. Proscribing offensive content on the Internet for all users just to protect children would be "burn[ing] the house to roast the pig."[31]

In his opinion for the Court, Justice Stevens wrote that "[t]he CDA, casting a far darker shadow over free speech, threatens to torch a large segment of the Internet community." The CDA went too far in reducing all material accessible on the global Internet to a level suitable only for children.

DEVELOPMENTS WITHIN THE EUROPEAN UNION

The European Commission launched a Communication Paper on "Illegal and Harmful Content" together with a Green Paper on the Protection of Minors and Human Dignity in Audio-visual and Information Services in October 1996.[32] The Communication Paper was the result of calls for the regulation of the Internet within the European Union dating from early 1996.

The European Commission documents followed a resolution adopted by the Telecommunications Council of Ministers in September 1996, concerning the dissemination of illegal content on the Internet, especially child pornography. While the Communication gives policy options for immediate action to fight against harmful and illegal content on the Internet, the Green Paper sets out to examine the challenges that society faces in ensuring that these issues of over-riding public interest are adequately taken into account in the rapidly evolving world of audio-visual and information services.[33] All these initiatives at the European level were adopted in a Resolution at the Telecommunications Council in November 1996.[34]

The European Parliament adopted a resolution following a report about the European Commission Communication in April 1997.[35] Following the resolution, the European Commissioner Martin Bangemann, stated in his view that "it is difficult to pass legislation at international level on harmful content on the Internet, but there is no cultural difference in what is illegal, and the response must be global."[36] Therefore solutions may not be limited to the EU level and a future involvement of other fora such as the OECD or G7 is likely in future.

---

[31] Quoted from *Sable Communications v FCC* 492 US 115 (1989).

[32] See European Commission Green Paper on the Protection of Minors and Human Dignity in Audovisual and Information Services, Brussels, 16 October 1996. An on-line copy is available at <http://www2.echo.lu/legal/en/internet/content/content.html>

[33] See also the European Commission Working Party Report (1996) "Illegal and Harmful Content on the Internet" at <http://www2.echo.lu/legal/en/internet/content/wpen.html>

[34] See <http://law-www-server.law.strath.ac.uk/diglib/lab/resol.html>.

[35] See Report on the Commission Communication on illegal and harmful content on the Internet (COM(96)0487—C4-0592/96) Committee on Civil Liberties and Internal Affairs, Rapporteur: Mr Pierre PRADIER—20 March 1997, available at <http://www.europarl.eu.int/dg1/a4/en/a4-97/a4-0098.htm>.

[36] Agence Europe, "MEPs want voluntary code of good conduct to guarentee freedom of expression, while protecting children," April 26, 1997.

RESPONSIBILITY OF INTERNET SERVICE PROVIDERS (ISPS)

It is not possible to access the Internet without the services of an ISP, and thus the role of ISPs in content regulation of the Internet is crucial. As a result they are obvious targets for enforcement authorities. ISPs have recently been charged with criminal offences of providing child pornography in both Germany and France. Access to "hate speech" on the Internet is of particular concern to the German government, and again the ISPs have been the "usual suspects" in investigations of provision of such material on the Internet.[37]

The UK Government's preferred option in relation to ISPs, like that of the EC, is one of self-regulation rather than control by legislation.[38] ISPs have been encouraged to produce codes of practice to control access to illegal and unsuitable material.[39] The Home Office stated that:

"it is important to distinguish between illegal material and material which is legal but which some would find offensive. Self-regulation is an appropriate tool to address the latter. Dealing with illegal material is a matter for the courts and the law enforcement agencies."[40]

Walker comments that:

"Self-regulation in this field has a number of advantages. Rules devised by the media are more likely to be internalised and accepted. In addition, it may avoid heavy-handed legal intervention which carries with it the spectre of government censorship."[41]

It should not however be forgotten that the prime responsibility for content lies with authors and primary content providers. Blocking access at the level of access providers was criticised in the EU communication paper discussed above on the ground that access is restricted to far more material than the limited category of illegal communications. Such a restrictive regime severely interferes with the freedom of the individual and the political traditions of Europe. There is a real need for the legal position of the ISPs to be clarified,

---

[37] Deutsche Telekom (DT), the national telephone company, in January 1996, blocked users of its T-Online computer network from accessing Internet sites used to spread anti-Semitic propaganda, which is a crime in Germany. The company was responding to demands by Mannheim prosecutors who were investigating Ernst Zundel, a German-born neo-Nazi living in Toronto. See "German Service Cuts Net Access" *San Jose Mercury News*, January 27, 1996.

[38] "Home Office Meeting of January 19th 1996" available at Cityscape manager Clive Feather's home page at <http://www.gold.net/users/cdwf/homeoffice/>.

[39] See for example the JANET Acceptable Use Policy, at <http://www.ja.net/documents/use.html>.

[40] See House of Lords, Select Committee on Science and Technology, "Information Society: Agenda for Action in the UK", Session 1995-96, 5th Report, London: HMSO, 23 July 1996, available at <http://www.parliament.the-stationery-office.co.uk/pa/ld199596/ldselect/inforsoc/inforsoc.htm>, para 4.63.

[41] Walker Clive "Fundamental Rights, Fair Trials and the New Audio-Visual Sector" [1996] *MLR* 59, 4, 517-539, pages 537, 538.

so that they need not, as at present, steer a path between accusations of censorship by users, and exposure to liability for the content they carry.

Self- regulation by ISPs—the Internet Watch Foundation[42]

The Internet Watch Foundation (IWF), was announced in September 1996 with the backing of the UK government. It follows a similar initiative in Holland although there are differences between the two hotline systems.[43] The IWF has an e-mail, telephone and fax hot-line so that users can report materials related to child pornography and other obscene materials.[44] The IWF undertake to inform all British ISPs once they locate undesirable content. The ISP concerned then has no excuse in law that it is unaware of the offending material, and the UK police will be entitled to take action against any ISP which does not remove the relevant content requested from IWF.[45]

Although the IWF proposals state that UK ISPs should bear responsibility for their services, and take reasonable measures to hinder the use of the Internet for illegal purposes, it is wrong to assume that ISPs should be held solely responsible for content provided by third parties on the Internet. The real problem will remain elsewhere; in the real rather than virtual world, where illegal materials are originally created. As long as such material is produced, there can never be a total solution to its availability via the Internet. The Internet is just another convenient tool for paedophiles who wish to traffic in these kind of materials. The formation of the IWF sets a dangerous precedent for privatised censorship on the Internet.[46] A better approach would have been a free confidential telephone hot-line not run by the industry itself, akin to that run by the Metropolitan Police in London to combat terrorism. Furthermore, removing materials containing child pornography from the Internet at a UK level only is near futile as material can always be accessed by UK residents from computers located abroad.

---

[42] See further Cullen, p. 216.

[43] While the Dutch hotline was established by the Dutch Foundation for Internet Providers ("NLIP"), Dutch Internet users, the National Criminal Intelligence Service ("CRI"), National Bureau against Racial Discrimination and a psychologist, the UK Internet Watch Foundation ("IWF") is predominantly industry based.

[44] See <http://www.internetwatch.org.uk/hotline/>.

[45] See Safety-Net proposal, "Rating, Reporting, Responsibility, For Child Pornography & Illegal Material on the Internet" adopted and recommended by the Executive Committee of ISPA—Internet Services Providers Association, LINX—London Internet Exchange and The Safety-Net <Foundation at http://dtiinfo1.dti.gov.uk/safety-net/r3.htm>.

[46] David Kerr, head of the IWF had been reported to state that "there is also a whole category of dangerous subjects that demand ratings" such as discussions advocating suicide, information about dangerous sports like bungee-jumping, and more common areas of concern such as drugs, cigarette advertising, sex, and violence. See Wendy Grossman, "Europe Readies Net Content Ratings," *Wired News*, 7 July, 1997, at <http://www.wired.com/news/news/politics/story/5002.html>.

There are further problems. Users of the IWF hotline will probably report material unacceptable according to their taste and moral views, but it should be remembered that what is obscene or illegal is a matter for the courts. The IWF also promotes and recommends the use of rating systems such as PICS (see below) but industry based organisations backed up by governments should not impose rating systems nor get involved in their development. The utility of the IWF will need to be monitored and perhaps re-assessed.

UK POLICE CENSORSHIP OF INTERNET NEWSGROUPS

Although the UK Government supports self-regulation with respect to the Internet, the UK police appears to wish to take a more pro-active regulatory role. In mid August 1996, the Clubs & Vice Unit of the Metropolitan Police sent a letter to the UK ISPs supplying them with a list of Usenet discussion groups that they believe to contain pornographic material. The list mainly covered newsgroups which carried child pornography such as "alt.binaries. pictures.lolita.fucking, alt.binaries.pictures.boys," but it also included such newsgroups as "alt.sex.fetish.tickling, alt.sex.fetish.wrestling, alt.homosexual," which might or might not include pornographic content. As many people post the same material to multiple newsgroups, it is possible to find child pornography in newsgroups not intentionally devoted to the topic but attracting a similar readership such as alt.sex.fetish.tickling.

The action taken by the UK police appears to have been ill-considered and will not do much to reduce the availability of pornographic content on the Internet. Furthermore, the list of newsgroups provided by the UK police includes much material that is not illegal, such as legitimate discussion groups for homosexuals, and discussion groups which do not contain any pictures, but contain text, sexual fantasies and stories. These would almost certainly not infringe UK obscenity laws. The action of the UK police also amounted to censorship of material without public debate in Parliament or elsewhere. Political action by the UK government would be preferable to random censorship by law enforcement authorities.

TECHNICAL SOLUTIONS AND RATING SYSTEMS

Platform for Internet Content Selections (PICS)[47] is a rating system for the Internet similar to the "V-chip" technology used to filter out violence or

---

[47] PICS has been developed by the World Wide Web Consortium at http://www.w3.org/ pub/WWW/PICS/, a non-profit making association of academics, public interest groups and computer companies that looks at the social consequences of technology. It has the backing of 39 global computer and communications companies. The WWW Consortium expects the vetting system to be in widespread use by the end of this year and 80 per cent of information on the Internet to be coded by the end of 1997.

pornography on the television systems. PICS is widely supported by various governments and industry based organisations such as the Internet Watch Foundation in the UK. PICS works by embedding electronic labels in the text or image documents to vet their content before the computer displays them or passes them on to another computer.[48] The vetting system can be applied to political, religious, advertising or commercial topics. PICS tags can be added by the publisher of the material, by the company providing access to the Internet, or by an independent vetting body. The most common scheme for screening material is that developed in the United States by the Recreational Software Advisory Council on the Internet ("RSACi"). This was originally a scheme for rating computer games.[49] It rates material according to the degree of sex, violence, nudity, and bad language depicted. It is usually this PICS/RSACi screening combination that people have in mind when they refer to PICS.[50] PICS/RSACi initiatives are strongly criticised in the UK by "The Campaign for Internet Freedom" organised by Living Marxism Online:

> "We do not have the freedom to make up our own minds. PICS is just the modern face of censorship. . . State bans are overt, public and contestable. By contrast, the censorship of PICS is covert; the ratings authorities are not democratically account-able; the ratings schemes are not publicly determined; and there is no room for dissent."[51]

According to Electronic Frontiers Australia, "the definitions used in determining the four categories were clearly chosen with computer games in mind and lack the flexibility required for a wider range of materials. It is ludicrous that such a system should be applied to novels, online libraries, art galleries, and other such resources."[52]

There will be many rating authorities, and different communities may consider the same web pages to be in different PICS/RSACi categories. Some rating authorities may eg judge a certain site as an offensive, even though it has a public purpose, such as Web sites dealing with sexual abuse and AIDS. There will be no opportunity for free speech arguments to be made if ratings have been applied by private bodies as the government itself will not be involved directly in censorship.

---

[48] See R Whittle's web site "Internet censorship, access control and content regulation" at http://www.ozemail.com.au/~firstpr/contreg/ for an explanation of the PICS system and how it works. See also for a critique of PICS by The Campaign for Internet Freedom, "Frequently Asked Questions about PICS and Censorship" at http://www.junius.co.uk/censorship/faq.html.

[49] See <http://www.rsac.org/>.

[50] See <http://www.junius.co.uk/censorship/PICS.html>.

[51] See <http://www.junius.co.uk/censorship/index.html>.

[52] See Electronic Frontier Australia, "Media Release: Internet Labelling System Condemned," 9 February, 1997, at <http://www.efa.org.au/Publish/PR970209.html>

PARENTAL CONTROL SOFTWARE

Filtering software products[53] are available to allow parents to implement their preferences as to content when making decisions for their own children. The vast majority of the material available on the Internet is related to everyday topics, such as politics, news, sports, and shopping, but just as in the real world, there are areas of cyberspace which may contain materials that are not appropriate for children. Blocking and filtering technologies are far more effective and far more flexible than any law. The tools are designed to be easy to use for parents who may not be as computer savvy as their kids.[54] The National Center for Missing and Exploited Children produces a brochure called "Child Safety on the Information Highway."[55] After explaining the benefits of the Internet, it also explains the risks of the Internet for children:

(a) Exposure to inappropriate material,
(b) Physical molestation,
(c) Harassment.

The brochure strongly emphasises the importance of parents and their responsibility for their children's use of on-line services. Similar brochures are also produced in the UK[56] and blocking and filtering software is available to limit or control children's access to adult oriented Internet sites.[57] By using such technology parents themselves have the chance to decide what is good for their children, and what is not, but do not inflict this choice on the rest of the world's Internet users. There are many programs available with parental control features including "Surf Watch,"[58] "Net Nanny"[59] and

[53] See Netparents.org which provides resources for Internet parents at <http//www.netparents. org>.

[54] See CDT Policy Post Vol 3 (10), July 16, 1997 at <http://www.cdt.org>. See also "Summary of the Internet Family Empowerment White Paper: How Filtering Tools Enable Responsible Parents to Protect Their Children Online," July 16, 1997, at <http://www.cdt.org/speech/ summary.html>. See the White Paper at <http://www.cdt.org/speech/empower.html>.

[55] NCMEC and Interactive Services Association "Child Safety on the Information Highway" 1994, available at <http://www.isa.net/isa>. See also the Interactive Working Report to Senator Leahy, "Parental Empowerment, Child Protection, & Free Speech in Interactive Media" July 24, 1995 available at <http://www.cdt.org/>.

[56] See British Computer Society, "Combatting Computer Pornography: Guidance Notes for the BCS Members" BCS, April 1995, National Council for Educational Technology, "NCET Information Sheet for Schools: Computer Pornography" NCET, February 1995 and Norfolk IT Team, "Organising IT in Schools: Computer Pornography" Norfolk Educational Press, 1994.

[57] See eg. Cyber Patrol available on the Internet at http://www.microsys.com/CYBER/.

[58] Surf Watch is designed to provide parental control for families who do not subscribe to commercial online services which is available at http://www.surfwatch.com/. Surf Watch allows parents to block their children" access to known Internet sites

[59] Net Nanny is designed to prevent children from accessing areas on the Internet that a parent deems inappropriate, prevent children from giving the name, address, telephone number, credit card, or other personal information to strangers via e-mail or chat rooms, and can log off an on-line service or shut down the computer when the child attempts any of these activities. Net Nanny is available at http://www.netnanny.com/netnanny.

"CYBERsitter".[60] Sometimes this kind of software is over-inclusive and limits access to or censors inconvenient web sites, or filters potentially educational materials regarding AIDS and drug abuse prevention.[61] Again, the companies creating this kind of software provide no appeal system to "banned" content providers, thereby "subverting the self-regulating exchange of information that has been a hallmark of the Internet community."[62] As one opponent of such systems put it:

> "A close look at CYBERsitter reveals an agenda that infringes on the rights of children, parents and teachers wherever the program is used. Despite the hype over 'parental control' as an alternative to government censorship, it is Solid Oak Software that takes control when CYBERsitter is running on your computer."[63]

CYBERsitter, it should be remembered, still relies upon an initial form of labelling outside the home, which can amount to unchallengeable censorship. It is better for such control to be placed wholly in the hands of parents who can set standards for the welfare of individual children.

CONCLUSION

By providing quick and cheap access to any kind of information, the Internet is the first truly interactive "mass" medium. It should not be surprising that governments around the globe are anxious to control this new medium,[64] and the Internet seems to be following a pattern common to the regulation of new media.[65] In reality, while the Internet tends to produce extreme versions of problems, it rarely produces genuinely new ones.

There is a real problem of availability of child pornography on the Internet (and elsewhere), as well as that of the availability of sexually explicit material to unsuitable audiences, such as children. But any regulatory action intended to protect children from being abused in the production of pornography, or from accessing unsuitable content, should not take the form of an unconditional prohibition of using the Internet to distribute content where that content is freely available to adults in other media.

[60] CYBERsitter is similar to the other two with an option to prevent children from accessing files on the home PC computer. It is available at http://www.solidaok.com/.

[61] It has been reported in December 1996 that CYBERsitter completely or partially blocks access to sites such as the National Organization of Women (<http://www.now.org>), and the Yahoo search engine (http://www.yahoo.com).

[62] From a letter sent to Solid Oak (CYBERsitter) by The Cyber-Rights working group of Computer Professionals for Social Responsibility, a group of computer and network users concerned about the preservation of free and open expression on computer networks in the USA, dated 18 December 1996. See Cyber-Rights at <http://www.cpsr.org/cpsr/nii/cyber-rights/>.

[63] See "Don't Buy Cybersitter" at The Ethical Spectacle Web page, http://www.spectacle.org and Peacefire web pages at http://www.peacefire.org

[64] See Human Rights Watch Report, "Silencing The Net: The Threat to Freedom of Expression On-line" [1996] *Monitors: A Journal of Human Rights and Technology* 8 (2), at <http://www.cwrl.utexas.edu/~monitors/>

[65] See eg. the Cinemas Act 1909, Broadcasting Act 1952.

At the moment bans or pre-censorship acts in relation to Internet pornography or sexual content are in any case be unworkable because of the diversity of pornographic sources. Following the introduction of the CDA 1996 in the USA, many WWW pages containing sexually explicit material introduced password protection schemes which required credit card numbers. For example, Adultcheck[66] is one of the main US based companies regulating WWW pages carrying sexually explicit content on the Internet. Its system requires that both the willing adults and the providers are registered by paying fees to obtain username and passwords. By means such as this, the pornography industry will regulate itself anyway. To do so is in their best interest, since they will wish to safeguard the substantial amount of profits made from the pornography industry each year.[67]

The prime responsibility for assuring an appropriate moral environment for children does not rest with Internet content suppliers or access providers. Instead parents and teachers should be responsible for protecting children from accessing sexual or other material which may be harmful to their development. Standards that are overly broad or too loosely defined will result if the job of rating is handed over to rating bodies with different cultural backgrounds, the software industry, or even the producers of pornography. It is not unreasonable to demand that parents take personal responsibility, when the computer industry is already supplying software which parents can use to regulate access to the Internet.

Child pornography is another matter. Its availability and distribution should be regulated, whether on the Internet or elsewhere. But the main concern of enforcement authorities should remain the prevention of child abuse—the involvement of children in the making of pornography, or its use to groom them to become involved in abusive acts— rather than victimless discussion and fantasy by adults. Child pornography not only consists of "crime scene photographs" of child sexual abuse and exploitation, but is also a possible tool for future criminal abuse and exploitation of other children. It is considered "illegal" in many countries, so there is no need to single it out in a special way because it is found on the Internet. The police should make no distinction whether the offence is committed in Oxford Street or on the Internet. Hotlines and monitoring of Internet content should however be encouraged, and police forces should take action if a content provider refuses to remove the illegal materials. Existing UK legislation is capable of fighting child pornography on the Internet and elsewhere, but many of the paedophiles act in international rings, and the targeted group should be the distributors rather than the possessors of child pornography (in some countries possession

---

[66] See Adultcheck at http://www.adultcheck.com

[67] It has been estimated that pornography, including child pornography, is an $8 to $10 billion a year business, and it is also said to be organised crime's third biggest money maker, after drugs and gambling. See US Senate Report 104-358, Child Pornography Prevention Act 1996.

of child pornography is not an offence)[68] and tougher sentences for the production of child pornography may be needed. Although the UK police succeeded with "Operation Starburst" in identifying an international paedophile ring, substantial collaboration at an international level is needed between various national police forces. All nations have an important part to play in the fight against child pornography. This can be achieved, as suggested by the European Commission, initially at the EU level.

There are no borders on the Internet, and actions by individual governments and international organisations can have a profound effect on the rights of the citizens around the world. The full potential for the development of the Internet depends on global society striking the right balance between freedom of speech and public interest considerations; between policies designed to foster the emergence of new services, and the need to ensure that the opportunities they create are not abused.

---

[68] The recent cases shown that many cases involved simple possession offences in the UK. See Cyber-Rights & Cyber-Liberties UK at http://www.leeds.ac.uk/law/pgs/yaman/yaman for a complete list of child pornography prosecutions in the UK.

PART 5

Electronic Evidence and Procedure

14

The Impact of Information Technology Upon Civil Practice and Procedure

W.S. GALE QC[1]

For the civil practitioner, the development of the Internet and other electronic means of transferring information has significant implications. The intention of this paper is to highlight a number of these implications, although discussion here cannot be exhaustive. This paper deals with Scots law only, although some comparative points from other jurisdictions will be highlighted.

PLEADING A CASE INVOLVING THE INTERNET

The civil practitioner requires to have a reasonable understanding of the technology now available for the electronic exchange of information. It is important to understand what the technology can do—not necessarily how it does it. The requirement to explain the Internet or other electronic technology will generally arise in one of two situations:

(a) Sales and other contractual relationships are increasingly concluded through the use of the Internet. It is therefore necessary to understand how a contract can be formed by an exchange of electronic messages.[2] Of particular interest to the civil practitioner are the evidential issues which arise. How is such a contract recorded? What is the proper form of electronic execution?[3]

(b) The Internet is particularly open to abuse by those who infringe intellectual property rights and those who issue defamatory material.

In both situations the civil practitioner will be required to place before the court an intelligible account of how the contract was concluded, or how the

---

[1] I would like to thank my wife, whose knowledge of the computer industry and the law relating thereto begins where mine stops, for her helpful comments on earlier drafts of this paper. Any errors are however the responsibility of the author.

[2] Forms of electronic contracting are discussed in detail in Davies, p. 97.

[3] See further Lloyd, p. 137.

offending material has been published, and how it can be accessed. The necessary starting point in such an account is a description of the technology. A particular example can be found in the (thus far) only Scottish case in which alleged infringement on the Internet has been considered—*Shetland Times Limited v Wills*,[4] in which Lord Hamilton was invited to consider, albeit at the stage of an application for interim interdict, a contention that the information made available by the pursuers on their Web site was a cable programme service within the meaning of s 7 of the Copyright, Designs and Patents Act 1988. Lord Hamilton accepted, perhaps not surprisingly, that the resolution of that issue was one which might turn on technical explanations not available to him at the interim stage, particularly the question of whether the cable programme was "interactive" and thus fell within the exception referred to in s 7(2)(a) of the Act.

In the *Shetland Times* case Lord Hamilton described the Internet as:

". . . a world-wide electronic system for the exchange of information . . . Information is accessed through computers in conjunction with the telephone system. Persons wishing to impart information or to advertise on the Internet can do so by establishing for themselves a web site. Access to the information available at a web site is gained by callers accessing a relative web address."

There will, however, be a need for further understanding and explanation. A comprehensive explanation of the creation of the Internet, the means by which individuals access the Internet, how communications over the Internet occur and the nature and function of the World Wide Web can be found in the judgment of the United States District Court for the Eastern District of Pennsylvania in *American Civil Liberties Union v Janet Reno*[5] (the well known case on the constitutionality of the US Communications Decency Act 1996). The findings in that case contain a definitive legal explanation of the history and basic technology of the Internet. As the terminology explored by the court is universal, the account is as relevant in Scotland as it is in the United States. It is not suggested that such references should, in the drafting of pleadings, supplant any technical information which accompanies the client's instructions, but they provide useful points of reference for the practitioner, and a wider understanding of the technology for the court.[6]

JURISDICTION

The rules of jurisdiction applicable to Scottish civil causes are found in the Civil Jurisdiction and Judgments Act 1982, Schedule 8. Present consideration

---

[4] 1997 SLT 669. The case is discussed in detail in MacQueen, p. 70.

[5] 929 F. Supp. 824 (1996). The case is discussed in detail in Akdeniz, p. 231.

[6] More information on the structure and origins of the Internet can also be found in this volume in Terrett, p 14; Davies, p 97.

is confined to those provisions of Schedule 8 which may have application to the likely causes of action arising out of the uses and abuses of the Internet.

Rule 1 provides that persons shall be sued in the courts for the place where they are domiciled. Persons may also be sued as follows:

Rule 2(2)—in matters relating to a contract, in the courts for the place of performance of the obligation in question.

Rule 2(3)—in matters relating to delict or quasi-delict, in the courts for the place where the harmful event occurred.

Rule 2(10)—in proceedings for interdict, in the courts for the place where it is alleged that the wrong is likely to be committed.

Rule 2(14)—in proceedings principally concerned with the registration in the United Kingdom or the validity in the United Kingdom of patents, trade marks, designs or other similar rights required to be deposited or registered, in the Court of Session.

A number of observations can be made in relation to these rules. It is to be noted that the rules do not refer to intellectual property rights beyond the restricted reference contained in Rule 2(14). Jurisdiction in relation to infringement of such rights could be based upon either the domicile of the infringer or, in the event that the remedy of interdict was sought, upon the place where the wrong is likely to occur. There is an obvious temptation to equate infringement of intellectual property rights with delict or quasi-delict, given that one can probably identify the place where the harmful event occurred,. Infringements of copyright, patents, design rights and trade marks are regulated by statute, and it is unclear as to whether they are to be regarded as delicts or *quasi* delicts for the purpose of Rule 2(3).

It is quite possible that wrongs committed through the use of the Internet may involve passing off and breach of confidence. There is no doubt that passing off in England is a tort.[7] The nature of the wrong in Scotland is less clear. The apparent acceptance by the Second Division in the case of *Lang Bros Ltd v Goldwell Ltd*[8] of the five essentials of the cause of action set out in the speeches of Lords Diplock and Fraser of Tullybelton in *Erven Warnink BV v J Townend & Sons (Hull) Ltd*,[9] including the essential of a misrepresentation, might suggest that passing off is to be regarded as a delict in Scotland.

In assessing the status of an action for breach of confidence, some assistance can be derived from the recent judgment of the Court of Appeal in *Kitechnology B vUnicor GmbH*[10] where Evans L.J., having observed that Article 5(3) of the Brussels Convention required to be given "an autonomous" meaning and that the classification accorded to a claim of breach of confidence in English law was not decisive, went on to say:

---

[7]   See Drysdale and Silverleaf *Passing Off: Law and Practice,* (2nd ed), Ch. 2.
[8]   1980 SC 237.
[9]   [1979] AC 731.

"It is clear in my view that such claims do not arise in tort. . . These claims are certainly non-contractual: . . .That the jurisdiction to restrain and, if necessary, award damages for breach of confidence was an equitable jurisdiction is clear beyond doubt."

In Scotland, the tendency has been to emphasise the duty of confidence as a contractual duty incumbent upon, for example, an employee, and in the event that a third party received the information in the knowledge that it had been originally communicated in confidence, then the person to whom the duty was owed would have a right of action against the third party.[11] There is considerable doubt as to whether an action for breach of confidence would be a matter of delict or quasi-delict, although it can be more readily seen as arising out of a contract. The position of a third party recipient would be more difficult to classify.

Accordingly there are difficulties in classifying the types of causes of action which the practitioner may encounter in the context of wrongs committed over the Internet. It is, however, apparent that in deciding whether the court has jurisdiction the practitioner requires to consider the following:

Is there jurisdiction over the defender by virtue of his domicile? In the event that the wrong is a delict or quasi-delict is there jurisdiction by virtue of the harmful act occurring within the jurisdiction of the Courts? (In *Kitechnology* (*supra*) the Court of Appeal held that the plaintiff had not shown that it had suffered any direct damage in England.) If interdict is being sought, is the alleged wrong likely to be committed in Scotland?

Consideration must therefore be given to the place of the wrong. Where a wrong is committed over the Internet, it should be clear to the wrongdoer that the information which he makes available on the Internet may be accessed by persons outwith the country in which he resides, and it may be, of course, that the wrongdoer intended to cause injury to a person within another country. If an individual makes available information over the Internet which causes injury to a person in Scotland, then it would seem that the harmful act occurs in Scotland, or alternatively Scotland may be the place where the alleged wrong is likely to be committed. The fact that the information is being made available to others outwith Scotland does not affect the location of the harmful event. In *California Software Inc v Reliability Research Inc*[12] it was held that California had jurisdiction over non-residents who used a nationwide computer bulletin board service to publish false statements about a company's right to market a computer program. The court held that the defendants had "made tortious statements which, though directed at third persons outside California, were expressly calculated to cause injury in California. The defen-

---

[10] [1995] FSR 767.
[11] *Lord Advocate v The Scotsman Publications Ltd* 1988 SLT 490 per Lord Justice-Clerk Ross at 502–3.
[12] 631 F. Supp. 1356.

dants knew that the plaintiffs would feel the brunt of the injury, i.e. the lost income in California."

It is apparent from the foregoing discussion of jurisdiction, that a practitioner should recognise that in respect of a wrong committed over the Internet there may be jurisdiction in more than one country. One should therefore consider carefully which jurisdiction gives an advantage to the client.[13] This is not simply an academic exercise. If the client's complaint is one of infringement of copyright, and where there is jurisdiction in both Scotland and England, it is important to appreciate that the available remedies, albeit in the context of a UK statute, may not achieve the same results. In Scotland there is doubt as to whether "additional damages" under Section 97(2) of the Copyright, Designs and Patents Act 1988 are punitive.[14] In England it is well established that the damages under that section are not compensatory, but are punitive.[15] If it is thought that the infringement was flagrant, and there is the possibility of jurisdiction in England, then it may be to the client's advantage to commence the proceedings in England.

PROCEDURE

The present Rules of the Court of Session came into force on 5 September 1994. The preparation of the Rules and their coming into force both predated the wider use of modern electronic document transfer technology. The framers of the Rules could not have anticipated the changes in technology which could have an impact upon the content of the Rules. It should also be remembered that the Rules were, in large part, derived from their predecessors.

The availability of modern technology to those who use the courts and to the courts' administration has clear implications for the exchange of information between the two, and accordingly there are potential implications for the Rules of Court. The innovation of facsimile transmission has been recognised. Practice Note No. 4 of 1994 makes provision for entering appearance and for the enrolling of motions and opposition thereto by way of fax, but it should be noted that the Practice Note makes clear that it is only these steps in process which can be carried out by way of fax.

Technology has the potential to impact on a number of areas of court procedure—the rules relating to service and intimation, the rules on the recovery of evidence, the rules dealing with the conduct of proofs are but examples. There is an increasing tendency for those who appear in the Court of Session

---

[13] For a discussion as to the advantages of such "forum-shopping" in the context of Internet defamation actions, see Edwards, p. 189.

[14] *Redrow Homes Ltd v Bett Bros. Plc*, Second Division, unreported, 14th March 1997; 1996 SLT 1254 (Outer House).

[15] *Cala Homes (South) Ltd v Alfred McAlpine Homes East Ltd* [1995] FSR 818, per Laddie J. at 841.

to have access to personal computers, yet the use of such equipment in Court remains at the discretion of the presiding judge. There are litigations in which such use is an obvious advantage to those appearing, particularly where such use reduces the paper chase.

It may now be thought appropriate to review the Rules of Court having regard to the developments in technology. That exercise should be a comprehensive one, involving the Courts' administration, solicitors, judges and counsel. As the progress of the technology has been so rapid within the past few years, the exercise should also call on the expertise of those involved with the development of the technology in order that any changes to the Rules can be sufficiently flexible to accommodate further developments in technology.

Service and intimation

Do the existing Rules of Court on service and intimation allow for the use of electronic document transfer technology? In England service of a libel writ by email has been allowed on at least one occasion. The writ was served on a defendant in Europe in an Internet libel case and receipt of the writ was proved by the use of email "return receipt" capability.[16] It is suggested however that electronic service is not appropriate, although a limited type of intimation might be permitted.

Rule of Court 16.1 specifies the means of execution of service of a document. The rule refers to (a) personal service, (b) leaving the document in the hands of a person or failing which depositing it at a dwelling place or at the registered office/place of business, and (c) post. Rule 16.1.3. requires that the party on whose behalf service has been executed must lodge in process proof of such service. Where service is carried out personally, or by leaving it in the hands of an individual, failing which by depositing it at a dwelling place or place of business, it must be carried out by Messengers-at-Arms, (Rule 16.3). When a document is served by post (which can be done either by a Messenger-at-Arms or by an agent) it requires to be sent by registered post or by first class recorded delivery service. The envelope requires to have on its face certain information and proof of execution requires a receipt of posting or a certificate of posting, (Rule 16.4)

The approved methods of service do not therefore admit of the possibility of service by e-mail (for example). Similarly they do not admit of service by way of facsimile transmission. Would a relaxation of these rules be appropriate to allow for service using the presently available technology? There are at least two good reasons to oppose this, the first relating to the legal significance of service, the second relating to practical difficulties involved in electronic service.

---

[16] See *Daily Telegraph*, April 30, 1996.

Service is a vital step in the process of litigation. The author of the commentary on Ch. 16 of the Rules of Court put the matter thus: "Service of a summons marks the commencement of an action. The cause is then in dependence." The court requires to be satisfied that the party upon whom service is required has knowledge of the existence of the document and its contents, and there has to be proof that this has occurred. There requires to be personal investigation of a person's residence or place of business. It seems appropriate that such investigation should continue to be required and it can only be achieved by human intervention. To appreciate the importance of service, one has only to consider the circumstances of a grant of interim interdict. Breach of the interlocutor may eventually lead to the imposition of punishment in the form of imprisonment or a fine. It is a requirement in any proceedings for breach of interdict (interim or perpetual) that the order has actually or presumptively been brought to the knowledge of the person charged with the breach.[17] The court will not find a party in breach unless satisfied that the service of the order has been made in accordance with the Rules of Court.

The other difficulty is a practical one. The recipient must have the appropriate equipment to receive the message. Even if that person has an e-mail address it may not be possible to ensure that the recipient can actually read the document attached to the e-mail message. Documents can be easily corrupted. In addition, it must be remembered that unless the recipient is running the same application program as was used to create the document, the recipient may not be able to read the document. There is a way around this, however, in that software is available which allows users to create what are termed PDF (portable document format) files. Macintosh, Windows, DOS and UNIX end users can all view, navigate and print any PDF files they receive.

Although e-mail programs do usually offer a "return receipt" or "acknowledge" facility, there is no foolproof method of establishing that the message has in fact been read by the intended recipient. Return receipts are, after all, as likely as any other email to be lost in transit. Furthermore email is not secure. It can be password protected, but the password can be used by anyone and is not unique in the way that a signature is. Unless an e-mail message is encrypted, it can be manipulated through intermediate computers, and a return receipt can be attached without the message having been read by the intended recipient.

There is also the additional difficulty of establishing that the document has actually been served or delivered to the correct place. Depending on the e-mail protocol some e-mail is accessed directly from the server. In the case of an individual it is unlikely that the server will reside where the individual does, and therefore the question arises as to where the electronic document has been left. For all these reasons it would seem both impractical and undesirable that service of a document should be made by way of electronic transmission.

---

[17] *Burn Murdoch on Interdict*, para. 446.

Intimation of documents is now conveniently divided into three categories:

(a) intimation of documents upon persons for the purposes of information
(b) intimation in accordance with a warrant to intimate
(c) intimation of a step in the process, such as the enrolling of a motion, or opposition thereto, or intimation to the Deputy Principal Clerk of Session that something has been done.

Categories (a) and (b), in general terms, require personal or postal intimation, and accordingly do not lend themselves to intimation by electronic transfer. The final category is dealt with in Rule 16.9 which provides that intimation may be made "by first class post or other means of delivery to that person". It would appear from the terms of the Practice Note No. 4 of 1994 that recognition has been given to intimation by fax as another method of delivery as referred to in Rule 16.9. Given the generality of the wording, it would probably be competent to intimate in terms of Rule 16.9 by way of e-mail. Those who do so, however, risk the practical difficulties referred to above, and it would seem prudent for the practitioner to await guidance, either in the form of an individual Practice Note or in the context of a more thorough review of the Rules of Court, before using this method for intimation.

Recovery of evidence

There can be little doubt that the electronic production and storage (and probably transmission) of documents will become the norm. It will be necessary for the practitioner to have some understanding the concept of electronic files and data.[18]

The present regime for the recovery of documents applies to documents stored electronically, but there are obvious specialities of electronic storage which give rise to particular problems. That said that the classic statement as to what documents are recoverable remains that contained in *Sheriffs Walker on Evidence* at p. 321.

> "Subject to confidentiality and relevancy a document is recoverable if it is a deed granted by or in favour of a party or his predecessor in title, or a communication sent to, or by or on behalf of a party, or a written record kept by or on behalf of a party"

In framing a Specification of Documents the practitioner must seek only documents which are relevant to the facts averred. A Specification seeking documents stored electronically can be no more a vehicle for a fishing expedition that a Specification seeking documents in paper form. In framing a Specification of Documents what factors require to be taken into account? It is suggested that regard is had to the following:

[18] A useful guide may be found in an American book, Patrick, *An Attorney's Guide to Protecting, Discovering and Producing Electronic Information* (1995).

(a) the fact that documents can be shared over a network;
(b) that files can be held on a server;
(c) that there are external means of storage;
(d) that back-up copies are regularly made;
(e) that documents may have been deleted.

With these factors in mind a Specification might be framed along the following lines:

> "All written files, documents, correspondence, memoranda, reports, etc., kept by or on behalf of X, in paper form, and/or all electronic files, documents, correspondence, memoranda, reports etc. kept by or on behalf of X and held or stored on any computers or network of computers, or on any server, or externally on floppy disk, compact disk, hard disk drive or magnetic tape, in order that excerpts may be taken therefrom at the sight of the Commissioner of all entries therein showing or tending to show. . . ."

Compliance with the terms of the Specification by the haver may be by production of printed copies of the documents kept on computer, or alternatively by the production of a compilation disk containing the relevant documents. It is quite probable that a source of stored electronic information may contain information which is not relevant to the litigation, or which is confidential. If confidentiality is claimed then the documents should be produced but marked as confidential and produced in a sealed envelope. If the matter proceeds to a Commission then the haver may make available to the Commissioner the various storage devices in order that the Commissioner can excerpt the relevant entries from the devices.

Documents and records can of course be deleted from computers. Such documents may not, however, be irretrievably lost, as deletion (rather than defragmentation) tends merely to remove the directory structure and *links* to information stored as files, and not the information itself. Software exists which can readily reconstruct and "undelete" files. If a party suspects that another party has indeed deleted entries from its computers, can the party seeking the documents take any action to recover?[19] In such circumstances the party claiming deletion would have to set out in his pleadings a full explanation of the basis of the belief. The court would not contemplate any step without being satisfied that the party has reasonable grounds for the belief that the entry had been deleted or otherwise altered. If a party does have reasonable grounds for such a belief, then he may apply to the court for orders under s 1(1) of the Administration of Justice (Scotland) Act 1972. If there is a reasonable basis for the belief that the device is to be tampered with so as to delete or otherwise alter a document, an order for preservation, custody and

---

[19] For a discussion of discovery of electronically held evidence in the criminal context, see Cullen, p. 219. Refusal to supply, or destruction of, electronic evidence in the face of a court order may be held to be contempt of court: see Lloyd, p. 147.

detention of the device may be sought. If it is thought that deletion has occurred then it may be open to the party alleging deletion to apply to the Court for an order for inspection in terms of Section 1(1) of the Act. An order for inspection must name the inspector.[20] In other jurisdictions, orders have been made allowing a party an opportunity to examine, through an expert, the hard disk drive of a computer in order to search for files which were thought to have been deleted.

REMEDIES

Interim interdict

It is quite likely that the civil practitioner will be asked to consider the possibility of seeking an *interim* interdict to prevent the commission or continuance of a wrongful act relating to the Internet. The prospects of success of such an application have to be considered by reference to the guidance given by Lord Fraser of Tullybelton in *NWL Ltd v Woods*.[21] The applicant for interim relief must satisfy the Court that there is a *prima facie* case of infringement (if one is dealing with intellectual property rights) and that the balance of convenience favours the granting of interim relief. Lord Fraser expressed the view that the strength of the *prima facie* case should be considered in weighing the balance of convenience. The importance of a grant of interim interdict is obvious in relation to a medium like the Internet, and in practice, may be determinative of the whole case. In general terms recall of an interim interdict granted in the face of a contradictor or a reclaiming motion against such an award presents an uphill struggle.

It is important that an application for interim interdict (or, indeed, its contradictor) is accompanied by a full factual account of the basis of the application or the opposition. The form in which that account is presented is important. The Rules of Court relating to Intellectual Property Causes (Ch. 55) give no guidance on the matter. Affidavits are both competent and useful in such circumstances. They can set out in some detail the evidence upon which the parties rely which should not properly form part of the pleadings. In general, an interlocutory hearing is not the place to conduct a detailed examination of the competing factual merits,[22] but notwithstanding that powerful *dictum*, where a conflict of fact exists it is important that the conflict is properly presented to the judge in an intelligible form, not least because an assessment can then subsequently be made as to whether the judge has made an error in fact in his or her determination of the application. Such presentation is best achieved through the use of affidavits, and in the event that one

---

[20] Rule of Court 37.6.
[21] [1979] 1 WLR 1294 at 1310.
[22] *American Cyanamid Company v Ethicon Ltd* [1975] AC 396.

is dealing with a wrong occurring over the Internet then an affidavit dealing with the nature and function of the Internet, as discussed above, would be appropriate. In suggesting an extended use of affidavits in the context of applications for interim interdict, one is conscious that such use will likely contribute to the court time which such an application will occupy, but every effort should be made to properly accommodate hearings for interim interdict.

Extra-territorial remedies

Wrongs committed over the Internet or by other means of electronic transfer clearly have the potential to cross jurisdictional boundaries. This raises the question of whether an order of the Scottish court prohibiting the commission of such a wrong can have effect beyond the territorial jurisdiction of the court. In English law it has traditionally been the position that it was not easy to obtain an injunction which sought to restrain a particular act both in England and in countries outside it. This was because of the "double actionability test" ie the requirement that there be a cause of action in respect of a trans-national tort under both English law (assuming England is the forum) and the law of the place where the delict was committed, before a remedy could be claimed in the English courts. The Private International Law (Miscellaneous Provisions) Act 1995 does away with this test[23] and thus makes it much easier for an English court to grant extra-territorial relief, both in the form of a final as well as an interlocutory injunction.[24]

There has been a similar reluctance on the part of the Scottish courts to pronounce orders which have effect beyond the territorial jurisdiction. The underlying reason for such reluctance seems not, however, to be rooted in the double actionability rule, but rather because the Court is likely to decline the exercise of jurisdiction "when a concurrent and perhaps more effective jurisdiction is possessed by the foreign courts."[25] It does appear to be the case, however, that the Court of Session can competently grant an interdict, interim or permanent, against the commission of a wrong which occurs or is likely to occur outwith the geographic boundaries of Scotland, where the Court has effective jurisdiction over the wrongdoer.[26] In recent years the Court of Session has granted interim interdicts to prevent the commencement or the continuance of proceedings in foreign jurisdictions,[27] although in both cases the court observed that such an order should be granted only with caution given that the order indirectly affects the foreign court.

---

[23] Except in relation to actions for libel or defamation, which are specifically excepted.
[24] See further Smith ed. *Internet Law and Regulation* (FT Law and Tax 1996), para. 2.5.5
[25] *Burn Murdoch on Interdict*, para. 12.
[26] *Liquidators of the California Redwood Co Ltd v Walker & Another* (1886)13. R. 819.
[27] *Pan American World Airways Inc. v Andrews and Others* 1992 SLT 268, *Shell UK Exploration and Production Ltd v Innes and Others* 1995 SL T 807.

The global nature of the Internet means that a person domiciled in Scotland and in respect of whom the Court of Session has jurisdiction, who commits a wrong through the use of the Internet, is likely to commit the wrong in Scotland as well as in other jurisdictions. (For example, material placed on a Web site in breach of copyright will be accessible in Scotland but also in many other jurisdictions.) Even where the wrong is aimed at a person or entity in another jurisdiction (eg as where defamatory comments are made on-line about the business activities of a foreign resident), it would appear competent for the Court of Session to grant an interdict restraining such conduct, notwithstanding that the principal intention of the wrongdoer is to cause damage outwith the jurisdiction of the Court.

It should be noted that the question of whether the Sheriff Court can pronounce an interdict restraining conduct outwith the territory of the Sheriffdom is currently the subject of two conflicting decisions by Sheriffs Principal.[28]

CONCLUDING THOUGHTS

This paper has concentrated upon the challenges which developments in information technology pose for the civil practitioner. One point not stressed thus far is that this technology may also prove an invaluable tool in preparing for litigation. The Scottish courts have shown a welcome tendency to utilise comparative legal material in assisting in the resolution of difficult issues and the Internet allows foreign legal sources to be accessed which were previously available only with difficulty. United Kingdom law is also on-line although the position is not quite so healthy as that in the US and Australia.[29] At present, only recent UK statutes are available (since January 1996)[30] and are moreover only available in the form in which they passed the Royal Assent. Unless and until that service is revised so as to provide the user with the amended text, it may provide potential pitfalls rather than benefits. It is also to be hoped that statutes other than recent ones will become available. On the case law front, the House of Lords has now made available the speeches of Lords of Appeal in Ordinary at its Judicial Business Page.[31] These are available within two hours of the speeches being issued, the service having begun

---

[28] *McKenna v McKenna* 1984 SLT (Sh. Ct.) 92; *Calder Chemicals Ltd v Brunton,* 1984 SL T (Sh. Ct) 96.

[29] For example, in the United States, the House of Representatives Internet law library contains extensive US Federal and State legislation and case law, as well as information and materials on other legal systems. The University of Indiana hosts an extensive Virtual Law Library which contains similar material together with academic works. In Australia the Australasian Legal Information Institute has made reported decisions and statutes available free of charge to Internet users.

[30] http://www.hmso.gov.uk/acts.htm.

[31] http://www.parliament.the-stationery-office.co.uk/pa/ld199697/ldjudgmt/ldjudgmt.htm.

in November 1996. There are also moves to place Court of Appeal judgements on line.[32] As yet no Scottish decisions (save House of Lords judgments) have appeared on the Web. Hansard reports of proceedings in both Houses of Parliament are also available, a service which may be of particular relevance post *Pepper v Hart*.[33]

Although this paper has focused on critical issues in current practice and procedure, information technology is likely to result in other, more startling changes in court procedure, sooner rather than later. There are already moves to provide real-time transcription of court proceedings in electronic form to both judges and counsel in the Court of Session, as is in place already in some US states, as well as a computerised court diary and case tracking system in commercial actions.[34] Many practitioners already make extensive use of litigation support software or case management technology, especially in complicated cases involving many thousands of documents or images. Other developments, such as the "virtual courtroom" where litigants, counsel and judge never meet in one room, but converse by means of video-conferencing, email or real time "electronic chat", may be further off, but cannot be ignored. The introduction of information technology into both courts and the legal workplace in general has the potential both to transform legal practice, and to challenge lawyers to develop new forms of legal services to meet new client needs.[35]

---

[32] The first Court of Appeal judgment was placed on the Web in April 1997 (see *Times*, April 29 1997) at the instigation of the panel of judges involved in the case of *Bannister v SGB*, because of the significance of, and urgent need for dissemination of, the judgment. See <http://www.open.gov.uk-lcd-lcdhome.htm.>

[33] http://www.parliament.the-stationery-office.co.uk/pa/ld/ldhansard.htm.
http://www.parliament.the-stationery-office.co.uk/pa/cm/cmhansard.htm.

[34] See 1997 SLT (News) 49.

[35] For some interesting speculation on the future of legal practice in the information technology society, see E Katsch *Law in a Digital World* (Oxford University Press, 1995); R Susskind *The Future of Law* (Clarendon Press, 1996).

Index